Embedded Librarians
Moving Beyond One-Shot Instruction

Edited by Cassandra Kvenild and Kaijsa Calkins

Association of College and Research Libraries
A division of the American Library Association
Chicago 2011

The paper used in this publication meets the minimum requirements of American National Standard for Information Sciences–Permanence of Paper for Printed Library Materials, ANSI Z39.48-1992. ∞

Library of Congress Cataloging-in-Publication Data

Embedded librarians : moving beyond one-shot instruction / edited by Cassandra Kvenild and Kaijsa Calkins.
    p. cm.
  ISBN 978-0-8389-8587-8 (pbk. : alk. paper) 1. Academic libraries--Relations with faculty and curriculum. 2. Information literacy--Study and teaching (Higher) 3. Research--Methodology--Study and teaching (Higher) 4. Library orientation for college students. 5. Academic libraries--United States--Case studies. I. Kvenild, Cassandra. II. Calkins, Kaijsa.
  Z675.U5E45 2011
  027.7--dc23
                  2011014802

Contents

Acknowledgments

The editors would like to thank ACRL for publishing this book. In particular, we thank Kathryn Deiss for her excellent guidance to two first-time editors and her thoughtful and warm advice. All of the authors included in this volume contributed excellent ideas and many hours of writing and revision; we are overwhelmingly grateful for their work.

We must thank our coworkers at the University of Wyoming Libraries. We especially thank Jamie Kearley, our department head, for allowing us flexibility for our embedded work and the time we have invested in developing this book. We also owe sincere thanks to Maggie Farrell, Dean of University Libraries and Lori Phillips, Associate Dean of University Libraries, for providing amazing support for our travel to present at national and international conferences.

Additionally, we are grateful to our University of Wyoming colleagues in the Department of English, the Outreach School, and the Synergy Program for partnering with us in the embedded projects that first got us started on the long path that led to this book.

Finally, we would like to thank our families for their love and support always.

Introduction

Embedded librarians work closely over extended periods of time with non-librarian groups, whether by joining a semester-long course, maintaining an ongoing presence in online courses, participating in broad curriculum planning efforts, or joining the staffs of academic departments, clinical settings, or performing groups. Barbara Dewey coined the term in 2004, writing: "Embedding requires more direct and purposeful interaction than acting in parallel with another person, group, or activity. Overt purposefulness makes embedding an appropriate definition of the most comprehensive collaborations for librarians in the higher education community."[1]

Embedded librarianship is a relatively new idea in the field, but its impact on instruction and its potential growth are already evident. By joining varied groups of patrons and assisting their research over the long haul, embedded librarians commit themselves to service in a very different way than they did in traditional one-shot bibliographic instruction. In this collection, we see librarians using the embedded model to become valuable collaborators, trusted instructors, and partners in shaping the curriculum and broad institutional goals beyond the boundaries of the library. In Chapter One, librarian Matthew Brower traces the evolution of embedded librarianship over the past decade and a half, providing detailed insight into early adopters of embedded models and how they defined their work.

Many early embedding initiatives were developed as a response to the library instruction needs of distance learners. For librarians serving off-campus students, the ACRL Access Entitlement Principle drove efforts to make library services available to all, whether they teach and learn in traditional classrooms or in new technological environments.[2] In asynchronous settings for online instruction, embedding librarians into class discussion boards and other areas of the online class made sense as the most straightforward solution to an existing need. Librarians at Regis University, the Community College of Vermont, and at the University of Wyoming were early adopters of the embedded model in order to reach off-campus teachers and learners. As the use of online course materials increases, and as we see enrollment in distance courses continue to grow nationally, embedding library instruction online will increasingly become the norm in academic libraries. Indeed, at libraries like the one described by Ann Schroeder in Chapter Five, online embedded library instruction has completely replaced traditional bibliographic instruction.

We would argue that the primary lesson learned by all of the authors in this collection is that collaboration is key to implementing an embedded librarian program. Without extensive collaboration with faculty members, with departments, with administrators, and with other stakeholders, successful embedding is impossible. In the case of online course management systems, librarians have succeeded in gaining access to courses by creating goodwill and forging partnerships with system administrators. Creating a culture of information literacy extends beyond the library's walls, and requires the participation of students, faculty, and administrators. Including institutional stakeholders in planning to embed librarians is crucial to success.

The idea of embedding online without synchronous contact extends beyond distance learning. As you will read in Chapter Six, Duke University Libraries now create a presence in the course management system for all of the university's courses—if not embedding an individual librarian, then embedding at least a library guide, a link to services, and contact information. Later in the book, Kristen Mastel discusses how she used embedded librarianship principles to collaborate online with Extension services to fulfill the mission of the University of Minnesota, a land grant institution. Corporate librarians use the same embedded principles to connect with far-flung staff, and David Shumaker makes a persuasive argument in Chapter Two about how to apply lessons learned from both corporate and academic examples to the future of embedded librarianship.

In addition to presence in online courses, librarians are also increasing their presence in the classroom. At many schools, the freshman composition class provides an opportunity to include a librarian's expertise in the daunting semester-long process of searching, writing, revising and citing. Rick Fisher and April Heaney, two composition faculty, describe here the value of embedded librarians to the success of their at-risk freshmen students. Other successful initiatives within the first year experience detailed in this book involve embedding librarians in Honors Programs, Writing Centers, and even the dormitories to provide a welcoming and constant presence of a librarian for instruction and assistance during the transition to college life. Scalability is a constant concern of librarians undertaking embedded initiatives, particularly when the projects involve working with large populations such as freshmen. However, many of the librarians you will hear from here use the lessons they learned from close interaction with a small group of freshmen to gain insight on larger issues and trends. In Chapter Four, Australian librarians Craig Milne and Jennifer Thomas reveal that an initial investment of time in creating a strong first-year embedded program can save future time in preparation and instruction. The knowledge librarians gain from small embedded initiatives has the potential to inform more traditional library instruction for the broader campus population.

Librarians are also successfully embedding themselves and their work in academic departments, in senior capstone courses and at the master's and PhD levels. Making librarians available to provide in-depth help over time as students explore subject-specific resources or complete their literature review is invaluable to them. Chapters Twelve and Thirteen describe successful examples of librarians and teaching faculty partnering in

upper-division disciplinary courses in Health Sciences at Monmouth University and Education at Harvard, respectively. Initiatives to embed librarians at the graduate level have been shown to be particularly successful in business schools, colleges of education, and the health sciences. Librarians from the University of Michigan detail in Chapter Eleven their embedded project working intensively with future MBAs at the Kresge School to complete multidisciplinary action projects.

The seemingly limitless sites for embedded librarianship are illustrated by the variety of initiatives and programs described in this book. In Chapter Seven, Christopher Miller describes how he physically embeds himself within his discipline by maintaining office space in the department of dance. Another innovative physical example of embedded librarianship is described by Jezmyne Dene in the final chapter, where she details the various approaches Claremont Colleges librarians use to work with the many colleges served by one centralized library.

The collaboration and the partnerships developed through embedded librarianship can help open doors to providing better library services and opportunities for collaborations across campus. Embedding in a class as a librarian requires increased knowledge of course, department, and institution-level goals, as well as facility with a variety of pedagogical techniques. Librarians must consider information literacy objectives as well as the primary instructor's student learning objectives when designing an embedded project. A scaffolded program of embedding across a department's offerings requires an in-depth understanding of curriculum goals and performance assessments. The librarian must consider at what points in a major field of study to introduce appropriate information skills and resources to students. Many of the librarians here found that after collaborating to embed themselves in one class, they increased their visibility in departments and were asked to participate in more courses and even in planning future goals and objectives of the curriculum. The more ambitious the program of embedding, the more opportunities arise for the libraries to be visible and persuasive influence across the curriculum.

Librarians are seeing a trend toward declining reference interactions at the same time we face dramatically increasing demand for instruction. The opportunity to shift our focus toward embedded librarianship has arrived, and we hope this book can serve as an introduction to models of successful programs. We look forward to seeing even more literature on assessing embedded models, and how best to manage concerns such as staffing and scalability. There is so much more to the story of embedded librarianship yet to be written.

Cass Kvenild & Kaijsa Calkins

NOTES

1. Barbara Dewey, "The embedded librarian: strategic campus collaborations," *Resource Sharing & Information Networks* 17:1/2 (2004): 5–17.
2. Association of College and Research Libraries (ACRL) "Standards for distance learning library services," (2008) http://www.ala.org/ala/mgrps/divs/acrl/standards/guidelinesdistancelearning.cfm

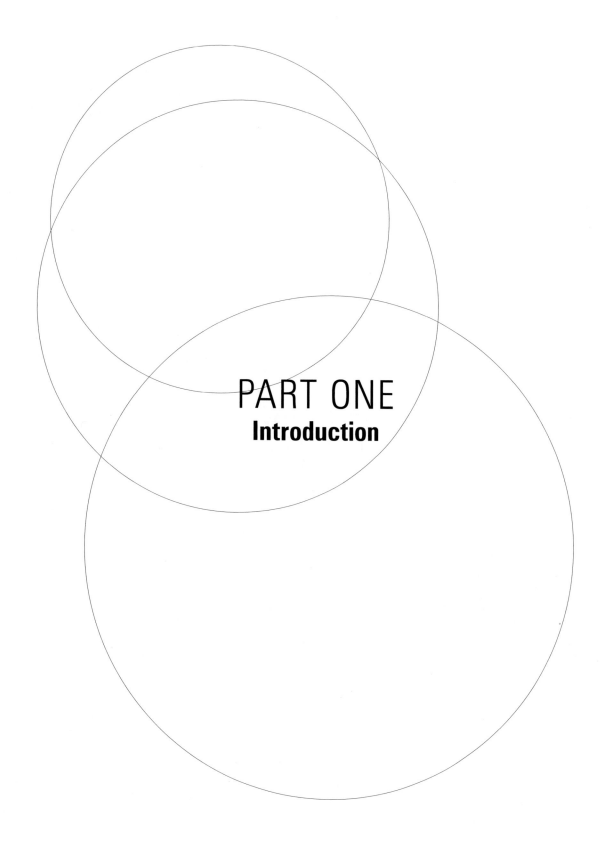

PART ONE
Introduction

 ONE

A Recent History of Embedded Librarianship: Collaboration and Partnership Building with Academics in Learning and Research Environments

Matthew Brower

Introduction & Scope of this Chapter

When many people hear the term *embedded*, they remember TV journalists embedded with troops in 2003 during the war in Iraq. Fortunately, embedded academic librarians work in an environment far from combat and, instead, are finding ways to embed their skills and services in physical and virtual environments. Librarians may have been embedded among researchers earlier than the phrase started appearing in the professional research literature. All of their experiences could not be justly addressed in one book chapter. Instead, this chapter includes the characteristics of embedded librarianship, an account of the origin of embedded librarianship, and follows with examples from library research literature about embedded librarianship at academic institutions.

Throughout my examination of research literature on embedded librarianship, I encountered many definitions of embedded librarianship. It is not my goal to reexamine the definition of embedded librarianship, but instead to focus on common characteristics I discovered while reading about embedded librarianship. In a recent SLA report, Shumaker & Talley write a concise and encompassing description of embedded librarianship:

> [Embedded Librarianship involves] "...focusing on the needs of one or more specific

groups, building relationships with these groups, developing a deep understanding of their work, and providing information services that are highly customized and targeted to their greatest needs. It involves shifting the model from transactional to high trust, close collaboration, and shared responsibility of outcomes. In order for an embedded librarian to achieve these goals, there must also be some long term planning between the customer and the librarian."[1]

This passage outlines many of the characteristics I will describe in the following section, but in the last sentence it also emphasizes the importance of *long term planning* with the customer, which is a crucial aspect to becoming a successful embedded librarian. Shumaker and Talley state that, "over half of embedded librarianship programs have been in existence for 10 years or more."[2] This indicates that many who have been practicing embedded librarianship have continued to use the strategy for a significant period of time. Developing embedded library services cannot be successful without a long-term strategy that addresses the needs of a user base. It is necessary to develop a long-term plan to address how librarians should interact with their users. With limited resources, it is easy to simply address the immediate needs of a user base. This practice does not incorporate a dialogue with customers to determine what they feel is most important. Shumaker and Talley suggest that librarians should be meeting with their customers to better understand their needs and planning their service goals accordingly. This type of conversation will inform a librarian's strategy for providing embedded library services.

Characteristics of Embedded Librarianship
Embedded Librarians Collaborate with their Users

Librarians who collaborate with their clientele often work with an individual faculty member on a specific project. Collaborating with a faculty member can involve the following activities: incorporating information literacy into class assignments, partnering to provide specialized research assistance to students over a semester, or helping a faculty member find resources supporting their research.

Form Partnerships on the Department and Campus Level

Partnerships involve a long-term strategy to embed library services or outreach efforts within an entire department or campus. For instance, a librarian may meet with a department chair to discuss a proposal that integrates a research component into the curriculum, or a library director may meet with an administrator to discuss placing librarians in offices near departmental faculty.

Provide Needs Based Services

Needs based services focus on customizing services to meet the specific needs of an individual user. Instead of anticipating what services or research materials users may need, this strategy focuses on having conversations with the user and providing specialized services For example, after a librarian provides an instruction session, he may setup research appointments with students closer to assignment submission deadlines when students are more likely to begin their research. Librarians also incorporate several web technologies that aim to reach users at the point of need. For instance, a chat window could be embedded in a library database to make it easier for students to contact a librarian.

Offer Convenient and User-Friendly Services Outside of Library Settings

This characteristic includes activities that embedded librarians perform outside of the library or its website. Since some users may not enter the library or its website to realize the value of the library's services and resources, hence it is necessary to embed services where users are more likely to find them. Some activities could include: holding office hours near the offices of faculty, giving presentations at the department's faculty meeting, or even joining faculty and students in class discussions or site visits.

Become Immersed in the Culture and Spaces of Users

Immersion in the spaces and culture of users is not based on the activity or service being performed by the librarian, but rather having a presence in places where students and faculty are conducting their research or other academic business. Reaching students may involve embedding services in places where students start their research. For example, a librarian may place their contact information or other library resources in a Course Management System. Attending departmental faculty meetings could help a librarian better understand the needs of a department, and therefore offer assistance when it is needed.

Understand the Discipline Including the Culture and Research Habits of their Users

Librarians with a deep understanding or background in a discipline can more easily approach and interact with faculty. When faculty trust that a librarian can correctly assess their needs, they are more likely to participate in collaborations with librarians involving their research and teaching. An understanding of the discipline can also help librarians anticipate the needs of faculty.

Overview of the History of Embedded Librarianship

Medical librarians first practiced embedded librarianship in the late 1960s and early 1970s.[3] Recognizing that doctors and patients could benefit from specialized research services; medical librarians started accompanying doctors on their rounds. Over the last few decades this practice has been adopted in some medical libraries. While academics have historically created branch libraries to serve specific disciplines, some universities began placing their reference librarians among the offices of faculty in the early 1990s.[4] It is during this time that physically embedded services are joined with new models of providing embedded services electronically.

As research became more easily accessible in online/virtual environments in the late 1990s and early 2000s, reference and instruction librarians began placing an emphasis on teaching information literacy skills to researchers. Librarians began proactively collaborating with faculty to include information literacy into research assignments and the curriculum. As online access to scholarly materials became more ubiquitous, librarians looked at how they could become embedded in virtual environments. In the early 2000s, several librarians documented their experiences embedding library resources into the university's course management system (CMS). Shortly after, several librarians wrote about their experiences providing virtual reference services, especially through email and chat reference. Later, the research literature documents some librarians' experiences participating in discussions with students in the classroom and through online platforms such as Wikis or Course Management Systems. Within the last couple of years, there have been several examples of librarians participating with instructors in the design and delivery of entire courses.

Librarians Embedded among Professionals in their Workplace

In early examples of embedded librarianship, librarians provided embedded research services by physically locating among faculty, professionals and students. Librarians who experimented with this concept realized that it was a step towards providing better service for their users. Taking on this form of embedded librarianship allowed librarians to more readily collaborate with faculty, provide specialized services, and utilize their discipline knowledge.

Embedding within Clinical Medical Libraries

Clinical Medical Librarians (CMLs) were some of the first to document how they evolved their service model to better meet the needs of their primary clientele, physicians. For various reasons, doctors were not using the library or librarians to help with research for patient treatment. Kay Cimpl explains that doctors did not use their services as much as they could for the following reasons: the library was closed when doctors weren't seeing patients, the doctor's time might not be best spent searching the literature, or the information they did retrieve might not be useable.[5] In other words, the library services were not convenient and did not address the needs of the doctors. When hospitals began patient health care teams in the early 1970s, it opened up an opportunity for librarians to use their discipline knowledge in the field to collaborate with doctors and other patient care team members.[6] Interacting with the physicians in the patient care setting made it much easier for doctors to bring up questions, and in turn for librarians to ask doctors questions.[7] After rounds were over, librarians could begin searching the medical literature and use their subject knowledge to find information relevant to the doctor's need.[8]

By joining the patient care team and providing doctors with valuable information from the medical literature, the clinical medical librarian's involvement provided the following contributions: "enhancement of patient care; physician, health care team, and medical student education; greater awareness of library services and resources; time saving for physician and health care team; exposure to a wider variety of journals; and information sharing among colleagues."[9] Since embedding clinical medical librarians on the patient care team was largely a success, it began to be practiced at other hospitals.

Even though the librarian's embedded presence had many positive outcomes, there were some barriers to implementing this new embedded model. While the librarian was on rounds there was a diminished librarian presence at the central library location.[10] Therefore it was integral that the outreach service become part of the library's mission, but also must include a cost-recovery plan.[11] The embedded model must be seen as a value added service that could be supported by supplemental funds.[12]

Over time, doctors became more aware of the research skills that librarians could offer, resulting in increased visibility and service expectations by the library's clientele.[13] New Clinical Medical Librarians (CMLs) were required to have expert searching skills, and an ability to understand and interact with clinicians. As embedded CMLs became standard practice in some hospital libraries, there was a need to establish a more formal training for new CMLs. Davidoff and Florance recognized this need, and suggested in an article that a CML training program be developed.[14] This proposed program would help CMLs develop a solid understanding of both information science and the essentials of clinical work.[15] More importantly, CMLs would learn practical skills such as how to retrieve and synthesize information, and how to interact with a clinical care team.[16] The desire for a CML program, and the increased visibility and appreciation for the new services are evidence that an embedded library presence on the patient care team was a successful pilot.

Embedding within Academic Departments

Many librarians working in the private sector receive some extra compensation for personalized research services. In hospital or academic research libraries, extra funding for libraries is rarely given unless through grants or other outside sources. When funding for new initiatives is scarce, finding partnerships with those in leadership positions can help achieve embedded services within a department. In an article in the Journal of the Medical Librarianship, Gary Freiburger and Sandra Krammer write about their experience collaborating with administrators and faculty during the planning phase of a new multidisciplinary research facility at the University of Arizona in Tucson.[17]

In the early stages of planning a new research facility, the library director believed that the librarians with education in medicine could be best utilized if they were stationed closer to the research and teaching faculty.[18] In consultation with the person planning the research section of the new building, it was decided that librarians would have designated areas to provide research services throughout the new interdisciplinary research faculty.[19] Some would be located in hallways connecting departments, while others were given offices among faculty.

Once the new facility was completed, these new service points helped librarians become more available to provide research services, and opened up more opportunities to interact with faculty.[20] As a result of being physically embedded in the department the librarians could collaborate with faculty more by participating in the following activities: grant research, teaching information literacy courses, and attendance at department faculty meetings.[21] Assisting with grant research would allow librarians to demonstrate their advanced subject knowledge and research skills to faculty. Meanwhile, teaching information literacy courses would help librarians reach out to students who may not have received library instruction. Finally, attendance at the department faculty meetings gave librarians a chance to meet other faculty and learn about research initiatives or curriculum changes. Freiburger and Kramer explain that it takes special service provider characteristics to collaborate with faculty, most importantly, strong interpersonal skills, discipline knowledge, and an understanding of the organization's culture.[22]

Since it is uncommon for academic librarians to locate extra funding for embedded librarianship programs, Freiburger and Kramer added that they were able to find support for the embedded librarian program by restructuring the staff within the library and consolidating service desks in the library.[23] In their library, restructuring the library was a much better alternative than diminishing the role of reference services within the library.[24] As with the earlier example in which clinical librarians were physically embedded among doctors, being physically embedded for these medical librarians meant being included with the faculty in the delivery of research and instructional services and potentially led to more funding for their services.

Embedding Information Literacy Instruction into the Curriculum

In response to a need for a curriculum-wide strategy to teach research skills, academic librarians formed partnerships with departments to design research and writing assignments. Academic librarians felt it was important to teach information literacy skills to students and expose them to the library's resources early in their academic careers. Designing assignments that required the use of library resources helped students to recognize the value of the library's resources for their course assignments. Embedded information literacy components also helped librarians share their knowledge of the research process.

In my experience teaching instruction sessions in upper division business classes, I regularly encounter students who tell me they wish they had known about the library's resources earlier in their academic career. At my institution, University of Colorado at Boulder, the librarians in the Leeds School of Business have integrated key business databases into the final project of an Introduction to Business Class. While this project is not comprehensive in terms of library resources, it does give the students an overview of important resources for their current and future business research. Even though some students may not retain what they learned in this course, others recognize the value of the resources and utilize them as they advance in their academic careers.

Embedded Librarians in the Core Curriculum

Librarians seek opportunities to instruct students early on in their college experience. Meanwhile, many academic departments offer classes that are specifically designed to introduce their students to the discipline. Since these introductory courses often include a writing or research component, faculty who teach these introductory courses may be willing to collaborate with librarians to integrate library resources into assignments. Callison, Budny and Thomes coauthored an article explaining how they partnered with the engineering department faculty to design a writing assignment that would introduce students to library resources and information literacy concepts.[25] This assignment also served a purpose for the engineering faculty and mentors since it assessed the students' writing skills. The librarians hoped the students would learn information literacy skills by completing this project, and could subsequently use these skills throughout their academic and professional careers.[26]

Callison, Budny and Thomes note that not all faculty may be inclined or accustomed to collaborate with others on projects.[27] For this reason, librarians may collaborate with faculty more successfully if they focus on shared interests.[28] In their case study, a writing project afforded faculty and student writing mentors the opportunity to evaluate their students' writing, while the librarians had the opportunity to include research resources that were highly relevant to the students' assignments and final project.[29] Students in this course recognized the library's resources as the best place to begin their research. They also learned teamwork and computer skills that would be beneficial later in their education and careers.[30]

Once both the faculty and the librarians saw the positive impact of this assignment on student learning, the librarians and engineering faculty developed the idea of designing a career education project.[31] The engineering faculty hoped this assignment would educate students at the start of their studies about an engineer's job functions and activities, and therefore help students decide if they were still interested in an engineering career.[32] The librarians saw this project as an opportunity to teach students database researching skills and information literacy concepts.[33] Since the assignments were designed to be completed over a few class sessions, the information literacy and research concepts were more deeply embedded in the course and students had more time to learn the research process and utilize critical thinking skills.[34]

The career writing project was preceded by three highly structured assignments.[35] The librarians met with the student writing mentors to discuss the desired learning outcomes, since the mentors evaluated the students' weekly assignments.[36] Later the final projects would be evaluated by the instructors and would constitute a percentage of the student's final grade for the course.[37] In the first assignment, students were expected to research what activities engineers did while on the job.[38] The last assignment was designed to help the students learn how to access scholarly articles.[39] The final project instructed students to write a technical paper for a conference and give a presentation about it.[40] The librarians presented a 45-minute instruction session accompanied by a detailed handout.[41]

In fields such as engineering, where research is increasingly available digitally, it is especially important for librarians to integrate the library's resources and research services into the curriculum. In addition to learning about information literacy concepts and the research process, the students were made aware of librarians and library resources and became accustomed to starting with the library for their research at the library (in person or online). The librarians showed students how library resources in the digital format they expected could meet their research needs. We learn from Callison, Budny and Thomes that partnering with a department to embed library research into the curriculum reinforces how important research skills can be for the students' educational and professional careers.

Embedded Librarians in a Course throughout a Semester

By collaborating with faculty, some librarians are afforded the opportunity to interact with and assist students over an entire semester. Engaging students over an entire semester allows librarians to better assess how much students use and retain research and information literacy skills. Russell Hall, a librarian at Pennsylvania State-Erie, Behrend College, writes about his full semester embedded presence in a class for which he had previously offered only a one-shot instruction session.[42] Reporting on a similar project, Mary Duggan writes about her involvement in an Agricultural Economics class with a semester long marketing plan project.[43]

A common problem for librarians is that students often do not retain some of the important skills taught to them in instruction sessions. Since students were not using the resources presented to them in a one-shot instruction session, Hall offered to take an approach that would encourage discussion about the information sources students used in research for their required presentations.[44] His goal was to promote critical thinking, and evaluate the students' use of information to enhance the quality of their speeches.[45] Since his involvement in the class would occur as the students were practicing their research skills, Hall could observe the students when they were more likely to need assistance, and could use this observation to inform his instruction of students in future classes.

Hall decided that the best approach would be to attend every one of the faculty member's class sessions.[46] Since this would involve a substantial added time commitment, Hall sought approval from his supervisor.[47] When pursuing an embedded presence similar to Hall's experience, where time commitments are substantial, it is vital to gain supervisor approval.

While Hall was attending the classes, he regularly participated in the discussions.[48] His main goal was to keep the students thinking about all aspects of information literacy.[49] Hall also presented two library instruction sessions that consisted of a short lecture and hands-on exercises.[50] When delivering these sessions, he felt his presence in sessions prior to his lecture gave him more credibility and led to a more engaging session with the students.[51] Additionally, he received more reference questions outside of the class.[52]

Hall felt his most important contribution to the class was to promote critical thinking.[53] Looking back on his experience he felt that he could have done more to participate in evaluating the students' work, and incorporated more measures of student satisfaction and learning outcomes in the class design.[54] These two additions would help him acquire firsthand knowledge of how students were using resources, and would provide him with more than anecdotal evidence that his contributions were having an impact on the students' speeches.

While Hall worked individually with an entire class, three Business librarians and an Agriculture librarian worked directly with three groups in an Agricultural Economics class at Purdue University throughout a semester to provide specialized reference services. Similar to Hall's experience,

the business librarians' goal was to improve research skills and knowledge of business information sources.[55] In her article, Duggan explains that in prior instruction sessions many students would simply lose track of librarians' efforts to teach them research skills since the sessions often took place weeks before students would be seriously engaged in research for a project.[56] Therefore, it seemed that an embedded presence for research assistance and careful collaboration with a faculty member in assignment planning could help students realize the need to learn research skills.

The librarians collaborated with a professor teaching an Advanced Agribusiness Marketing class where the main project for the class was to develop a marketing plan to sell surplus meat.[57] One new strategy the librarians undertook with this assignment was to have a research consultation with student groups at the point of need, rather than weeks before the students would do the research for the project.[58] In order to better evaluate the students' progress, the assignments were structured so that one part would be due every 4–6 weeks.[59] The librarians and the faculty member decided that requiring the students to complete research throughout the semester would result in a more refined marketing plan by the end of the term.[60] Students were motivated to produce a better product since the group with best plan would be entered in a national competition.[61] Since each of the librarians was assigned to a group, this eliminated the need for students to explain the background of their project to a librarian.[62] Throughout the semester librarians scheduled meetings with students and wrote students follow up emails asking if the students needed further help.[63] This type of personalized service made the librarians more approachable.

Interestingly, Duggan's experience seemed to parallel some of the results that Hall found in his experience with the speech class. Most notably, Duggan wished the librarians would have participated more in the evaluation process. Similarly,

Duggan felt that their approach with the students may have been too passive, since the students did not ask for help and may not have realized they were not using appropriate sources.[64] Therefore, Duggan emphasizes that it is important to discuss with the faculty member in planning phases how much interaction and involvement the librarians will have with the students.[65] As noted earlier by Callison, et al., it is important to set goals that align with the faculty member's, such as improving the students' research skills.[66] Duggan makes a few suggestions for fostering interactions with the students, such as setting appointments with the students before assignments are due, monitoring the students' progress, and participating in the evaluation of the students' projects.[67] In addition to careful planning at the beginning of the course, the librarians' specialized knowledge of the subject also contributed to the success of this collaborative project.

While participating in courses over an entire semester may not be scalable for every class in a department and would clearly involve an increased workload, the librarians who have experienced an embedded presence over an entire semester feel that this approach has great potential to help students retain the skills we try to teach them in information literacy sessions. These interactions with students address learning at the point of need rather than trying to anticipate their needs by reviewing an assignment before giving an instruction session. Librarians may seek an embedded presence in classes for which they have offered instruction previously, and anticipate that the course could be offered regularly in the future. By collaborating with an instructor to integrate a librarian into the course project, the librarian will develop better relations with the faculty member and students. Likewise, this experience may help a librarian better realize how students could best learn research skills, and could inform any future sessions and interactions that a librarian would have with students from this particular class. To implement an embedded pres-

ence in a class, Hall suggests that librarians look for opportunities to become embedded in a class that is discussion or project based, since it gives the librarian a clear avenue for participating in the class.

Partnering in Teaching and Evaluation

Partnering with instructors to participate in the evaluation of students' assignments can help librarians determine whether or not students apply information literacy skills in their assignments. Michael Hearn writes about a collaborative effort with a faculty member that allowed him to teach information literacy skills to students and participate in the evaluation of students' work.[68] This collaborative teaching effort also added an online component in which the students communicated and submitted assignments through the Blackboard Course Management System.[69]

While planning the class, Hearn and the faculty member decided that a combination of electronic and print research skills would best serve the students' research needs.[70] Hearn conducted library activities in eight separate library instruction sessions that focused on illustrating a research strategy and how it could be applied to the assignment.[71] This close connection between the research strategies and the class assignments helped students realize the importance of research skills, especially the evaluation of information resources. Hearn explains that in order for students to retain research skills, it was necessary to teach and build upon skills learned over an entire semester.[72]

Hearn was also heavily involved in individual consultations and evaluating the students' work. A unique component of Hearn's embedded presence was his ability to administer a pre and post-test to measure the students' ability to perform academic research.[73] One of the elements he measured was the students' ability to select appropriate sources (the primary reason he was embedded in the course).[74] Hearn learned that after he provided the instruction sessions, students were better able to select acceptable sources for research.[75] The pre and post-test indicated the students were no longer relying solely on broad Internet searches, and were able to select credible websites.[76] Another major benefit of the pre and post-test was that it gave a more concrete method for deciding what research skills should be emphasized in future classes.[77]

The benefit of this type of collaboration was significant since he was subsequently invited to participate in other activities within the department, and therefore increased the awareness of the library among the writing faculty.[78] Hearn argues that this increased awareness weighs positively against the time investment.[79]

Hearn, Duggan, and Hall all recommend discussing partnerships with faculty to incorporate information literacy into their classes. Their examples demonstrate how to move beyond a one-shot presentation and develop an embedded librarian presence. They have worked with faculty to include library resources into the assignments for the class. Hall highlighted his experience of becoming immersed in class discussions. By providing research assistance to specific groups of students over an entire semester, Duggan and other librarians offered convenient, needs based services. Finally, by evaluating students' work and instructing a large portion of the class, Hearn successfully demonstrated to faculty how librarians can improve students' research skills through their teaching and knowledge of the research process.

Embedded Resources and Services in Virtual Environments

Over the last decade, librarians have increasingly documented their experiences embedding library resources and services in virtual environments. Today most colleges and universities use online Course Management Systems. Over the last five years, there have been many articles describing how to integrate library resources into a CMS. Models of embedded librarianship in virtual environments seek to deliver resources and services

to users when they are most needed. Embedding the library into virtual environments can open up opportunities to collaborate with distance learning faculty, and since faculty often need to grant a librarian access to their course pages in a Course Management System (CMS), collaborating with faculty may be a necessary step to help librarians become immersed in the virtual classroom.

Distance Learning Courses and Course Management Systems

As more distance learning courses are offered at universities, librarians should be looking for ways to include these students in their service base. Librarians can help distance faculty by supplementing a faculty's course with online research guides, virtual reference services, and contributing valuable research skills and sources to online discussions. In a paper published in the proceedings of the 22nd Annual Conference on Distance Teaching and Learning, Jim Kinnie identifies some helpful advice for collaborating with faculty to develop an embedded presence in distance courses.[80] First he advises librarians to meet with the faculty member and determine how they could best contribute to his or her class.[81] He cautions that some faculty may be resistant to adding library resources and may consider it more of a burden, but he suggests that librarians should focus on how incorporating library resources can be mutually beneficial for the students, the faculty member and librarians.[82] In his experience, Kinnie found that students were even more likely to seek research assistance when their assignment recommended or required the use of library resources.[83]

In a 2003 article , Shank and Dewald provide an overview about how librarians can become more embedded in virtual classrooms through a CMS.[84] They suggest incorporating some of the following services into an online classroom: virtual reference-desk services, catalog and database links, pathfinders and help guides and document delivery services.[85] These services provide increased visibility for the library and convenient access for both students and faculty. Librarians should provide customized, needs-based guides for each class in a CMS. As librarians build a valuable presence in distance learning classes, they should also seek involvement at the institutional level in order legitimize the library's role.[86]

Shank and Dewald explain that collaborating with faculty to develop course assignments that incorporate the library's resources will generate more use of the resources and tools the librarians develop for a course.[87] Additionally, the library materials should be provided in the Course Management System to coincide with times the students are working on their research.[88] To offer research assistance to distance education students, Shank & Dewald recommend embedding multiple avenues for contacting a librarian including: email links, phone numbers, or chat reference widgets within the course research guides.[89] George & Martin also offer guidelines for collaborating with faculty who are eager to embed library materials in a course page on a CMS: "...discuss details of research assignments, the type of library instruction that would best suit the class and how they can be integrated into the CMS".[90] As always, it is important to remember that the class assignments should define the role of library instruction in the course.

It is also important to note that many faculty who teach on-campus classes with a standard lecture format also use a Course Management System to organize various aspects of their classes. Since faculty who use a CMS are already inclined to use technology to provide their students with course materials, librarians should seek out these faculty and find out how the library can support them with an embedded presence in the CMS. Emily Daly, a librarian at Duke University, explains how to personalize an embedded library presence in a CMS.[91] She suggests adding the librarian contact info, social bookmarking, and help for citing sources.[92] She also recommends looking at course assignments and syllabi that are viewable in the CMS

to identify faculty who may benefit from a library presence in their class.[93] Posting resources and providing answers to research questions on discussion boards in a CMS is a method some librarians have experimented with to provide more specialized research assistance to students. Participating in class discussions can also allow a librarian to pose important critical thinking questions to students about their research for an assignment. Jacqueline Corinth conducted both an in person instruction session, and offered her input on weekly class discussions facilitated by the instructor in the CMS.[94] In another case, Ann Schroeder explains that an introduction by the faculty member helped explain to students her role in the class and made students feel more comfortable asking Schroeder questions about research.[95] Schroeder notes that participating in multiple class discussions helped her answer common reference questions more quickly.[96] Schroeder states that having discussion boards can save the librarian time because students can view others questions and get help if they have a similar type of question.[97]

Embedding in virtual environments is an area where librarians are experimenting and developing best practices, but moving forward there are several ways to improve an embedded presence. If it is a priority to reach out to distance education students, partner with the faculty on an individual and system-wide level. Also be sure any assistance or materials provided are needs based. Meanwhile, students may be able to better identify with the library if the librarian finds ways to immerse themselves in the class, whether through participating in class discussion or evaluating students assignments.

Conclusion

Librarians have adapted their practice of embedded librarianship as users have changed the way they access and use research. Despite changes in the way embedded librarianship is practiced, the main characteristics of embedded librarianship remain constant. As I close the chapter, I will review how and why librarians practiced embedded librarianship, and mention some future directions.

Embedded Librarians Collaborate with their Users

Librarians providing collaborative embedded services often participate in the following activities: finding resources to support a faculty member's research area, or designing assignments with faculty to include information literacy and library resources. Librarians can more easily collaborate with faculty if they are physically located near their workspace, have a background in a related discipline, and are familiar with that discipline's research needs and habits. Collaborating with faculty can help build relationships with a department, which may lead to important political and fiscal support for the library. In the future librarians may look for ways to collaborate with PhD. students on research. Building relationships with PhD. students will help them better understand the services librarians provide as they become future faculty members.

Form Partnerships on the Department and Campus Level

Embedding information literacy and research resources into class assignments is the most common way librarians have partnered with academic departments. Working with faculty to develop a structured presence in the curriculum can ensure that students are aware of the library and its resources. Since it would not be possible at many institutions to have individual instruction for all students, building partnerships to promote library instruction can help the students avoid overlooking the library as a resource. Similarly, partnering with departments to support embedded librarians in faculty workspace can help librarians promote their research skills and knowledge of the discipline by providing faculty with specialized research assistance. In the future, academic libraries may want to partner with campus Information

Technology departments. Partnering with IT departments could aid the delivery of content and services in new and innovative methods, which many students expect since they are early adopters of emerging technologies.

Provide Needs Based Services

Librarians need to find out how users prefer to access our resources and services. If librarians are not curious or interested in trying innovative ways to provide services and resources that match user preferences, they risk not being useful to those who may need assistance. Librarians could explore other innovative ways to provide assistance. Since students are often early adopters of technology, perhaps librarians will experiment with methods to provide new reference services as they have done with text messaging.

Offer Convenient/User-friendly Services Outside of Library Settings

Many librarians still work from an office in the library, but those who have moved to an academic department have found that faculty in the department appreciate the convenience of having a librarian easily accessible. Librarians may want to be available to faculty since engaging in projects with faculty helps librarians best utilize their subject knowledge. Faculty members can also help librarians more easily reach out to students. Librarians can explore more ways to reach out to students through the mobile computing environment.

Become Immersed in the Culture and Spaces of our Users

Librarians have participated in several activities where they are immersed in the culture of the customers including: having an office in an academic department, embedding resources in a CMS, or participating in an off campus class. Finding ways to immerse the library in the culture of the users helps the library become more visible, and can decrease unfamiliarity with the services it can provide. For instance, a librarian may attend a major conference with a faculty member from a discipline they serve.

Understand the Discipline including the Culture and Research Habits of their Users

Librarians may be involved with the research of faculty through finding articles to supplement their research, or coauthoring articles with faculty members. Some librarians may even publish regularly in the disciplines they serve. To learn more about the culture of an academic discipline it might be helpful to become involved in the professional organizations of a discipline. Librarians may continue their education in the discipline by taking a class or reading important works in the field to stay current on research trends. Librarians could also attend the presentation of an invited speaker hosted by an academic department.

The cases described in this chapter are just a few of many examples of embedded librarianship throughout the profession; please see the Resources section at the end of the book for more articles on embedded librarianship.

Notes

1. Shumaker, D., & Talley, M. (2009). *Models of Embedded Librarianship Final Report* Special Libraries Association. http://www.sla.org/pdfs/EmbeddedLibrarianshipFinalRptRev.pdf : 9.
2. Shumaker & Talley, *Models of Embedded Librarianship*, 6.
3. Ibid., 8.
4. Ibid. 6.
5. Cimpl, K. "Clinical Medical Librarianship: A Review of the Literature." *Bulletin of the Medical Library Association* 73, no. 1 (1985): 21.
6. Ibid.
7. Davidoff, Frank and Valerie Florance. "The Informationist: A New Health Profession?" *Annals of Internal Medicine* 132, no. 12 (06/20, 2000): 996.
8. Cimpl, "Clinical Medical Librarianship," 21.
9. Ibid., 24.
10. Ibid., 26.
11. Ibid., 27.
12. Ibid.
13. Ibid., 26.
14. Davidoff & Florance, "The Informationist," 997.
15. Ibid., 997.
16. Ibid., 998.
17. Freiburger, Gary. "Embedded Librarians: One library's Model for Decentralized Service." *Journal of the Medical Library Association* 97, no. 2 (2009)
18. Freiburger & Kramer, "Embedded Librarians," 140.
19. Ibid.
20. Ibid.
21. Ibid., 141.
22. Ibid.
23. Ibid., 140.
24. Ibid.
25. Callison, R., D. Budny, and K. Thomes. "Library Research Project for First-Year Engineering Students: Results from Collaboration by Teaching and Library Faculty." *The Reference Librarian* 43, no. 89 (2005): 93–106.
26. Callison, Budny & Thomes, "Library Research Project," 94.
27. Ibid., 95.
28. Ibid.
29. Ibid., 96.
30. Ibid.
31. Ibid., 98.
32. Ibid., 99.
33. Ibid.

34. Ibid.
35. Ibid., 100.
36. Ibid.
37. Ibid.
38. Ibid.
39. Ibid., 101.
40. Ibid.
41. Ibid.
42. Hall, R. A. "The 'embedded' Librarian in a Freshman Speech Class." *College & Research Libraries News* 69, no. 1 (2008): 28.
43. Dugan, M. "Embedded Librarians in an Ag Econ Class: Transcending the Traditional." *Journal of Agricultural & Food Information* 9, no. 4 (2008): 301–309.
44. Hall, "The 'embedded' Librarian," 28.
45. Ibid., 29.
46. Ibid.
47. Ibid.
48. Ibid.
49. Ibid.
50. Ibid.
51. Ibid., 30.
52. Ibid.
53. Ibid., 29.
54. Ibid., 30.
55. Duggan, "Embedded Librarians in an Ag Econ Class," 306.
56. Ibid., 305.
57. Ibid., 304.
58. Ibid., 306.
59. Ibid., 305.
60. Ibid.
61. Ibid., 306.
62. Ibid.
63. Ibid.
64. Ibid., 307.
65. Ibid.
66. Ibid.
67. Ibid.
68. Hearn, Michael R. "Embedding a Librarian in the Classroom: An Intensive Information Literacy Model." *Reference Services Review* 33, no. 2 (2005): 219
69. Hearn, "Embedding a Librarian in the Classroom," 220.
70. Ibid.
71. Ibid., 221.
72. Ibid.
73. Ibid., 224.
74. Ibid.
75. Ibid., 225.
76. Ibid.
77. Ibid.
78. Ibid.
79. Ibid., 226.
80. Kinnie, J. "The Embedded Librarian: Bringing Library Services to Distance Learners."2006.
81. Kinnie, "The Embedded Librarian," 1.
82. Ibid.
83. Ibid., 2.
84. Shank, John D. and Nancy H. Dewald. "Establishing Our Presence in Courseware: Adding Library Services to the Virtual Classroom." *Information Technology and Libraries* 22, no. 1 (2003): 38–43.
85. Ibid., 38.
86. Kinnie, "The Embedded Librarian," 4.
87. Shank & Dewald, "Establishing Our Presence," 41.
88. Shank & Dewald, "Establishing Our Presence," 42.
89. Ibid., 41–42.

90. George, J. and K. Martin. "Forging the Library Courseware Link: Providing Library Support to Students in an Online Classroom Environment." *College & Research Libraries News* 65, no. 10 (2004): 596.

91. Daly, E. "Embedding Library Resources into Learning Management Systems." *College & Research Libraries News* 71, no. 4 (2010): 208.

92. Daly, "Embedding Library Resources," 209.

93. Ibid., 209.

94. Corinth, Jacqueline. "The Lurking Librarian Project." *Academic Exchange Quarterly* 7, no. 1 (Spring 2003): 278–281.

95. Matthew, Victoria and Ann Schroeder. "The Embedded Librarian Program." *Educause Quarterly* 29, no. 4 (2006): 61.

96. Matthew, Victoria and Schroeder, "The Embedded Librarian Program," 62.

97. Ibid.

 TWO

Beyond Instruction: Creating New Roles for Embedded Librarians

David Shumaker

Introduction

The revolution is well underway. The role of librarians in the instructional process in American higher education is changing dramatically, and for the better. Librarians are transcending the old model of one-shot library orientation and bibliographic instruction programs. They are establishing an ongoing presence in the classroom—be it real or virtual. They are delivering instructional services directly related to course content and directly supporting student learning objectives.

There is an extensive body of literature that documents the growth and success of these embedded library instruction programs. There has been a proliferation of conference papers, journal articles, blog postings, website listings, and all manner of discussion on the topic of embedded librarianship. Surely this growth demonstrates expanding interest and widespread implementation of these services. It shows that they are being tried, tested, and proven successful. These services are pointing the way forward for academic librarians seeking to redefine their role in the world of anytime, anywhere digital scholarly information.

So, can we say, "mission accomplished"? Can we say that the role and value of embedded academic library services have been established? Well, maybe not. In fact, research into the practice of embedded

librarianship indicates that there's much more work for academic librarians still to do. Embedded library services have not achieved their full potential in colleges and universities. The task of developing the embedded librarian's role is not finished.

In this chapter, we will explore the nature of this unfinished business, and define new approaches and new roles that are waiting to be seized by academic librarians. We will review the state of practice of embedded library services in higher education and contrast it with embedded services in other professional settings, presenting a summary of results from a recent research study and a survey of the literature. We will identify the practices, roles, and functions that some embedded librarians are adopting that go beyond embedded instruction on demand. We will discuss the outlook for higher education, and the reasons why academic librarians will need to take on some of these practices, roles, and functions as well. Finally, we will offer suggestions to those seeking to initiate or strengthen embedded library service programs.

How Academic Embedded Services Are Different: Recent Research Results

During 2008 and 2009, my co-investigator Mary Talley and I conducted an extensive multi-modal research project on embedded librarianship, sponsored by the Special Libraries Association.[1] Our primary research goal was to identify factors that contribute to the success of embedded library services programs. We hoped to offer suggested practices to librarians who want to initiate or strengthen their embedded services. However, along the way we collected a considerable amount of information about embedded librarianship as practiced in different segments of the profession.

Our results show that embedded librarianship in higher education differs significantly from embedded librarianship in for-profit, nonprofit, and government settings. Although embedded services are more prevalent in academe, the range of services is narrower. Academic embedded services are heavily concentrated on instruction, while in other sectors librarians deliver a broader range of research and content management services. Further, the nature of collaborative relationships with non-librarian groups appears weaker in academe than in other sectors. These differences suggest both an opportunity and a threat for academic librarians.

The research project included two surveys, the first of which was intended to identify embedded librarians and gather basic information about the services they provide. Invitations to participate were sent to a randomly selected sample of 3,000 members of the Special Libraries Association, and 1,001 responded, for a response rate of 33%. Of the 1,001, 961 were currently employed. Of that number, 19% were employed in academic libraries.

Academic librarians were found to be more likely than librarians in other types of organizations and industries to provide embedded services. We asked librarians who were directly responsible for delivering library and information services whether they provided specialized services to specific customer groups. Twenty-eight percent (28%) of those answering yes were academic librarians—a proportion significantly higher than their representation in the overall sample. Analyzed another way, 61% of academic librarians responding reported being embedded, in the sense of providing

specialized services, versus 35% of academic librarians who said they were not. (Four percent weren't sure.) While many librarians in several other sectors also reported providing specialized services, a Chi-square test for association between variables found a significant relationship between providing specialized services and type of organization ($p < 0.0001$).

In our second survey, we explored the types of services delivered by embedded librarians in various types of library and information service settings. We asked about three broad categories of services:

- Reference, research, and resource development services—including in-depth topical research; current awareness or news alerting; evaluating, synthesizing, and summarizing the literature; evaluating resources; and negotiating with vendors
- Technology-related services—including content management for web, intranet and wiki sites
- Training and educational services

Across all library types, it was found that reference, research, and resource development services were most commonly provided, training and educational services next most common, and technology-related services least common. These patterns were consistent—with one significant exception. Embedded librarians in higher education were much more heavily involved in training and educational services than librarians in other sectors, and less involved in providing other services.

Over eighty percent (80.5%) of academic librarians stated that they "Provided training on information resources or information management tools away from library facilities, such as in customer's office, a conference room, or classroom." This percentage contrasts with proportions between 50% and 65% for for-profit, nonprofit, and government sector librarians. The difference was found statistically significant at levels of $p < .01$.

We found other significant differences between the types of services provided by academic librarians and others. Embedded academic librarians were less likely to provide reference, research, and information management services than others. They reported providing all of the following services less often than their counterparts in for-profit, nonprofit, and government organizations (all statistically significant; p values as noted):

- Interlibrary loan / document delivery (p=0.0167)
- Evaluating, synthesizing, and summarizing the literature (p=0.0005)
- Current awareness, news alerting (p=0.0254)
- Competitive intelligence (p=0.0000)
- Data analysis, such as trends, industry research (p=0.0000)
- Structured database development and/or management (p=0.0016)
- Computer and/or network systems management (p=0.0277)
- Information architecture (p=0.0467)
- Document repository management (p=0.0000)

Clearly, according to this research, embedded academic librarians are focused very heavily on their instructional role. The implications of this difference will be discussed in detail below.

In the initial survey, we also asked about activities that would help establish relationships, develop collaboration, and ensure that the librarian's work was well aligned with the needs of the customer group. A significant finding was that academic librarians seem less likely to participate in the kinds of activities that strengthen their relationships with non-librarian colleagues, and provide opportunities to improve their responsiveness to those colleagues' needs. We asked respondents whether they had engaged in any of ten activities related to both task-oriented and social communication and interaction.

Academic librarians reported engaging in four of the ten less often than members of other organizational sectors. All differences were statistically significant (p values as noted):

- Met with a customer manager to review my performance (Academic less likely than For-profit (p=0.0020); Academic less likely than Not for profit (p=0.0074))
- Met with senior members of your customer group to discuss information-related needs and services (Academic less likely than For-profit (p = 0.0287); Academic less likely than Not-for-profit (p = 0.0131))
- Attended your customer group(s)' meetings to learn about their work and information needs (Academic less likely than Government (p = 0.0271); Academic less likely than For-profit (p = 0.0006))
- Collaborated on or contributed to your customer group's work (Academic less likely than Government (p = 0.0024); Academic less likely than For-profit (p = 0.0000); Academic less likely than Not-for-profit (p = 0.0034)

The presence or absence of these behaviors does not directly characterize the strength of the relationships or the responsiveness of the services, of course. However, we speculate that these kinds of activities would tend to occur more commonly in strong collaborative relationships, and that they would tend to ensure that the librarian's contributions were well aligned with the needs of the customer group.

To sum up, the indications from this research project are that, while academic libraries have adopted an embedded model of delivering specialized services to a greater degree than corporate or government libraries:

1. Academic embedded librarians are much more heavily focused on instructional services than other embedded librarians are—and therefore may be missing opportunities to deliver other valuable

contributions to the academic community, and

2. Academic embedded librarians are not building their relationships with customer groups (such as the leaders and faculty of academic departments) as actively as other embedded librarians—and therefore may be less well integrated and aligned with those groups' activities and needs than they could be.

Embedded Library Services: Examples from the Literature

Examples from the recent professional literature confirm the research findings. Published descriptions of embedded services delivered by embedded librarians in higher education predominantly discuss information literacy instruction, while descriptions from other sectors present a range of research and content management services as well as instruction. In harmony with the teaching mission of the university and the longstanding instructional orientation of academic library reference services, academic librarians have focused on replacing in-library orientations and bibliographic instruction presentations. They have substituted visits to class meetings, and sometimes even regular attendance at classes. In doing this, they have embedded the library in the instructional process—but not in the academic enterprise as a whole.

A few examples will illustrate this emphasis. Ramsay and Kinnie discussed outreach initiatives to distance learning faculty in their 2006 article in Library Journal.[2] They applied the term "embedded" to their initiative to "reach out to distance learning faculty by offering library assistance to their students." Russell Hall applied the term "embedded" to his experiences as a regular participant in a first-year Speech and Communications course. He presented two information literacy lectures, contributed to class discussions, and counseled individual students on their research papers.[3] Other librarians, including Bozeman, Deitering, and

Ferrer-Vinent, have embedded guides, pathfinders, virtual reference services and tutorials into courseware both for distance education and as a supplementary resource for face to face classes.[4-6] They have also served as research consultants to student teams. Dugan provides a vivid example of the information literacy consultant role at the undergraduate level,[7] and Berdish and Seeman describe such services in a graduate professional school.[8] In Dugan's case, the librarian consulted with students doing market research for an Agricultural Economics course, while Berdish and Seeman work with MBA students. The level of students reaches even to the Ph.D. level, and the nature of collaboration to full co-teaching of courses. In an article illustrating both points, Garson and McGowan describe their collaboration in teaching a research methods seminar for Ph.D. students at the Harvard Graduate School of Education.[9]

In short, embedded instructional services have been developed and delivered for audiences of students at every level of higher education in both distance learning and traditional classroom settings. Where the terms "embed" or "embedded" are used, the embedding is generally occurring in the instructional process.

No matter the academic discipline involved or the level of student in the audience, the common thread of all these services is that information literacy instruction is delivered within the context of the course. Services are delivered at the information seeker's point of need, which may be a physical or virtual classroom. Just as important, services are customized to the information seeker's need. While initial lectures may present generic information literacy concepts, as in Hall's case, follow-up involvement ensures that the general principles are applied to the students' immediate, course-related tasks. Instructional services are not truly embedded if all the librarian does is take a generic bibliographic instruction presentation that used to be delivered in the library, and deliver it in the English 101 classroom. It must be customized.

Examples from the literature of other sectors of librarianship discuss a much broader range of services. The special library sector uses the term "embedded" to encompass any situation in which a librarian establishes a close, ongoing working relationship with a group of information users, such as a law firm practice group, engineering project team, or medical specialty group. Recent research and examples from the literature provide many examples of the roles and value that librarians deliver. Here are three examples that illustrate the diverse professional contributions of embedded librarians.

Writing in 2006, Moore describes his embedded role in the MITRE Corporation.[10] Hired by the MITRE library in 2002, he was assigned to manage a special collection of technical materials on the discipline of systems engineering, used primarily by the staff of the corporation's Systems Engineering Process Office (SEPO). His position was funded by the SEPO, but managed by the library management. Moore reports that initial progress was slow, as he had only two designated contacts in the SEPO staff and struggled to learn enough about systems engineering to manage the collection effectively.

Then everything changed. He says his office, formerly in the library, was "relocated to an office on the same hall with the SEPO team, and things changed quickly." He continues:

> Once I was co-located with SEPO, I met the rest of the 15-person team. I was invited to their meetings. I saw how my work related to their ongoing activities. I began to participate in conversations about how the library is organized and managed. People dropping in with a quick question became a common occurrence, and overhearing (and being brought into) discussions about upcoming projects became part of my day. Over time, I gained opportunities to expand my role.[11]

Moore continues by summarizing the varied roles he took on and contributions that he made to SEPO's work. They include:

- Stewarding digital content; tagging and linking digital information resources
- Delivering customized news alerts on systems engineering topics
- Serving as rapporteur at technical meetings to record and make accessible the essence of the knowledge shared by the participants[12]

Jill Stover Heinze describes the evolution of her role in a for-profit corporation.[13] Hired initially as a competitive intelligence researcher to support the Marketing Department, she felt somewhat disconnected from her customers until the company president asked her to move her office into the office area of the Brand Communications group. Her new physical proximity to this key group gave her opportunities to participate in their work and new insights into what they needed from her. Her functional role continued to be news alerting and carrying out research and analysis projects, but her effectiveness was heightened because of her increased understanding of the organization's information needs. She also found herself brought into meetings on corporate strategy, and helping to make decisions on marketing tasks. Not coincidentally, her own promotional materials benefited as her new colleagues in Brand Communications gave her brand a makeover.

A third case study comes from an international law firm. The Chief Library and Records Officer of the firm described embedded services at his firm in an interview reported by Shumaker and Talley.[14] The firm has a network of embedded and centralized library and information services. Four types of embedded services are provided:

- Knowledge Management Analysts. These Analyst librarians work collaboratively with Knowledge Management Attorneys to provide knowledge management services to legal practice groups.

- Global Services Librarians. These librarians "focus on marketing and competitive intelligence research and analysis" worldwide, working with the firm's business development department and senior executives.
- Merger and Acquisitions Virtual Team. These librarians, who are neither co-located with one another nor with attorneys in the firm's mergers and acquisitions practice, are on-call specialists in research related to mergers and acquisitions projects.
- Company Representation Practice Embedded Services librarians. These librarians serve as web content stewards and managers. They post highly relevant and timely information on access-controlled internal websites, tracking corporate regulatory activities. Their work is closely coordinated with designated attorneys who are specialists in the companies and industries they track.

Embedded services in this organization thus encompass a variety of research and content management roles and functions, but little if any instructional involvement. The Chief Library and Records Officer fosters the program through participation in senior-level meetings and programs, and strong ongoing relationships with the firm's executives. Individual librarians in turn are responsible for developing and maintaining collaborative relationships once they are given an embedded role. A typical model is that employees are hired into the centralized library service and later promoted into an embedded position after they have gained experience and knowledge of the firm's work and personnel. At this firm, embedded positions depend little on physical co-location; distance and virtual collaboration are the norm.

Finally, no survey of embedded librarianship would be complete without a discussion of embedded librarians in health sciences and medical facilities. It may be said that the medical library community originated the embedded service model—though the word "embedded" has rarely been used in the medical library literature. The term "clinical librarianship" has been employed to describe service initiatives dating to the 1970s, when Gertrude Lamb, a medical librarian, decided to "move medical reference librarians out of the stacks and onto clinical services."[15] Davidoff and Florance proposed the title "Informationist" for these information specialists who, according to their vision, would "become a part of [embedded in] almost every clinical staff and service."[16]

The initial and primary role of such clinical medical librarians or informationists was to provide expert literature research and analysis to the doctors, nurses and other medical professionals responsible for patient treatment and care. However, the range of tasks has become quite broad. Rankin et al. reviewed the literature and noted a wide range of reference, research, analysis, technological, training, and educational roles of informationists in various settings. Among other things, they conclude that "an embedded informationist is more likely to achieve credibility, acceptance, and sustainability than an impersonal information service provided at a distance."[17] Shumaker and Talley interviewed an embedded librarian in an academic health sciences center whose responsibilities include:

- Web content management: Overseeing web content for a Genetics Institute website
- Knowledge management: inviting university faculty to affiliate with the Genetics Institute and organizing seminars and symposia
- Research consultation services, especially in the fields of molecular genetics and microbiology
- Embedded instruction and co-teaching for undergraduate Biophysical Chemistry and Genetics courses, a junior pre-med Honors program, and Ph.D. Bioinformatics course, among others

The history and development of embedded medical library services demonstrates the range and diversity of potential embedded services.[18]

Taken together, these examples contrast sharply with those from the academic sector and demonstrate the range of services that embedded librarians can deliver. But is it appropriate for academic librarians to engage in these other research and content management services? There are a few examples in the literature of academic librarians doing just that, suggesting that these activities may be untapped opportunities for others.

These examples are sometimes provided by "liaison librarians" or under other titles such as "field librarian." The embedded librarian should not be equated with the traditional liaison librarian, however. As Stoddart notes, "Traditionally, library outreach and liaison work have focused on collection development..."[19]

Using the term "field librarian", Johnson and Alexander describe a "close consultation" of the library management with three academic departments and schools at the University of Michigan. Their consultation resulted in a job description for librarians to engage in "traditional collection development, participation on library committees, reference service, and instructional initiatives," each focusing on the needs of single academic department. The field librarians are co-located with the departments they work with, and have developed differing emphases on instruction, research, or collection development work depending on the needs of the departments.[20]

Johnson and Alexander cite several precedents for their "field librarian" initiative.[21] Among them is the "College Librarian" program of Virginia Tech, which has been described by Seamans and Metz.[22] As at Michigan, Virginia Tech College Librarians are not only assigned to specific academic units, but also co-located with them. Their roles include:

- "reference librarian
- Instructor in library and information literacy skills

- Builder of library collections
- Web master for relevant library resources
- Colleague in the life of the college
- Provider of technical support ..."[23]

This list bears a strong resemblance to the list of embedded librarian roles found by Shumaker and Talley.

In one of the few articles to use the term "embedded" to encompass services other than instruction in an academic setting, Bartnik describes the dramatic changes in her relationship with the faculty and administration of the College of Business and Public Affairs at Murray State University following the move of her office from the library to the College.[24] She notes that her roles grew to encompass service and research involvement as well as embedded information literacy instruction. Soon after her move, she was assigned to participate in the re-accreditation work of the College. Of her involvement in research, she says that "I've been given research problems as a colleague that challenged me". She sums up her experience by saying that "I am now a strong advocate for embedded librarianship."[25]

Relationship Building: A Key Element of Embedded Services

We have seen that the literature and the research findings are consistent with regard to the range of services delivered by embedded librarians. Similarly, the literature also offers support for the research finding that academic librarians have paid less attention to the nature of their collaborative relationships with customer groups than librarians in other sectors.

In the non-academic reports cited in the previous section, relationships loom large. Moore cites the working relationships that developed after his office was co-located with the SEPO group.[26] Similarly, Heinze notes the opportunities for informal communication and collaboration that were created when her office was moved to the area of the Brand Communications Group.[27]

The Chief Library and Records Officer of the international law firm highlights the importance of his participation in senior level meetings where firm-wide operations are reviewed and strategy is decided. Through interactions at these meetings and the opportunities for relationship building that they afford, he is able to identify opportunities for librarians in his organization to take on important new assignments.

By contrast, most reports of academic embedded services, including those cited above, say little or nothing about the working relationships between subject faculty and librarians.

There are, however, some counterexamples that address relationship building. Owens describes a joint initiative of a librarian and a business writing instructor who obtained approval from a vice president and a dean to embed the librarian in the writing course. She emphasizes the importance of collaboration and the need for both parties to adjust their attitudes and thinking.[28] Hearn recounts the process by which the librarian and subject instructor collaborated in planning the course: "The faculty member and the librarian met to determine what facets of research were to be covered, how to effectively present the material and which resources should be used …"[29] Hearn further explains that this collaboration in instructional design led to an expanded role for the librarian in the evaluation of overall student progress.[30] At the end of her article describing the experiences of a librarian embedded in an agricultural economics course, Dugan recommends that the embedded librarian and the subject instructor meet before the beginning of the term to plan, and during the term to make mid-course adjustments.[31] Garson and McGowan have described in detail their collaborative approach to research methods instruction at the Ph.D. level.[32] Finally, Black et al. have devoted an article to their successful experiences in fostering collaboration between subject faculty and librarians to incorporate information literacy instruction in the curriculum.[33] They say that "Librarian-faculty collaboration … is fostered by the creation of strong interpersonal relationships between librarians and teaching faculty, and through both informal and formal faculty development sessions."[34]

In a survey of library outreach methods and initiatives, Rudin says that "The embedded approach often uses as its foundation the liaison model that already exists in many university settings whereby a particular subject specialist 'owns' the corresponding academic department."[35] She incorporates publicizing library resources and services, promoting information literacy in courses, and collection development in the job description of the embedded librarian. She identifies the Michigan "field librarian" and Virginia Tech "College Librarian" initiatives as examples of a "more intense version of the embedded model" in which the librarian metamorphoses from a visitor to the academic unit to "becoming a member of the family."[36]

These examples demonstrate that, while overshadowed by the emphasis on embedded information literacy instruction, there are successful models of embedded library services in higher education, in which librarians have developed close collaborative relationships and also extended their roles beyond instruction to encompass research collaboration and academic service.

There are those who are skeptical of the prospects for librarian-faculty relationship-building and collaboration. Badke avers that "…effective collaboration simply is not the norm."[37] He proposes that instead of collaborating with subject faculty to embed information literacy in existing courses, librarians develop and teach standalone information literacy courses attuned to various subject departments: an English information literacy course, one for History, Biology, and so on.[38] Without going into the many obstacles to such an approach—some of which Badke discusses—we conclude that the examples presented above, in conjunction with the research data showing the prevalence of collaborative behaviors in other sectors of librarianship, suggest that expanded faculty-librarian collaboration is within the reach of many academic librarians.

Calls for Change: The Future of Academic Library Reference Services

There is no shortage of leaders crying out for reform and new directions in academic library reference services. These calls seem to have increased markedly about the time that the Internet became available to society in general, and the first visionaries recognized the impact that digital information technologies would have on traditional library missions and methods. Writing in 1992, Campbell advocated replacing present-day Reference Librarians with "Access Engineers" who would "continue to be our predominant medium of contact with the public, but … will move beyond the current role of primarily answering questions and begin analyzing consumer information needs and desires."[39] David Lewis, recognizing the need for academic libraries to "find and articulate their roles in the current and future information ecology", proposes a five-point strategy.[40] Point 4 is, "Reposition library and information tools, resources, and expertise so that they are embedded into the teaching, learning, and research enterprises."[41] As he explains his strategy, Lewis goes on to state, "Libraries must preposition in-person interactions so that they are used to responding to the most complex and difficult problems. The aim should not be to replace in-person interactions and the relationship [sic] that are built through them, but rather to find ways to enhance them and to build stronger relationships."[42] Yet he concludes his discussion of this point by stating his uncertainty about what should replace our traditional concepts of the reference desk and reference services.[43]

McAdoo implicitly recognizes the need for improved collaboration between subject faculty and librarians.[44] He notes that when providing passive reference services—answering questions at the reference desk—librarians are often required to "interpret an assignment in order to bridge the gap between student and instructor expectations."[45] In these situations, the librarians are handicapped by the fact that they are not familiar with the assignment; they have not been involved in developing it and do not know its relationship to course activities and objectives. McAdoo says that librarians can improve not only their own success but the success of students and instructors by "working with the instructor to create more effective assignments."[46] He concludes by offering ideas on how to go about establishing collaborative relationships with faculty.[47]

Barbara Dewey has perhaps articulated the most comprehensive vision of the potential role of embedded librarians in higher education. In her 2004 article, "The Embedded Librarian: Strategic Campus Collaborations", she presents "the imperative for academic librarians to become embedded in the priorities of teaching, learning, and research in truly relevant ways."[48] She sees that librarians can indeed contribute to all aspects of the mission of higher education, and that the "most effective collaborations are multi-dimensional."[49] She recognizes the new demands that this type of collaboration places on librarians, and notes that to increase librarians' participation in research "requires a deeper level of embeddedness than casual contact."[50] She also suggests some means by which librarians can build the relationships required by their new roles. She advocates that librarians become actively involved in campus initiatives—which may not directly bear on the library—as a way of establishing professional credibility and strong working relationships with faculty and administrators. In closing, she sums up her vision by asserting that "The embedded librarian, who is truly integrated into the academic, administrative, athletic, cultural, research, teaching, and learning arenas of the university, provides quality and depth to the total campus experience."[51]

Dewey provides a succinct statement of the potential value of the embedded librarian, delivering uniquely valuable and highly customized information services that contribute to multiple core missions and goals of the educational enterprise.

Embedded Librarians and the Future of Higher Education

Some readers may still be wondering whether more academic librarians should emulate those at Murray State, Michigan, and Virginia Tech as well as their colleagues in corporate and health sciences organizations, and expand their conception of the embedded library services role. Another way to approach this question is to analyze the changes taking place in higher education, and to consider the opportunities and threats they may pose for librarians.

We've seen that so far, embedded services in academic librarianship are heavily concentrated on information literacy instruction. So what's wrong with that? After all, institutions of higher learning exist to teach, don't they? Well, not entirely. The German model of higher education, adapted by American society over the past century, articulates a three-part mission for the academy. This mission is commonly formulated as "Teaching, Research, and Service". Every junior faculty member knows that the path to tenure requires attention to all three. The professor aspiring to become tenured must demonstrate skill in teaching, the ability to conduct research that will gain the respect of academic peers and be published in prestigious peer reviewed journals, and the capacity for service: to the department, the university, the academic society.

The research mission of the university has grown in importance because of shifts in the business model and revenue stream of higher education. For example, Reyes has noted that the state of Arizona's direct funding of the University of Arizona declined from 36% of the university budget in 1997 to about 25% in 2004.[52] Recent economic conditions have not reversed this trend. As state budgets shrink and students resist perennial increases in tuition and fees, universities look to their research programs as revenue generators. Grants have become an important source of funds for salaries and assistantships. Institutions have opened Technology Transfer Offices to cash in on patents and other forms of intellectual property they own. For the individual tenure-track faculty member, the pressure to "publish or perish" often translates into a requirement to attract grants that help fund not only the individual's research, but the institution as a whole. Thus economic necessity, as well as the mutual reinforcement that occurs between teaching and research, have elevated the research mission in many institutions of higher learning. Yet the embedded library services model pays little if any attention to it.

The faculty's service mission, while not undergoing such dramatic change, is no less real. Faculty are expected to contribute to the operation of the university through committee service and sometimes quasi-administrative duties, to their discipline or profession by volunteering for leadership positions in associations, and often to society at large by contributing their expertise to socially valuable activities. These tasks are analogous to the managerial, promotional, and social responsibility functions of corporations. Whether we like it or not, universities are operating more and more like businesses. As Campbell notes, "higher education, in 1992 and today, remains one of the last multibillion dollar markets that has not been fully commercialized or commoditized."[53] The presumption is that academic institutions are and will be undergoing this change. Like businesses, they are affected by external pressures that they can't control: rapid technological changes, social changes, the rise of distance education leading to increased competition for available students, for-profit higher education. The managers of an institution in this complex, dynamic environment need sophisticated and effective information systems such as environmental scanning and competitive intelligence. These kinds of information services help them make sense of what's going on around them, and formulate their institutional strategies. In the academic environment, this need affords opportunities for librarians to collaborate with faculty and administrators in pursuit of these institutional goals.

In this context, it seems strange for academic librarians to focus exclusively on the teaching mission of the academy, and to concentrate solely on the delivery of embedded information literacy instruction. Librarians have unique skills in information management, delivery, and analysis that can contribute to the research mission and serve the business strategy of the higher education enterprise. Why would we not wish to explore the ways to align them with the needs of our academic communities in every way we can? Indeed, it is the thesis of this essay that academic librarians should be exploring ways to become active collaborators (not just to "serve" or "support") in the research and institutional strategy missions of their institutions. To do so will strengthen our role, add value, and if we are good at what we do, make an enormous difference. These new roles can become important elements of the future of academic librarianship—if we have the energy and vision to pursue them.

There is much debate about the future of academic libraries, just as there is much debate about the future of academe in general. Educause Quarterly has featured essays on the impact of information and communications technologies (ICTs) and distance education, and on the development of open access to course materials and scholarly publications. Lev Gonick, CIO at Case Western Reserve University, has said that "the learning enterprise for students is changing, most likely forever."[54] Meanwhile, researchers and academic administrators are finding equally fundamental shifts in the role of libraries. Housewright and Schonfeld have found a decline in faculty regard for what they call the "gateway role" of academic libraries.[55] They find a trend toward disintermediation—direct use of scholarly digital library resources and general search engines by faculty—and away from dependence on librarians for assistance in using traditional library resources.[56]

At the same time, shifts in the patterns of research activity suggest that the need for librarians' unique skills may be greater, not less, in the new research environment. Writing in the same issue of Educause Quarterly as Gonick, Deana Pennington, Research Associate Professor at the University of New Mexico, addresses problems in the increasingly common patterns of cross-disciplinary research.[57] She notes not only the diversity of disciplinary perspectives and backgrounds that researchers bring, but the diffuse nature of the literature they use.[58]

These changes in funding, technology, and style of work all dovetail well with the expansion of the embedded librarian's role in the academic enterprise.

How to Change: Success Indicators for Embedded Services

Shumaker and Talley identified practices that differentiated successful embedded library services (those that experienced growth) from others that were less successful, and did not experience growth.[59] In all, they found twenty-two attributes that differed significantly between successful and less successful programs ($p < 0.05$). They grouped these attributes into four themes:

1. Marketing and promotion
2. Service evaluation
3. Services provided
4. Management support[60]

Successful programs were more likely to engage in active marketing and promotion, especially taking advantage of word-of-mouth promotion; use of printed promotional materials such as brochures, fliers, or posters; and promotion through presentations at formal new-employee orientations. In the academic environment, the last of these could encompass both orientations for entering students, and presentations for new faculty. The presence of word of mouth promotion is interesting, because it typically occurs only as a result of successful performance and the development of a positive image and relationship.[61]

These programs were also more likely to engage in self-evaluation, and to communicate the results of their evaluations to decision-makers as justification for the continuation of embedded services. Seven distinct differentiators were identified at the p<0.05 level. The most significant of these were that financial outcomes, such as Return on Investment or cost avoidance, are measured; and that the Service metrics are used to justify the continuation of services. Other factors included the collection of anecdotes about the impact of services, and traditional statistics such as libraries often collect. Since most academic institutions are nonprofit entities and like other nonprofits place less emphasis on conventional financial measures, perhaps embedded librarians can substitute other measures of impact on institutional goals: contributions to improved learning outcomes, increased publication and impact factors of publications, or success in winning grants, for example.[62]

The research also found that successful embedded services delivered six services more commonly than less successful programs. All but one of these can be characterized as sophisticated contributions in which the librarian adds a great deal of value through specialized knowledge. They are: in-depth research, competitive intelligence, training that is held away from library facilities, shared instructional responsibility with subject faculty, and data analysis. Of these, two are included in the current focus of academic librarians on embedded information literacy instruction, while the others would come about as librarians participate in research and institutional service activities.[63]

The fourth and final differentiating factor is Management Support. Specific factors that were significant in this area include:

- Authorization from any level of management in the organization *was not* required prior to the initiation of specialized services
- A manager/leader of the customer group facilitated the integration of the service provider into the group

- The customer group contributes feedback to the librarian's performance review
- A written agreement exists between the customer group and the service provider group
- Authorization was required from the library/information group manager for the initiation of specialized services
- Continuing education related to the customer group's area of specialization is required of the embedded librarian[64]

Taken together, these factors suggest that a good working relationship and commitment of both library management and customer group management (i.e. academic deans or department heads) are associated with success. Embedded services that have been established solely based on the interest of a single faculty member and a single librarian may be more tenuous, because of the lack of senior customer support for their establishment and sustainment. Instead, the model that seems to be associated with success is that the customer manager and the library manager, acting autonomously, agree to support the embedded relationship. The agreement is documented (perhaps through an email exchange) and the commitment is visibly implemented by the customer manager helping to integrate the librarian into the group, and the library manager soliciting and using customer input on the librarian's performance.

Conclusion

Academic librarians have made great progress with embedded information literacy instruction, but there's more to be done. Both the nature of collaborative relationships with teaching faculty, and the range of services that librarians provide to their institutions can be improved.

Imagine, for example, an undergraduate curriculum in which certain courses are designated to have a strong information literacy component. Librarians who have strong teaching skills and a familiarity with the subject matter are assigned as co-instructors with subject faculty for these courses. Course goals developed in collaboration include learning outcomes related to information literacy as well as the subject domain. Librarian and subject faculty share instructional responsibilities and the task of evaluation student performance.

Imagine, further, that these collaborations lead to other collaborations. The subject faculty involve the embedded librarians in their research projects. The librarians join research teams, participate in grant-funded investigations, perhaps serve as co-principals on grants from time to time. What they contribute are their information services and information management skills, made valuable by their understanding of the research topic and their ability to provide information that is analyzed, focused, and highly relevant.

Some may say that these imaginings are unrealistic in the extreme—pipe dreams that librarians will never realize, and certainly not in these times of economic slowdown and reduced budgets. The answer to the naysayers is twofold. First: if information is as important as we say, and if information literacy is truly a critical skill for the Twenty-first Century, can we librarians afford to set anything less as our goal? And second: the research and the literature demonstrate that these visions can be achieved. There are librarians, within academe and in other sectors, who are achieving them.

The task of embedded librarians now is to follow these pioneers, learning from them and each other, to make these visions of a stronger embedded librarianship a reality in more and more academic institutions.

Notes

1. David Shumaker and Mary Talley, *Models of embedded librarianship: Final report.* Alexandria, VA: Special Libraries Association, 2009; William B. Badke, "Can't Get No Respect: Helping Faculty to Understand the Educational Power of Information Literacy," *The Reference Librarian* 89/90 (2005), 63–80.

2. Karen M. Ramsay and Jim Kinnie, "The Embedded Librarian," *Library Journal* 131, (2006), 34–5.

3. Russell A. Hall, "The 'Embedded' Librarian in a Freshman Speech Class: Information Literacy Instruction in Action," *College & Research Libraries News* 69, (2008), 28–30.

4. Dee Bozeman and Rachel Owens, "Providing Services to Online Students: Embedded librarians and Access to Resources," *Mississippi Libraries* 72 (2008), 57–9. ; Dee Bozeman, "Embedded librarian: Research Assistance Just in Time. Paper presented at 24th Annual Conference on Distance Teaching and Learning, Madison, WI, 2008.

5. Anne Marie Deitering and Sara Jameson, "Step By Step Through the Scholarly Conversation: A Collaborative Library/ Writing Faculty Project to Embed Information Literacy and Promote Critical Thinking in First-Year Composition at Oregon State University," *College & Undergraduate Libraries* 15, (2008), 57–79.

6. Ignacio J. Ferrer-Vinent and Christy A. Carello, "Embedded Library Instruction in a First-Year Biology Laboratory Course." *Science & Technology Libraries* 28, (2008), 325–51.

7. Mary Dugan, "Embedded Librarians in an Ag Econ Class: Transcending the Traditional," *Journal of Agricultural and Food Information* 9, (2008), 301.

8. Laura Berdish and Cory Seeman, "Spanning the Straits of Business Information: Kresge Library's Embedded Librarian Program for MAP (Multidisciplinary Action Program)," Paper presented at Special Libraries Association Annual Conference, 2008.

9. Deborah Garson and Elaine McGowan, "Co-Teaching: Why Two Heads are Better Than One," Paper presented at Special Libraries Association Annual Conference, Washington, D.C., 2009.

10. Michael F. Moore, "Embedded in Systems Engineering: How One Organization Makes it Work," *Information Outlook* 10, (2006), 23–5.

11. Ibid

12. Ibid

13. Jill Stover Heinze and Kimberly Kortash. "Navigating Through Turbulent Times: How the Corporate Special Library and Brand Communications Work Together to Forge a Path to the Future," Paper presented at Special Libraries Association Annual Conference, Washington, DC, 2009. http://www.sla.org/pdfs/sla2009/navigatingturbulenttimes_heinze.pdf.

14. Shumaker and Talley

15. Frank Davidoff and Valerie Florance, "The Informationist: A New Health Profession?," *Annals of Internal Medicine* 132 (2000), 996–8.

16. Ibid

17. Jocelyn A. Rankin, Suzanne F. Grefsheim, and Candace C. Canto. "The Emerging Informationist Specialty: A Systematic Review of the Literature," *Journal of the Medical Library Association* 96 (2008), 194–206.

18. Shumaker and Talley

19. Richard A. Stoddart, Thedis W. Bryant, Amia L. Baker, Adrienne Lee, and Brett Spencer, "Going Boldly Beyond the Reference Desk: Practical Advice and Learning Plans for New Reference Librarians Performing Liaison Work," *The Journal of Academic Librarianship* 32 (2006), 419–427.

20. Brenda L. Johnson and Laurie A. Alexander, "In the Field: An Innovative Role Puts Academic Librarians Right in the Departments they Serve," *Library Journal* 132 (1 February 2007), 86.

21. Ibid

22. Nancy H. Seamans and Paul Metz, "Virginia Tech's Innovative College Librarian Program," *College & Research Libraries* 63 (2002), 324–32.

23. Ibid

24. Linda Bartnik, "The Embedded Academic Librarian: The Subject Specialist Moves into the Discipline College," *Kentucky Libraries* 71 (2007), 4–9.

25. Ibid

26. Moore

27. Michael R. Hearn, "Embedding the Librarian in the Classroom: An Intensive Information Literacy Model," *Reference Services Review* 33 (2005), 219–27.

28. Rachel Owens, "Where the Students Are: The Embedded Librarian Project at Daytona Beach College," *Florida Libraries* 51 (2008), 8–10.

29. Hearn

30. Ibid

31. Dugan

32. Garson and McGowan

33. Christine Black, Sarah Crest, and Mary Volland, "Building a Successful Information Literacy Infrastructure on the Foundation of Librarian–Faculty Collaboration," *Research Strategies* 18 (2001), 215–25.

34. Ibid

35. Phyllis Rudin, "No Fixed Address: The Evolution of Outreach Library Services on University Campuses," *The Reference Librarian* 49 (2008), 55–75.

36. Ibid

37. Badke

38. Ibid

39. Jerry D. Campbell, "Shaking the Conceptual Foundations of Reference: A Perspective," *Reference Services Review* 20 (1992), 29.

40. David W. Lewis, "A Strategy for Academic Libraries in the First Quarter of the 21st Century," *College & Research Libraries News* 68 (2007), 418–34.

41. Ibid

42. Ibid

43. Ibid

44. Monty L. McAdoo, "Be the Bridge: Librarians Can Span the Gap Between Students and their Instructors," *American Libraries* 40 (2009), 38–40.

45. Ibid

46. Ibid

47. Ibid

48. Barbara Dewey, "The Embedded Librarian: Strategic Campus Collaborations. *Resource Sharing & Information Networks* 17 (2004), 5–17.

49. Ibid

50. Ibid

51. Ibid

52. Verónica Reyes, "The Future Role of Academic Librarians in Higher Education," *Libraries and the Academy* 6 (2006), 1–9.

53. Jerry D. Campbell, "Still Shaking the Conceptual Foundations of Reference: A Perspective," *Reference Librarian* 48 (2007), 21.

54. Lev Gonick, Lev, "Future of Higher Education," *Educause Quarterly* 33 (2010).

55. Ross Housewright and Roger Schonfeld. *Ithaka's 2006 Studies of Key Stakeholders in the Digital Transformation in Higher Education.* (New York: Ithaka, 2008).

56. Ibid

57. Deana Pennington, Deana, "Enabling Science and Technology Research Teams: A Breadmaking Metaphor. *Educause Quarterly* 33 (2010).

58. Ibid

59. Shumaker and Talley
60. Ibid
61. Ibid
62. Ibid
63. Ibid
64. Ibid

PART TWO
Embedding in the
First-Year Experience

 THREE

A Faculty Perspective: Strengthening At-Risk Students' Transition to Academic Research through Embedded Librarianship

Rick Fisher and April Heaney

For most students, the transition from high school to college is a huge leap. For at-risk students, the leap is even more challenging, requiring them to acquire a wide range of new skills, to reconsider old values, and to navigate a series of systems which are completely unfamiliar. In general, students are considered "at risk" if their likelihood of degree completion is statistically lower than other students. Factors which are associated with higher risk of departure include low entrance exam scores, low high-school GPA, and low-income, minority, and first-generation status. Additionally, males are statistically less likely than females to complete a college degree. In our experience teaching at-risk and provisionally-admitted students at the University of Wyoming (UW), we also find that many come from familial or cultural backgrounds where post secondary education was not well understood or valued. Importantly, national studies have shown that underprepared students struggle with reading and information literacy to a higher degree than other students, and the gap continues to widen as the students progress through secondary and post-secondary schooling.[1]

To improve the success of at-risk students at the college level, many schools have implemented creative first-year programs—especially learning community models—which support development of critical thinking, information literacy, and study skills during this important transitional period. Current research suggests that the most successful programs for at-risk students, including the University of Wyoming's Synergy Program, help these students navigate this transitional period by creating strong mentoring relationships between students and more experienced members of the academic culture (including peer mentors, supportive instructors, and guest visitors such as authors and community members). This approach seeks not only to develop students' *skills* but also to create relationships which model the *habits of mind* that can lead to college success. However, little of the research regarding student persistence has explored the ability of university librarians to positively impact campus retention of at-risk students. We argue in this chapter that embedded librarians offer a natural extension to current strategies, and we believe that university libraries can more strongly advocate for the value of embedded librarianship by aligning it with campus-wide retention goals.

This chapter is divided into five sections. First, we explain the underlying cultural attitudes and values that define many at-risk students' prior experiences. Then we briefly explain current best practices for at-risk populations and explain how embedded librarianship fits naturally within these practices. Third, we describe several examples of embedded librarianship with at-risk students from our home institution, the University of Wyoming. Fourth, we identify the key benefits that have emerged from these embedding efforts, and finally, we present tips to help other librarians and teaching faculty design embedment approaches that support the unique characteristics of at-risk students.

Part I. Below the Surface: The Less Visible Struggles of At-Risk Learners

There is no single "face" which accurately depicts all at-risk learners. The financially struggling student who finished high school with a low GPA because he worked long hours to help support his siblings falls into the at-risk category. So does the student who comes from a relatively affluent blue-collar family but is the first to go to college. So too is the oft-cited traditional slacker, the student who just had little motivation and engagement and slid through much of his high-school experience.

Beneath these surface differences, however, these students often share a lack of academic cultural capital for post-secondary success. While cultural capital is frequently associated with concrete learning experiences and exposure to knowledge, at-risk students may misunderstand or undervalue the type of *involvement* that facilitates entry into a new discourse community.[2] Alexander Astin defines student *involvement* as "the amount of physical and psychological energy that the student devotes to the academic experience:"[3]

A highly involved student is one who … devotes considerable energy to studying, spends much time on campus, participates actively in student organizations, and interacts frequently with faculty members and other students. Conversely, a typical uninvolved student neglects studies, spends little time on campus, abstains from extracurricular activities, and has in-

frequent contact with faculty members or other students.[4]

Most at-risk students, by this definition, might be categorized as "uninvolved." However, this characterization may ignore the underlying issue.

It's important not to over generalize here: we do not mean to suggest that students struggle only because they lack the habits of mind necessary for college success. Many students have difficulties in reading comprehension, mathematical skill, and in the ability to develop schema for structuring new information, and these challenges certainly factor into their persistence, too. But at-risk students often struggle not because they lack the abilities to succeed but because they lack experience with applying skills to unfamiliar tasks and texts within a new academic discourse.

At our university, for example, students coming from first-generation, blue-collar, or rural backgrounds may receive messages from their families and communities that are actively anti-intellectual. Alfred Lubrano, in *Limbo: Blue Collar Roots, White Collar Dreams*, describes students from these backgrounds as "Straddlers,"[5] and he suggests they enter post-secondary institutions with barriers to success, both in terms of skills and in terms of attitudes:

If you're from the middle-class, you do not feel out of place preparing for college. Parents and peers help groom you, encourage you, and delight in your progress. Of course, when you get to freshman year, the adjustments can be hard on anyone, middle-class and working-class kids alike. But imagine going through freshman orientation if your parents are ambivalent—or hostile—about your being there, and your friends aren't clear about what you're doing.[6]

This type of experience is reflected in comments from conditionally-admitted students at UW. In fall 2003, for example, one conditionally-admitted student commented on the conflicting messages he received from his parents about college: "My mom wanted me to go to college but now that I am away they want me to come back home. Growing up, my dad always taught that owning your own business was the ultimate success. He never had an education. My parents want to have me work in their business just like my dad."[7]

An additional issue, Lubrano points out, is that more traditional or conservative families often fear the changes that will happen to their children as they pursue higher education. For example, he says, acclaimed social critic bell hooks' parents

> worried when she went to Stanford University because they feared she would not hold onto their ways and beliefs. The proper life, hooks' parents believed, was centered on family and God, with the rare good day thrown in. There is value in the day-to-dayness of it, and little need for "fancy ideas." (59)

Elsewhere in his writing, Lubrano discusses attitudinal characteristics of families who don't promote a clear path to post-secondary education. In those families, says Lubrano, "where conformity is the norm, all opinions are dictated by group consensus. … There's one way to do everything, one way to look at the world. Since all opinions are shared, there's never a need to explain thought and behavior. You talk less. Language in such a home … is implicit."[8] This characterization provides a way of understanding a key difference between college-ready students and those who struggle in their first years of school: the language of students who come from non-academic families is often more concrete, more focused on immediate concerns, more binary, and more practical than the language of students who come from backgrounds where collaborative, deliberative, abstract language is modeled.

As a result of this difference, at-risk students enter college with skills and knowledge that may have served them well in other settings but which leave them unready for the evidence-based thinking that is a hallmark of the academy. In particular, James Gee, Glynda Hull, and Colin Lankshear argue that the previous experiences of such students may actually lead teachers to perceive these students as "illiterate" by university standards. For Gee, Hull, and Lankshear, literacy is "*understanding* a particular *type of text* in a *certain way*,"[9] and they argue that such literacy is socially and culturally embedded:

> A way of reading a certain type of text is acquired *only* when it is acquired in a 'fluent' or 'native-like' way, by one's being embedded in (apprenticed as a member of) a *social practice* wherein people not only *read* texts of this type in this way but also *talk* about such texts in certain ways, *hold certain attitudes and values* about them, and *socially interact* over them in certain ways. (3, emphasis in original)

Until students understand the "native" view of academic discourse, they are likely to regard schoolwork with suspicion, and to regard the curriculum of college as an irrelevant exercise in bureaucracy.

Additionally, as Gee, Hull, and Lankshear stress, texts can be read differently by different groups. Their extended example is worth repeating:

> Consider the following sentences from a brief story in which a man named Gregory has wronged his former girlfriend Abigail: "Heartsick and dejected, Abigail turned to Slug with her tale of woe. Slug, feeling compassion for Abigail, sought out Gregory and beat him brutally."

In one study … some readers, who happened to be African-Americans, claimed that these sentences "say" that Abigail told Slug to beat up Gregory. On the other hand, other readers, who happened not to be African-Americans, claimed that these sentences "say" no such thing. These readers subsequently claimed, in fact, that the African-Americans had *misread* the sentences. The African-Americans responded: "If you turn to someone with a tale of woe and, in particular, someone named 'Slug,' you are most certainly asking him to *do* something in the way of violence and you are most certainly responsible when he's done it."[10]

In other words, reading is "a *plural* notion… and we can dispute how the sentences ought to be read (and we can ask *who* determines the "ought" and why)."[11] In the case of at-risk college students, their home literacies may lead them into ways of thinking and encountering texts that are deemed as "misreading" by the academic community. The first-year transition for these students (and indeed for many other students) is as much about adopting new ways of thinking as it is about learning new information. And, as Gee, Hull, and Lankshear point out, becoming fluent in those new discourses requires engagement in "native-like" ways—opportunities to see members of those discourses talk about and socially interact in ways that are accepted by the academic culture.

Part II. A Natural Extension: The Potential Role of Embedded Librarians

Based on studies of at-risk learner characteristics, a broad variety of strategies have been implemented at the post-secondary level. Many of those efforts have focused on helping students not only develop *skills* for college success but also *experiences* and *attitudes* that can help them feel more comfortable interacting with and ultimately imitating native members of the academic learning culture. Nationwide, several programs aimed at supporting conditionally admitted students have implemented learning communities centered on college reading, writing, and research. Some of the most well-known models include the University of Alabama at Birmingham's "University 101," Trinity University's "Future Focus," San Francisco State's "Literacy Unleashed" program, and the University of Wyoming's Synergy Program. In addition to increased training for instructors, these programs provide support for at-risk students in reading and research tasks through multiple courses. UW's Synergy Program, for example, offers three linked courses that highlight information literacy within traditional first-year courses including composition, public speaking, and a research-based first-year seminar.

Perhaps more importantly, however, all of these models employ heavy mentorship and relationship-building within the learning community. Peer mentors, faculty mentors (fostered through smaller class sizes and increased conferencing), and advising mentors often work together to assess students' progress and offer meaningful help when students face problems. Rather than assuming that underprepared students will be motivated by straight achievement or future-focused success, these connections build on the values that many first-generation and low-income students bring with them to college., For example, students from homes that lack academic cultural capital often possess an element of working class culture which privileges group consensus and loyalty to community much more than they value individual achievement.[12]

While our society, in general, holds ambition in high esteem, a community-focused mindset which downplays individual status brings powerful advantages of its own. In a nationally funded research study of three flagship universities, Hurtado et al. report that students who achieved the highest scores on tests were "significantly less likely to see the world from someone else's perspective," and concluded that "high test scores do not translate into more complex thinking needed for participation in a diverse democracy."[13] On the other hand, instructors in the Synergy Program report that at-risk students excel at the kind of complex and empathetic thinking that develops effectively when individuals are less concerned with modeling dominant mores and mindsets.

Characteristics of at-risk learners, therefore, are often more suited for support practices that prioritize relationships and minimize incentives that are connected solely to grades or long-term career/educational rewards. While there is a need for more research on the influence of mentoring on at-risk college students, several studies show significant gains in academic success and retention where peer or faculty mentoring is a key ingredient in the support system.[14] Rather than entering a new discourse through the incentives of individual success or future status, a relationship-based model allows students to establish comfort with new academic discourse on a personal level—and feel invested in new modes of thinking or learning largely because of the relationships that form around this discourse.

Given the positive impact of mentoring on at-risk students, it is not surprising that recent studies on information literacy instruction offer compelling evidence that a team-taught model of librarian embedment leads to significant gain in at-risk student mastery of IL skills.[15] In a team-taught model, students are able to form a bond with the librarian and interact with the same person throughout a unit or module. When underprepared students perceive the librarian as both "expert" and "member of the community," their investment in learning increases. In one example from the University of Northern Colorado, the composition program piloted a team-taught model of information literacy within a first-year composition course for at-risk students. The results of a pre- and post-tests and analysis of students' annotated bibliographies

revealed significant gains in student performance and ability to select resources based on relevance when compared to previous classes.[16]

While the most popular embedment models involve librarians as co-designers of outcomes or assignments,[17] these models can fall short of fostering an authentic mentorship between librarians and students most at-risk of failure or departure from the university. It is important for students to see the mentoring model carried over into their information literacy unit through meaningful connections with librarians beyond the one-time visit. Because underprepared students don't automatically value information literacy skills, and may in fact fear or resist altering their habits of mind regarding these skills, they require an approach that honors the affective and community-centered learning methods these students value.

Part III. Theory into Practice: Examples of Embedded Librarians within At-Risk Communities

At the University of Wyoming, instructors and library staff have pursued a number of embedded librarianship opportunities with at-risk populations that highlight a mentor-learner relationship. Primarily those strategies have been implemented within the Synergy Program, but other efforts have been located within other programs as well. In the next section, we discuss a selection of the approaches that have been used on our campus.

Approaches within the Synergy Program

Synergy's cohort-model includes four general education courses in the first year: first-year composition, U.S. and Wyoming government, introduction to public speaking, and a research-and-reading focused course titled "Critical Reflection in Intellectual Communities." With the exception of the government course, the learning community courses work together to integrate reading, writing, and academic research with the ultimate goal of helping students transfer (and reinforce) the skills in new contexts. Beginning in 2005, various instructors have worked with library staff to capitalize on the potential benefits of embedded librarianship with at-risk learners:

• Composition teachers in the Synergy Program have bolstered librarians' involvement in the course's final research unit. Typically, the embedding happens over three or four class days, usually including a day of relatively typical library instruction followed by two or three days of more intensive, one-on-one, in-class time with students. In some courses, several librarians have participated on the intensive research days. Also, in some courses a follow-up research day has also been included *later* in the unit, in order to promote the idea of research as iterative/recursive rather than as "stage one" of a linear process.

Within this model, a few other features are worth highlighting. First, students typically come into the initial library session with a research proposal already written. When possible, the teacher may have already commented on the proposal, helping raise additional questions that the student should consider exploring during the research phase. This step helps ensure that the student already knows many of his or her specific research questions. Second, it has been helpful for instructors to require some intermediate assignment(s) during this extended research time, in order to pull students along in the process. Otherwise, students may see several days in the library as repetition of the same activity rather than as progressive support through several research steps. Along with small assignments, it has also been useful to give each library day a clear objective/focus in order to minimize the impression that multiple research days are merely repetitive. For example, one three-day embedded librarianship collaboration was broken down to include short mini-lessons about locating information (day 1), evaluating and summarizing research (day 2), and citing research (day 3). Finally, a key value of this approach is that extended individual or small-group time allows li-

brarians to serve as representatives of the "research ethos"—that is, the task of librarians in these settings is not only to help students *find* information but also to help students think through *how* and *why* they should want to find this information. In this model, librarians can become important models talking through the academic thinking process.

• In addition to classroom-based embedding, at least one Synergy instructor has planned student conferences which embed a librarian into this part of the research process. As with in-class strategies, this type of approach can help students to see research as a dialogic process—about which there can be disagreement both about perspectives on a topic as well as about what counts as evidence. These conversations can take the form of collegial, collaborative building of new knowledge rather than "experts" talking to "novices." This approach—if used *after* initial research, can also help reinforce the notion of research as a recursive, ongoing process. Students are often impressed to discover how quickly they can retrieve relevant material if they've been guided during conferences to develop specific follow-up research questions.

• As of 2010, the Synergy cohorts were not typically sharing assignments across courses, though teachers generally encourage students to apply research from one project towards assignments in other courses. However, the university libraries have begun coordinating "cross-course embedding," which assigns a single librarian to all courses within a Synergy cohort. This means that students will see the same librarian for all Synergy-related instruction throughout an entire year—an approach which strengthens the relationship between student and librarian. Additionally, since the librarian has a stronger sense of what students have learned in previous visits to the library, this approach also helps limit students' perception that each library visit is essentially covering the same ground.

Other Approaches at UW

In addition to the Synergy-based approaches discussed above, our local research also revealed two other institutional efforts which we felt recognized the special opportunities that embedded librarianship can provide to at-risk students:

• Student Success Services, a federally-funded program for first-generation, low-income, and minority students, incorporates a low-stakes, *reflective* visit to the library for first-year students, early in the fall semester. There is no research assignment directly related to this visit (though the visit does look ahead in a general way to other projects for other courses). This first visit is designed primarily to help students identify their assumptions and expectations about the purpose of library research. This approach both acknowledges that students may have apprehension about the research process as well as assumptions about library-based research which can be revised.

• Our university's Writing Center provides a drop-in workshop time for all students enrolled in the first-year composition course. During the final research unit of the course, reference librarians are available at the three-hour, once-a-week workshop time to answer student questions about the research process. Much of the success of this partnership has come during the topic-selection stage of research, when both librarians and writing consultants can work together to help students select interesting and appropriately narrow topics. Though this approach is not restricted to students considered "at-risk" by standard definitions, the drop-in workshop was developed based on concerns that freshmen students, in general, seem more hesitant to schedule time with support staff. We believe this hesitancy may come, in part, from generational trends as well as from a perception (based in part on secondary-school culture) that seeking help with schoolwork is a sign of weakness or inability.

These examples share a common thread: the role of the librarian is not only to serve as "information expert" but also as a "guide to academic literacy"—nearly all examples show the librarian taking on some kind of affective, mentoring role which helps to model the "talking about" and "social interacting with" that Gee, Hull, and Lankshear argue are so essential to successful adoption of new literacies. In these examples, the strategies often help librarians to move beyond an "outsider" role in order to help students see a more *unified* academic support structure. Library instruction becomes less about "inoculation" against information illiteracy (as one reference librarian termed it) and more about "initiation" into the community of academic discourse participants.

Part IV. Benefits for At-Risk Students

To date, neither instructors nor librarians at UW have undertaken extensive assessments of the impact of embedded librarianship on at-risk populations. However, several of the practitioners at UW have continued to informally assess, revise, and share their practices. One instructor-librarian pairing collected student feedback about their seven-week embedded approach and compared student final research essays to those from previous classes. Additionally, a focus group of three librarians and three instructors provided feedback about specific benefits of the team-taught approaches they've developed. Finally, Synergy's extensive, ongoing programmatic assessments (first-year surveys, entry characteristic analysis, and focus groups) gather a variety of data which indirectly measure students' growing familiarity with academic research practices. Based on these assessments, we believe that the following benefits result from embedding librarians into courses for at-risk students:

• Greater willingness to ask questions about the research process. During one-shot instruction sessions, at-risk students, especially, often hesitate to ask questions of someone who is unfamiliar. As they begin to feel a closer connection to librarians, however, instructors report that the students become more willing to seek advice about moving forward with their research.

• More focused research topics. Greater interaction with librarians also brings opportunities for students to receive more feedback about what constitutes an appropriately narrow, sophisticated research topic. Even when instructors provide information about how to select research topics, many at-risk first-year students still see academic research primarily as an act of gathering information rather than assembling evidence in support of their own claim. Extended conversations with students to draw them to the conflict or disagreement of an issue can help them arrive at a clear, guiding research question. In turn, this level of focus typically promotes more advanced composition skills/strategies.

• Increase in follow-up consultations. Librarians report that students who have participated in embedded librarianship approaches are more likely to request individual follow-up consultations with subject-area librarians.

• Greater ownership of librarians, and an increased view of librarians as "teachers" and "consultants" rather than merely "visitors" to their courses. One former Synergy student, speaking at an end-of-year conference, identified the embedded librarian as one of his first-semester teachers, even though she was not officially responsible assessing his work. This perspective of librarians may suggest that students are beginning to associate their learning with effective guidance rather than only with the act of grading.

• Greater appreciation for necessity of research. By reinforcing the library as location for various stages of the writing/thinking process, embedded librarianship approaches help students to see evidence-gathering as a more natural step of all academic activity. In turn, this effort also seems to increase students' comfort level with the library in general; in Fall 2007 survey of Synergy students, for example, participants indicated that the library was one of the "most important places where I spend time outside of class" (third only to "Dorm room" or "Friend's room/house").

Part V. Implications for Embedment with At-Risk Populations

Given the potential of embedded librarianship efforts to increase student retention, we believe that universities committed to open access should count librarians as natural allies in achieving this goal. Not only can guided research opportunities lead to better learning, but they can also lead to students who more fully understand the purposes and values of the academic culture. While we acknowledge the difficulties in developing scalable and effective embedded librarianship strategies, we believe that these encounters have the power to reverberate far beyond the individual classrooms in which they initially take place. We close this chapter with a number of considerations which we believe can help improve the acceptance and effectiveness of library collaborations with at-risk students.

1. Recognize the affective perceptions of at-risk students. Embedded librarianship, through closer connections between students and librarians, offers the opportunity to help students overcome fear and unfamiliarity about library-based research. Allowing time for students to explicitly voice their concerns, assumptions, and previous experience with library research may provide a way to strengthen the sense of a supportive learning environment, while also honoring the background experiences they bring with them to college.

2. Work with instructors during the planning stages of assignment design. If possible, promote inquiry-based projects, situated within a relevant student context, and promote assignments that develop contextualized issues which create the need for specific, genuine research. Since research indicates that at-risk students benefit from curricula perceived as relevant,[18] instructional design is a critical component to a successful information literacy assignments.

3. See the goal of information literacy instruction as process- rather than product-based. For students who don't have a clear understanding about *why* research is an integral part of academic

thinking and composing, it's important to help students see how research fits within a larger cultural context. Embedded librarianship can create opportunities to show research as dialogic, not merely black/white—and this shift in emphasis can show academic disciplines as sites of contested knowledge rather than only as repositories of accepted information.

4. Seek opportunities to embed within learning communities. The most challenging element of the team-taught/embedded model is the sustainability factor; given the time and effort required of both instructor and librarian, this model is often piloted with a subset of first-year students but rarely institutionalized. In addition, faculty frequently balk at giving up time to a more integrated IL unit involving team-teaching.[19] A learning community model offers perhaps the most effective and lasting platform for instituting an embedded librarian experience with at-risk college students.

5. Consider location. Depending on the extent of embedding and the level of technology available, it may make sense to bring the librarian into the classroom rather than bringing the students into the library. Classroom-based embedding can help reinforce the librarian as part of the learning community, in a space that is already comfortable. On the other hand, encouraging students to visit the library—both during and outside of class time— can help students expand their conceptions about appropriate learning spaces.

6. Build in assessment of the embedded librarianship component. Front-end discussions of objectives for the embedment can help ensure that assessment *will* take place. Evaluating student work, implementing pre- and post- surveys or exams, and conducting focus groups with students, faculty, and librarians leads to important revision as well as validation of effective strategies for continued administrative support. Additionally, such assessment provides information that can promote streamlining of the embedment, which in turn al-

lows librarians and faculty to increase scalability of these efforts.

7. Articulate embedded librarianship projects using language from comprehensive, university-wide plans. At our university, for example, *The Creation of the Future: University Plan 3* serves as the framework for our institution's priorities, and the document provides language that can help both teachers and librarians argue for the importance of our collaborative efforts even when ground-level job descriptions don't provide a clear mandate for embedded librarianship. Our institutional plan notes that

> Access without a reasonable chance at success is a hollow benefit. UW must work across the spectrum of Wyoming's educational system to ensure that students enter college with the right preparation, begin their college careers with the right courses, and have access to the right tools and resources to succeed.[20]

To affect the goal of improved retention, the plan calls for "a student retention strategy that includes at least five elements," including "a transition program to promote success among first-year and transfer students."[21] By seeking ways to align embedded librarianship efforts with long-range planning efforts, libraries may both take a more central role in instructional design and become a more obvious partner for university-level retention efforts.

Conclusion

As faculty interested in student retention efforts, we appreciate librarians' recognition of the cultural and contextual factors that influence students' ability to develop information literacies. However, we believe that many embedding approaches overlook their potential to more fully promote students' broader understanding of academic research culture. Additionally, we believe that embedded librarianship provides a route by which libraries can more directly align their reference-related activity with broader university goals such as retention. And, most importantly, we find that embedded librarian strategies provide a natural extension to programming which can increase the success of at-risk students.

Notes

1. Rebecca B. Sipe, *Adolescent Literacy at Risk? The Impact of Standards* (Urbana, IL: NCTE, 2009); Gayle B. Bray, Ernest T. Pascarella, and Christopher T. Pierson, "Postsecondary Education and Some Dimensions of Literacy Development: An Exploration of Longitudinal Evidence," *Reading Research Quarterly* 39, no. 3 (July/August/September 2004): 306–330, http://www.jstor.org/stable/i388085 (accessed June 7, 2010).

2. Pierre Bourdieu, and Jean-Claude Passeron, *Reproduction in Education, Society, and Culture*, 2d ed. (London: Sage, 1990).

3. Alexander W. Astin, "Student Involvement: A Developmental Theory for Higher Education," *Journal of College Student Development* 40, no. 5 (Sept/Oct. 1999): 513.

4. Ibid., 518.

5. Lubrano, Alfred, *Limbo: Blue-Collar Roots, White-Collar Dreams* (Hoboken, NJ: Wiley, 2005), 8.

6. Ibid., 56.

7. Quotation is excerpted from a series of focus groups conducted with fall 2003 first-year, conditionally-admitted Synergy students.

8. Lubrano, *Limbo*, 55.

9. James P. Gee, Glynda Hull, and Colin Lankshear, *The New Work Order: Behind the Language of New Capitalism* (New York: Perseus/Westview, 1996): 3. Emphasis in original.

10. Ibid., 2.

11. Ibid., 2–3.

12. Lubrano, *Limbo*, 19–20.

13. Sylvia Hurtado, Sylvia, Mark Engber, Luis Pnjuam, and Lisa Landreman, "Students' Precollege Preparation for Participation in a Diverse Democracy," *Research in Higher Education* 43, no. 2 (2002): 175.

14. George M. Colton, Ulysses J. Connor, and Eileen L. Schultz, and Linda M. Easter, "Fighting Attrition: One Freshmen Year Program that Targets Academic Progress and Retention," *Journal of College Student Retention: Research, Theory, and Practice* 1, no. 2 (1999–2000): 147–162.; Angelo Atondo, Mauro Chavez, and Richard Ragua, "A Study of the Puente Project, 1983–1986," San Jose/Evergreen Community College District. (ERIC Document Reproduction Service, no. ED 278 448, p. 2.); Martin Ober, Kim Francis, and Robyn Wishengrad, "Combining of Traditional Counseling, Instruction, and Mentoring Functions with Academically Deficient College Freshmen," *Journal of Educational Research* 70, no. 3 (1977): 142–147.

15. Meagan Bowler and Kori Street, "Investigating the Efficacy of Embedment: Experiments in Information Literacy Integration," *Reference Services Review* 36, no. 4 (2008): 438–449. http://www.emeraldinsight.com/Insight/ViewContentServl et?contentType=Article&Filename=Published/EmeraldFullTextArticle/Articles/2400360409.html (accessed May 25, 2010); Nancy Origer-Poole, "Team-teaching: Trends among Business Librarians," *Academic BRASS* 4, no. 2 (2009), http://www.ala.org/ala/mgrps/divs/rusa/sections/brass/brasspubs/academicbrass/acadarchives/vol4no2/acadbrassv4no2teamteaching.cfm (accessed May 25, 2010).

16. Bette Rathe, "Teaching Information Literacy to At-Risk Students," *Academic Exchange Quarterly* (December 2004), http://www.thefreelibrary.com (accessed May 25, 2010).

17. Rachel Owens, "Where the Students Are: The Embedded Librarian Project at Daytona Beach College," *Florida Libraries* 51, no. 1 (2008): 8–10, http://search.ebscohost.com (accessed May 25, 2010).

18. Gayle Bray, Ernest Pascarella, and Christopher Pierson, "Postsecondary Education and Some Dimensions of Literacy Development," 324.

19. Heidi Julien, and Stuart Boon, "Assessing Instructional Outcomes in Canadian Academic Libraries," *Library & Information Science Research*, 25, no. 2 (Spring 2004): 121–139, www.sciencedirect.com (accessed June 7, 2010).

20. *The Creation of the Future: University Plan 3*. University of Wyoming Office of Academic Affairs, May 8 2009. http://uwadmnweb.uwyo.edu/AcadAffairs/univ_plan/up3.pdf (accessed May 25, 2010): 8.

21. Ibid., 11–12.

Additional Resources

Campbell, Corbin M., and Jessica Mislevy. "Students' Perceptions Matter: Early Signs of Undergraduate Student Retention/ Attrition." (Forum paper for Association of Institutional Research 50th Annual Forum, Chicago, May 29–June 2, 2010), https://www.irpa.umd.edu/Presentations/2009NEAIR_UG_Attrition_paper.pdf (accessed June 2, 2010).

San Francisco State's "Literacy Unleashed" description: http://www.fipse.aed.org/grantshow.
cfm?grantNumber=P116B011242

University of Alabama at Birmingham's "University 101" overview: http://main.uab.edu/Sites/undergraduate-programs/general-studies/university101/

University of Wyoming's Synergy Program: http://uwacadweb.uwyo.edu/synergy/

 FOUR

Embedding a Library Program in the First Year Curriculum: Experiences and Strategies of an Australian Case Study

Craig Milne and Jennifer Thomas

Setting the Context*

The Queensland University of Technology (QUT) located in Brisbane, Australia, is a medium-sized university with approximately 40,000 students across the seven faculties of Built Environment and Engineering, Business, Creative Industries, Education, Health, Law, and Science and Technology. It is one of three universities that have a major presence in Brisbane.

QUT's Graduate Capabilities state that every QUT course aims to develop graduates who are able to demonstrate a capacity for life-long learning, including the ability to search for and critically evaluate information from a variety of sources using effective strategies and appropriate technologies.[1] At QUT such information literacy (IL) skills

are traditionally the domain of the Library.

In this chapter we case study the embedding of IL skills into a first year unit, *BEB100 Introducing Professional Learning*, of the Faculty of Built Environment and Engineering (BEE), which has average yearly enrollments of 1300 students.[2] The BEE faculty consists of three Schools:

1. Urban Development
2. Design
3. Engineering Systems

Combined, these Schools teach across 19 disciplines, represented in table 4-1.

At QUT Library, a Liaison Librarian is assigned to each of the BEE Schools and, with the assistance of a Reference Librarian, form the Faculty's library liaison team.

*Glossary of terms	
Faculty	At QUT, Faculties typically comprise a number of Schools. Some countries such as the U.S.A. refer to faculty being the individual academic staff members. In Australia, we typically refer to these as academics.
School	At QUT, a School is the fundamental organizational teaching unit comprising a group of academics and led by a Head of School. Other institutions may call this a Department.
Unit	At QUT, a Unit is the fundamental delivery package of content. Some institutions refer to these as Subjects or Courses.
Course	At QUT, a Course is the collection of units, which forms what is also known as a Degree program. Some institutions use the term Course to refer to a Subject or Unit.
Liaison Librarians	At QUT, Liaison Librarians are the Library's direct link with academic s within the faculties. Other institutions may refer to Faculty Librarians or Subject Librarians.

Table 4-1. BEE Disciplines	
School	Disciplines within each School
Urban Development	Construction Management, Quantity Surveying, Property Economics, Spatial Sciences, Urban Regional Planning, Civil, Civil and Construction, Civil and Environmental
Design	Architecture, Landscape Architecture, Interior Design, Industrial Design
Engineering Systems	Aerospace Avionics, Electrical Engineering, Infomechatronics, Mechanical Engineering, Medical Engineering, Software Engineering

QUT Library, part of the Division of Technology, Information and Learning Support, is well respected within the university and considered to be a helpful place offering outstanding service. Liaison Librarians have a good reputation, and with their transferable skills are often called upon to take on more responsibilities.

QUT Library is a hub of Information Literacy (IL) activity and with strong leadership, has pursued and developed many initiatives in this area. IL is delivered through traditional means such as the Library Help Desk and generic and discipline-specific IL classes, however, the delivery of academic skills has recently entered the IL portfolio and we now talk about integrated literacies as encompassing information literacy and academic skills. Academic skills include (but are not limited to) time and task planning, note-taking, reading and comprehension, critical thinking and creating an argument, writing, group work and exam preparation,

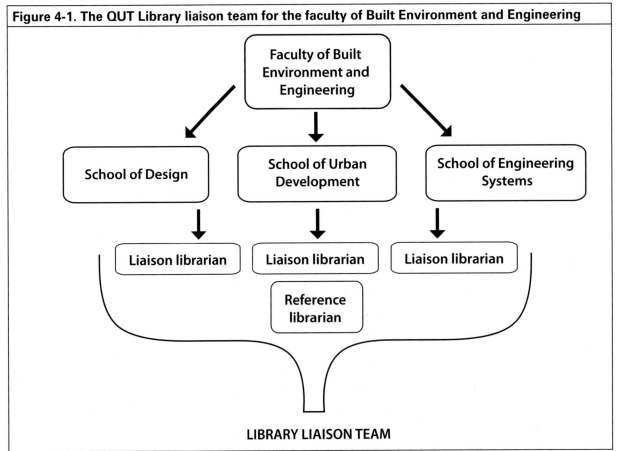

Figure 4-1. The QUT Library liaison team for the faculty of Built Environment and Engineering

and are now offered via the Library's service points as well as an online portal called *Studywell*.[3]

For a variety of reasons, some academics are more responsive to including IL instruction in the curriculum than others. One argument that often arises is that it is difficult to fit IL into an already crowded curriculum although if you are truly embedding this shouldn't be a problem. Fortunately, the first-year BEE unit coordinators are strong advocates of the library and sought involvement from the library liaison team for BEB100, a large first-year unit of approximately 1,300 students.

BEB100 as a faculty-wide unit was developed in 2006 as a way to introduce BEE students to foundational professional knowledge, values and skills such as project management, communication strategies, ethics and teamwork.[4] IL skills also fea-

tured in the curriculum and, in 2006, our library predecessors delivered IL skills via a single lecture.

In 2007, 2008 and 2009, library involvement in the unit escalated massively in size and scope via a number of different strategies. When we came on board we saw BEB100 as a golden opportunity to embed IL into the built environment and engineering disciplines. By ensuring that common foundation skills were taught in the first year across the 19 faculty disciplines, we could assume basic knowledge in later years, which would enable easier scaffolding of IL skills when we engaged with the students in individual discipline-specific units. An additional benefit of having foundation skills taught to all first year students across the disciplines meant there would be a consistent approach from which all students would all gain a

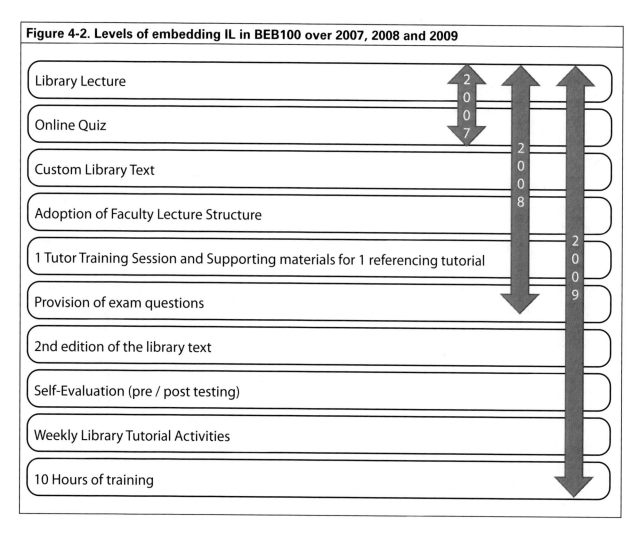

Figure 4-2. Levels of embedding IL in BEB100 over 2007, 2008 and 2009

- Library Lecture
- Online Quiz
- Custom Library Text
- Adoption of Faculty Lecture Structure
- 1 Tutor Training Session and Supporting materials for 1 referencing tutorial
- Provision of exam questions
- 2nd edition of the library text
- Self-Evaluation (pre / post testing)
- Weekly Library Tutorial Activities
- 10 Hours of training

core skill set, and allowing them to later change disciplines if they found there were better suited to other areas.

Our involvement over three years has resulted in a significant amount of embedding where the unit coordinators and tutors can deliver the IL content themselves in the years to come, as we will demonstrate.

Stages of Embedding—2007

Our involvement in embedding IL into BEB100 started in 2007. Based on feedback on the first iteration of BEB100 in 2006, the BEE Faculty was planning some significant changes to the content and structure of the unit. In 2007 we undertook two main activities:

- A library lecture
- An online quiz

Although library lectures could be described as bread and butter work, if it is done in collaboration with academics and you can demonstrate that you add value you will find that more doors open enabling further embedding. This was certainly true in our case as the work we undertook in developing the library lecture and the quiz in 2007 enabled us to develop a strong working relationship with the academic teaching team, which led to opportunities for substantial embedding in later years.

The Library Lecture

In 2007 there was a very short lead in time from being asked to deliver a lecture to getting the material ready and this limited the extent of embedding possible. Due to the size of the cohort and a desire to keep the unit in context with the 19 disciplines as much as possible, we had to deliver three lectures tailored to the three schools of Design, Engineering Systems and Urban Development. It was important to tailor each lecture for the Schools as the assignment requirements were all slightly different, but at the same time it was important to keep the core basic skills and format to each lecture.

One of the issues with using a lecture as the primary method for delivering IL instruction is that time is limited and yet the expectations of what should be delivered in 50 minutes can be high. In 2007 the lecture had to include:

- A general introduction to the library
- The importance of information literacy for BEE professions
- Skills to effectively search the catalogue, databases and the internet for reliable information for the unit assignment
- An understanding of the importance of referencing, and
- Where to find additional library resources

Not much for a student in week 2 of their first semester at university to take in, let alone deliver! We tried to keep the lecture simple and communicate the key points, but it can be very difficult to cut down to the essentials.

The search skills and knowledge imparted during a lecture are more likely to be retained if they are put to use. In 2006, to address this issue there was an attempt at delivering hands on instruction by providing library-run tutorials. Our predecessors advised against attempting this again in 2007 due to the large number of students, small training lab sizes (capable of accommodating 50 students at most) and only three liaison librarians and a reference librarian available to deliver the training. For the library team to take on this level of commitment in conjunction with the generic library programs and additional teaching to second, third and fourth year students was logistically burdensome and impractical. Our alternative solution was to develop an online quiz, which doubled as a self-paced tutorial within QUT's Learning Management System (LMS).

The Online Quiz

While QUT Library had tools such as the online information literacy tutorial PILOT,[5] academics felt that library training should be more faculty focused and blend in more effectively with the unit.

Students had to see the relevance of IL skills to their disciplines and terminology suited to their skill areas.

We developed an online quiz with questions focused towards the BEE disciplines. The questions linked to supplementary material, which students could access before answering the questions. These links enabled students to seek further instruction or undertake a short learning task to gain the knowledge that they required to answer each question. All of the supplementary information and learning tasks already existed as modules within PILOT or on the QUT Library website so we made effective reuse of existing resources and saved time by not reinventing the wheel.

The content of the online quiz from 2007 can be found on *QUT ePrints*.[6] Results from the quiz were positive and showed that students had undertaken the activities, gained new skills, and applied knowledge from the lecture and supplementary materials. Embedding the quiz in the LMS, within the normal domain of the unit, meant that the library and IL skills were seen as an integral and necessary part of the unit.

Through our work in 2007 we had created a core foundation skills lecture which could be tweaked for individual cohorts saving time and resources, and the online quiz enabled us to engage students in self-paced learning activities where needed, without the need for the library to deliver tutorials to over 1000 students. The work with the lecture and our willingness to develop custom resources, specifically the online quiz, established us as part of the teaching team and really built the foundations for embedding in this unit in future years. To borrow the title of a Kev Carmody and Paul Kelly song it is true to say that "From little things big things grow" as we will illustrate in the rest of this chapter.

Stages of Embedding—2008

Access to feedback is a valuable and critical aspect to moving forward with embedding and teaching IL skills within a curriculum. It is essential to understand what resources are working, what aren't and how they can be improved. QUT runs the Learning Experience Survey (LEX) at the end of every semester to capture feedback on individual units and teachers. In the case of BEB100 in 2007 the students in the middle of semester also undertook an evaluation survey. A question about the library lecture revealed that 86% of students (764 out of 891 respondents) **agreed** or **strongly agreed** that the library lecture was helpful in searching for, evaluating and referencing material for the assignment. A summary of all the LEX data for BEB100 for 2007 to 2009 can be found in Table 7 of Smit and Murray.[7] We were also able to make use of the FAQs that were developed throughout the unit in 2007 in response to students' questions to inform areas for development in 2008.

We were able to text mine the feedback for qualitative comments by searching for the mention of words such as "library". Some of the comments included: "the library lecture was difficult to follow in a non-interactive environment" and; "….one (lecture) that I believe was helpful was the library one which showed us how to look for information on the library website, however it was still boring and dragged out." We would argue that the "boring" comment was probably partly due to the nature of the material and the way it was delivered (not embedded) which encouraged us to liven things up. One comment reflected on the self paced PILOT resource: "I found that the best source of learning about information literacy was to spend some time going through the PILOT project." While we considered all the feedback, we found it important, especially with qualitative information, to consider comments in the bigger picture and to remember that one negative comment is not necessarily the view of all 1200 students.

The second important factor in successful embedding is early planning and preparation as the time required to create effective resources for embedding can initially be high although there is long term gain for students, academics and librarians. The planning for the third iteration of BEB100 started shortly after the exam period in 2007 giving a lead in time of 6 months for BEB100 2008. As a result of having a good lead in time and reviewing all the feedback, the activities undertaken in 2008 (in addition to those undertaken in 2007) were:

- Writing a custom library text
- Adoption of the faculty lecture format (enabling better blending of the lecture)
- Preparation of some tutorial material for delivery by academics
- Provision of final exam questions (30% of final exam) giving significant weight to the library content

A Custom Library Text

Students gave the text book aspect of LEX, for BEB100, a very low rating in 2007, a reflection that there was no one text covering all the material taught and indicating that students desired a text to accompany the professional skills delivered in the unit. The academics selected the text *Writing for the Technical Professions*[8] as the text that would address the majority of the professional skills taught in this unit, but commented that there was still a gap in library and research skills particularly from a QUT context. The Faculty teaching team suggested, over a coffee in a faculty tea room (where the most productive liaison work often occurs) that perhaps we could write a chapter to be added to the chosen textbook. This was a major opportunity that was seized upon and a lot of work was undertaken over a short period of time to meet the required publication deadlines. During the writing process we sought feedback from academics to ensure that our content would meet their expectations and we received some valuable input. The result was *Researching for the Built Environment and Engineering Professions*.[9]

QUT is very proactive in the Open Access field and librarians promote it on a regular basis, so we were careful to ensure that we retained the copyright for our material and issued a non-exclusive license to the publisher for the context of BEB100. By doing this we ensured that we could freely reuse and re-purpose our resource and could make it available via *QUT ePrints*. This was not only beneficial to students from an equity viewpoint (they could get a free copy) but also enabled re-use of the text in other units without the need for students to purchase a copy. The text is now a backbone resource for many other faculty units. Since we made the text available on *QUT ePrints* there have been 1285 combined downloads of the text in addition to the printed copies which were bundled with the text book which students purchased from the University book shop.

The text was primarily structured around the content we were delivering in the lecture. The main content covered included:

- planning for research
- search strategies
- search tools (catalogue, databases and the web)
- evaluating information, and
- referencing

The text is a great resource to deal with information overload, as it allows us to reduce the content of the lecture and to focus on the core, critical points. Students can expand their knowledge by reading the detail (unlikely to be retained from a lecture) in their own time and at point of need. It also means that students have a text covering basic IL that they can refer to during their 4 years at university. We are pleased to still see copies of the first edition, with their distinctive bright orange covers, used during assignment times. The library copies are also well used. In 2008 the text included referencing examples of resource types that the students were likely to use for their assignment. In 2009 QUT Library launched a new writing and referencing guide called *Cite|Write*,[10] which had the engineering referencing examples included. Following the rule that it is better to use existing resources that are well developed and widely supported, we removed the referencing table and included links to *Cite|Write* in the second edition of the text in 2009.

Developing the Lecture and Other Resources

After the text had been finalized we took the initiative and set up a meeting with the teaching team in late 2007 to plan how we could engage in the unit in 2008 and how we could best leverage the library text book. Academics have much more teaching experience than librarians and through true collaboration they provided us with a wealth of support in the development of our lecture and strategies for engaging with students in large lecture theatres. The academics were keen for us to reference the library text as much as possible in our lecture so that students would use the text and value it as a useful resource. To do this we mentioned page numbers continually throughout the lecture and on the PowerPoint slides. Other enhancements to the lecture included the addition of a short movie we created to capture the importance of IL skills to future BEE professions (rather than just having a librarian talk about it). This was very effective and engaging—it runs for just over two minutes (without sound) and yet we still had silence in a lecture theatre of 500 students. We also hoped the use of media would alleviate some of the "boring" stigma from 2007. The movie clip, lecture slides and other supplementary material that we used can be accessed on *QUT ePrints*.[11]

Other refinements to the lecture saw a second librarian driving the presentation and demonstrating the searches while the primary librarian maintained eye contact and engaged with the students. We also had a third librarian and reference librarian in the audience with microphones so that they could participate in any discussion.

At our meeting we also raised how we could best add value based on the feedback in 2008 and we were requested to provide assistance with de-velopment of the Criterion Referenced Assessment (CRA) for 2008 in relation to referencing and search skills. We were also keen to try and engage students more in the tutorials and we collaborated with the academics on creating some tutorial resources on referencing for use by Faculty tutors. The text was also the basis of supporting information for the library tutorial for which we carried out a "train the tutor" session in 2008. This led to further tutorial involvement, which is described in more detail in 2009 section.

Online quizzes were again used in 2008 but in a new Learning Management System (LMS) and using questions randomly selected from a bank of questions we provided. In addition, we were asked to develop a bank of questions for the mid-semester quiz and for the final exam. Also following the faculty lecture series format we established some week 2 tasks for students which included reading the library text, completing the online quiz and going to the library and borrowing a relevant book to take to the tutorial.

Without the advance planning for 2008 it is fair to say that there would never have been time to create resources and effectively blend IL into the unit. There was a high level of collaboration with academics when we created the resources but we ensured that we were not taking over the teaching of the unit and tutorials. Probably one of the trickiest balances in embedding is the fine line between truly embedding and providing resources for the academics to use, or just doing the work for them.

Stages of Embedding—2009

Over the years of our involvement with BEB100, we have had many discussions with the unit coordinators about the ways we could improve IL content and delivery. In 2009, two major additions were added which dramatically increased our involvement in the unit:

- Pre- and post- testing of student IL skills
- Weekly library tutorial activities and delivery of tutor training

Pre- and Post-testing of Students' IL Skills

For some time, academics and librarians have observed students entering university with inflated estimations of their own skills and abilities in information seeking. While we are resigned to students' initial belief that everything can be found on Google—which is unsurprising given its easy, intuitive interface and relative certainty of finding *something* on a topic—we wanted to evaluate their perceptions of their information skills and test the reality of their skills. Thus we developed a pre- and post-testing strategy in an attempt to achieve this. The premise of the strategy entailed:

- Pre- testing student IL perceptions and skills early in the semester
- Analyzing the results for strengths and weaknesses
- Providing feedback on the strengths and creating interventions based on the weaknesses, and
- Post-testing student IL perceptions and skills at the end of the semester, to see whether there had been a measurable improvement.

There was some debate over what to call the strategy. The university and unit coordinators are concerned that students should not be subject to too much "testing" or "surveying", so we settled on calling our strategy a "self evaluation of skills" which we blended into the operation of the unit—it wasn't tagged on or optional. For the purposes of this chapter, we will refer to the self-evaluation as a pre- and post- test.

The Pre-test

The pre-test was undertaken during the tutorial in week two of semester, prior to any formal IL instruction in the unit. It was completed during the tutorials as student attendance at tutorials is compulsory, resulting in a larger response rate than an online quiz. Questions were presented to students on a PowerPoint and their answers were recorded on a paper multiple choice question (MCQ) answer sheet. These answer sheets were identical to the ones the students would have to use for the final exam, and therefore they were getting practice in filling them out, as they aren't overly intuitive. The final number of respondents was 1,153; a large sample size from which to draw some conclusions and observations.

The pre-test consisted of 20 questions in five categories set out in the Australian and New Zealand Information Literacy Framework, also known as the "ANZIIL standards".[12] It tested the areas of planning, searching, evaluation, referencing and ethical use of information. Each of the five categories was introduced by a question testing student perception of their IL skill levels—see table 4-2.

Each perception question was then followed by three competency questions testing the actual skill. For example, for the category of referencing, students were asked to choose the correct answer from five possible answers for the following questions:

1. Look at the following reference for a book and identify what information is missing
2. What type of reference is this?
3. In this reference, what is the title of the journal?

Results of the perception questions revealed that the majority of students thought they were **OK** or **Good** at all of the categories. Full analysis of results including the competency questions revealed that in reality, students were good at planning, evaluating and ethical use, but less successful at searching for information and referencing. Consequently, we targeted most of our intervention in those two areas throughout the semester.

The Intervention

In 2009 the pre- and post-testing strategy was introduced to obtain evidence of the value of an embedded IL program, which built upon 2007 and 2008 library involvement to include:

- Two lectures—in past years the lectures were given as early as week 2, when stu-

Table 4-2. Student Perceptions of their IL skill level in week 2 (sample 1153 students)		Poor	Could be Better	OK	Good	Expert
Skill Area	In Your Opinion	Poor	Could be Better	OK	Good	Expert
Planning	How would you rate your ability to plan searches for information you need?	1%	9%	42%	44%	3%
Searching	How familiar are you with search tools needed to find information?	1%	10%	38%	46%	5%
Evaluating	How would you rate your ability to evaluate whether information is correct, reliable and of high quality?	0%	7%	35%	53%	5%
Referencing	How would you rate your ability to reference (or cite) items such as books, articles, websites and so forth?	5%	24%	36%	29%	6%
Ethics	How would you rate your ability to find and use information responsibly and legally?	1%	8%	29%	52%	10%

dents were "green" and generally unable to conceive the importance of library skills to their academic careers and assessment tasks. The two lectures in 2009 each addressed weaknesses revealed in the pre-test results and were scheduled for later in the semester to come in line with assessment deliverables:

- lecture 1 (in week 7)—finding information
- lecture 2 (in week 9)—referencing
- A second edition of the textbook, with minor updates to reflect changes to the library website and resources and based on feedback and FAQ's in 2008
- Interactive online resources for the BEB100 Blackboard site, including resources to assist with learning call numbers and referencing
- IL skills built into the CRA for the group assignment, including demonstrating use of a wide variety of sources and correct referencing style
- Weekly sample exam questions to give students a sense of the types of questions they would be asked in the final exam
- A bank of assessable multiple choice questions for the mid-semester quiz and final exam.

These materials were supplied for self-help, to support the content being actively delivered in the lectures. However, the significant addition in 2009 was the introduction of weekly library tutorial activities and the delivery of tutor training.

Weekly Library Tutorial Activities and Delivery of Tutor Training

In collaboration with the BEB100 unit coordinators, we increased library involvement by appropriating half an hour of each two-hour tutorial, with the remaining time dedicated to a half hour writing activity and revision of the weekly unit content. The exception to this schedule was in weeks seven and nine—the weeks we delivered our library lectures—where the full two hours were dedicated to library content.

We developed the library's tutorial content around the unit content taught each week. Table 4-3 lists these tutorial activities.

Most of the library tutorial activities were supplemented with readings from the library text and interactive flash objects embedded into the BEB100 Blackboard site. Students were also encouraged to bring along laptops to the tutorial that, due to the size of the cohort, could not be held in fully equipped computer labs.

We developed seven hours of new weekly tutorial activities in total, but the real breakthrough

Table 4-3. Schedule of library tutorial activities in 2009		
Week of semester	**Weekly topic/content**	**Library tutorial activity**
1	Knowing the built environment and engineering professions	Internet searching—using Google Advanced Search to locate professional associations and accrediting bodies
2	Ethics	Pre-test of student IL skills
3	Cultural issues & writing	Searching of library catalogue – keyword and subject searching for books on any topic covered in the unit to date
4	Graphics	Referencing images and diagrams, both the in-text citation and the reference list
5	Camp week	Nil
6	Team work	Provide feedback from week two pre-test and identify any issues that need addressing further
7	Library lecture – finding information	DEDICATED 2-hour library tutorial. • Locating and searching relevant databases • Locating a full text article from a journal citation
8	Writing reports	Search the web for officially published, professional examples of technical report writing.
9	Library lecture – referencing	DEDICATED 2-hour library tutorial. • Recognizing different reference types • Identify missing elements from references • Creating in-text citations and end references
10 – 12	Preparing and delivering oral presentations	Nil
13	Preparing for exams	Post-test of student IL skills
Exam period	Multiple choice exam	Assessable IL questions form approx. 30% of exam

came with the weekly hour-long tutor training sessions. We attended these sessions at the request of the unit coordinators to instruct the tutors in carrying out the library tutorial activities. The tutors found this beneficial as they could ask us questions while we were on hand to help and we also distributed detailed instruction sheets for tutors to consult during the tutorials. This delivery of IL skills by the tutors has been the most important step towards fully embedding such skills into the first year curriculum.

The Post-test Strategy

As mentioned, the premise of the pre- and post-testing strategy was not only to gauge student perception versus the reality of their IL skills, but also to tailor library involvement based on the results of the pre-test in an attempt to improve these skills. Therefore, to gain evidence of the effectiveness of our involvement with the unit, the post-test was conducted at the end of semester. The perceptions were tested in week 13 tutorial, and the reality was tested via the library questions asked in the final exam.

Once again we delivered the perception questions in the tutorials. Even though tutorials are compulsory, the response rate was significantly lower at 475 as attendance rates tend to drop off throughout the semester. However, when matched to the same sample from week 2, we still found this a decent-sized sample from which to draw conclusions.

The same perception questions were asked in the post-test. Across the five categories tested, there was a combined increase of 14-24% in the

Good and **Expert** categories, indicating that students believed they had improved their IL skills throughout the semester.

However, the reality of students' IL skills at the end of the semester would be the true indicator of improvement. As in 2008, we developed a bank of assessable multiple-choice questions for the final exam, and it was from the results of the final exam that we could analyze the reality of their IL skills. However, the exam questions were not evenly split across the five categories as some areas had been targeted with more intensive instruction than others. Therefore, one competency question from each category in the pre-test was mapped to a question in the final exam that tested the same skill but was asked in a different way. This was beneficial as it prevented rote memory of answers to questions asked in the pre-test, and the final exam also tested the skills at a deeper level than in week 2 which if answered correctly, indicated true gaining of skills.

Across the categories of planning, searching, evaluation and referencing, there was an improvement of between 22–32%. The category of ethical use of information could not be directly mapped, however, the average percentage of correct answers to questions testing this skill was 91% indicating a high level of comprehension.

Through the pre- and post-testing strategy, we have been able to prove that a structured and thoughtful approach to embedding IL skills within a curriculum can have a positive impact on student learning outcomes. While great efforts were involved in preparing library materials and content for BEB100 in 2009, these initial efforts have resulted in materials that can easily be reused, and with some updating and training of the tutors each year, embedding can continue and may even be adopted by other disciplines.[13]

Issues, Strategies and Experiences

Over the three years we have embedded into the first year engineering curriculum we have gained some useful insights on the issues that arise and

as a result, developed some strategies that we now employ in other teaching-related areas of our work. In hindsight, many of these would have been good to have known at the outset of our endeavours and so we have listed these for the consideration of any librarian attempting a program of embedding.

Conduct an Environmental Scan—Locally, Nationally and Internationally

Keeping an eye on the literature (such as reading a book like this) and attending IL conferences is a great way to start. The idea for the movie in our lecture originated from attending the ANZIIL conference in Hobart, Tasmania in 2007 as did the idea of trying to gauge the value of our work. A local scan is also worthwhile—by asking other liaison librarians about their experiences with IL testing and quizzes we were able to gather a good selection of questions for our quizzes, which we adapted, to the BEE context, saving time and effort.

Contextualize the IL Content to the Discipline

It is hard to think that liaison librarians are not already effectively contextualizing IL content to their disciplines. However, we found that a small amount of extra research connected our IL content not only to the curriculum and the university's graduate capabilities, but also to the professional competencies of professional associations and accreditation bodies such as Engineers Australia and the Accreditation Board for Engineering and Technology.[14] Thus we were able to point out these connections to students in the lecture, giving them some relevant context around the importance of IL skills.

Collect Feedback

Collecting feedback on what is going on around you is essential to make improvements to your embedding program. Be proactive in sourcing the feedback early and making changes. The feedback we were able to collect from students through surveys, Learning Experience Survey (LEX), and the pre- and post-testing strategy was key in targeting areas of weakness and ultimately improving our content.

Re-use Materials and Resources

When embedding it is important to re-use as many existing resources as possible so that you can direct energy and efforts into other areas. Our rather simple quiz enabled us to develop a tailored learning experience based on substantial existing resources. Having lots of resources available to supplement and aid the academics is key to embedding.

As mentioned, a big challenge for us was fitting all the required information into a 50-minute lecture. The temptation is to teach everything but the reality is that this can't be done. Less is more, and re-usable resources can be created and embedded within other areas of the curriculum to support the lecture.

Publish the Findings of your Work

It is important to publish the findings of your work, otherwise no one will know what you are doing. Through publishing at conferences and in journals, others can find out what works well, what doesn't, and can leverage existing resources you have created. It is also important to avoid "preaching to the converted" and for this reason, we presented our work at the Australasian Association for Engineering Education (AAEE) conferences in 2008 and 2009, attended mainly by engineering academics. Share your successes with your colleagues but more importantly, with academic staff. Attending and presenting at the AAEE conference in 2008 allowed us to demonstrate to academic staff, the value of embedding, and using their terminology, proving the value that it can have in their domains.

Summary and Future Directions

Embedding IL is a long process and the time we dedicated to the task increased as our involvement has increased. Over the three-year period, the teaching team contributed the following approximate amounts of combined preparation and teaching time:

- 2007—30 hours
- 2008—54 hours
- 2009—154 hours

The 2009 total seems extravagant, but in 2010, the total combined time of preparation and teaching has been reduced to approximately 53 hours, similar to 2008 levels but retaining the same amount of involvement as 2009. This is good evidence that our embedding strategy is just that—embedded, with our initial investment in time paying off as we had hoped.

As librarians it is increasingly necessary to build evidence to prove the value of what we do, as academic teaching staff cannot be expected to take a "leap of faith" in including IL if they don't have the space in the curriculum or are dubious about the benefits. So when planning for embedding, carefully consider how you will collect data, either directly or indirectly, as proof of the value of your work and the benefits of an embedded IL program is required if you are to maintain an ongoing program. Teaching and library staff change over time and if the value of your contribution is not clearly visible then you will have a harder time remaining embedded. Keep any data that you can, present your work at conferences and publish what you have done for others to learn and to gain credibility about your motives.

Additionally, embedding is not possible without the advocacy and support of academics. We were fortunate to collaborate with academics who valued information skills enough to feature them in the curriculum and had confidence in our abilities to develop effective materials. We had countless conversations behind the scenes, in person and via email about the unit and how it could be improved. We believe that collaboration between librarians and academics is essential for embedding to occur. Additionally, support from the academic teaching team can assist in gaining buy-in from students and changing preconceived notions about the value of information skills. In our case, there was a positive and measurable change not only in their perceptions of IL skills but more importantly an improvement in their actual skills.

An unexpected indication of the value of our work occurred when the teaching team discussed our efforts with the team in charge of QUT's First Year Experience program. As part of this program, a successful "transitions in" strategy to prevent attrition rates by aiding students identified as "at risk" was implemented, and there were discussions that the results of our week two pre-test might be used confidentially to assist in identifying these students, thus revealing another benefit of our work.

We also found that a key part of embedding was training the tutors to deliver library activities. By creating resources for tutors to use, providing backup support where necessary and continually updating the resources in line with the curriculum, there was a shift from spending our time in lectures to spending our time on resource creation and tutor training as a complement to the lectures.

With all this in mind, the real test of our hard work came when the BEE faculty underwent an external review of its large units, including BEB100. The review arose from the faculty's continual strive to improve its LEX results. We provided a written submission to the review panel demonstrating the value the library provided to BEB100 and we also attended focus groups to discuss our thoughts in person. Ultimately the review panel recommended removing the faculty umbrella and returning the unit to the control of the three Schools. While the unit would still be core for all BEE students, there would be three discipline-specific approaches to the content.

Future Directions

In 2010, BEB100 ceased being a faculty-wide unit and is now offered separately by each of the three Schools. It is still a core unit called *Introducing*

Professional Learning, but the three new unit coordinators each have a degree of free reign over the amount of discipline-specific and library content included in:

- UDB100 Introducing Professional Learning—School of Urban Development
- DEB100 Introducing Professional Learning—School of Design
- ENB100 Introducing Professional Learning—School of Engineering Systems

At the end of 2009 before this split, the BEB100 unit coordinators requested feedback from the tutors for unit content that should be introduced, retained or removed.

Fortunately the tutors flagged the library content as too important to remove and there was general agreement that the weekly schedule used in BEB100 in 2009 should be retained for the new units in 2010. The exception to this is the lecture on referencing which is placed earlier in the semester as students find it helpful for their other units.

While there was some reduction of the library content in ENB100, both UDB100 and DEB100 have each continued with the 2009 schedule. In fact, in DEB100 the embedding has been so successful that library assistance has only been requested for minor updates to the content. The week 2 pre-test was administered and the results analyzed without library assistance, and the tutorial materials have been so self-explanatory that tutor training hasn't been required. There has even been another small addition to each of the 2010 units with the lecture on report writing being given by one of the library's Academic Skills Advisors. This has helped to reinforce the library's expertise in supporting academic skills and strengthening the library's IL portfolio.

It is hoped that some further analysis of final exam data from 2007, 2008 and 2009 will be undertaken in 2010–2011 involving detailed examination of the 35 questions used to test student IL skills in the end of the semester exam In addition, we will attempt to cross-analyze these final exam results to determine if the large increase in library involvement over the three years has resulted in positive outcomes for students, however, as we didn't have a plan for a longitudinal study of results in place in 2007 this may prove difficult.

With the decision to change BEB100 to a School-based offering in 2010 our goal posts were moved, but we are confident that our efforts to develop comprehensive and effective methods for embedding IL into the first year engineering curriculum at QUT have paid off. With increased involvement over the 2007, 2008 and 2009 iterations of BEB100 and via the pre- and post-testing strategy delivered in 2009, we were able to prove the value that a tailored and constant IL presence had on improving student information skills.

Acknowledgements

We would like to acknowledge the substantial work of Marvin Van Prooijen, Reference Librarian, in assisting with the creation of resources for BEB100 and for his work as acting Liaison Librarian (Urban Development) in 2009 and 2010 and Graham Dawson, Liaison Librarian for Engineering Systems. It is also important that we acknowledge the support and collaboration of the BEB100 Faculty teaching team and tutors without whom the embedding would not have been possible.

Notes

1. Queensland University of Technology, *Manual of Policies and Procedures: C/4.3 Graduate Capabilities*. Available at http://www.mopp.qut.edu.au/C/C_04_03.jsp. [Accessed 12 May 2011].

2. Deborah K. Smit and Martin H. Murray, "Finding Order in Chaos: A Problem Based Collaborative Assignment for 1300 Students Across 19 Disciplines" (paper presented at the Australasian Universities Building Education Association Conference, Adelaide, South Australia, July 7-10, 2009). Available at http://eprints.qut.edu.au/26097/. [Accessed 12 May 2011].

3. Queensland University of Technology, "Studywell." Available at http://www.studywell.library.qut.edu.au/. [Accessed 12 May 2011].

4. Smit and Murray, "Finding Order in Chaos."

5. Queensland University of Technology, "PILOT—Your Information Navigator." Available at https://pilot.library.qut.edu.au/index.jsp. [Accessed 12 May 2011].

6. Craig Milne and Jennifer Thomas, "Embedding a Library Program in the First Year Curriculum: Experiences and Strategies of an Australian Case Study." Available at http://eprints.qut.edu.au/32393/. [Accessed 12 May 2011].

7. Smit and Murray, "Finding Order in Chaos."

8. Kristen R. Woolever, *Writing for Technical Professions*, 4th Ed. [New York: Pearson Longman, 2008].

9. Craig Milne and Jennifer Thomas, *Researching for the Built Environment and Engineering Professions* [French's Forest, N.S.W.: Pearson SprintPrint, 2008]. Available at http://eprints.qut.edu.au/15668/. [Accessed 12 May 2011].

10. Queensland University of Technology, "Cite|Write." Available at http://www.citewrite.qut.edu.au/. [Accessed 12 May 2011].

11. Craig Milne and Jennifer Thomas, "Embedding a Library Program in the First Year Curriculum."

12. Alan Bundy, *Australian and New Zealand Information Literacy Framework: Principles, Standards and Practice* Second edition. [Adelaide: Australia and New Zealand Institute for Information Literacy, 2004]. Available at http://archive.caul.edu.au/info-literacy/InfoLiteracyFramework.pdf. [Accessed 12 May 2011].

13. Craig Milne, Jennifer Thomas, and Graham Dawson, "Sampling Perceptions; Testing Reality : An Evidence-based Approach to Measurably Improve Information Literacy and Student Research Skills (paper presented at the Australasian Association for Engineering Education Conference (AAEE): Engineering the Curriculum, at The University of Adelaide, Adelaide, December 6-9, 2009). Available at http://eprints.qut.edu.au/29125/. [Accessed 12 May 2011].

14. Craig Milne and Jennifer Thomas, "Are Your Foundations Sound? Information Literacy and the Building of Holistic Professional Practitioners" (paper presented at the 19th Annual Conference for the Australasian Association for Engineering Education: To Industry and Beyond, Yeppoon, Queensland, 2008). Available at http://eprints.qut.edu.au/16899/. [Accessed 12 May 2011].

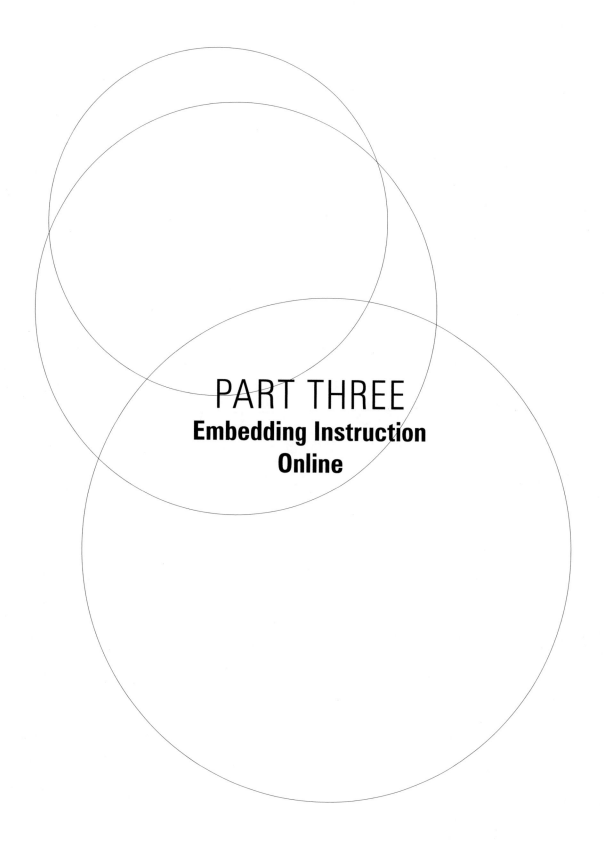

PART THREE
Embedding Instruction Online

 FIVE

Replacing Face-to-Face Information Literacy Instruction: Offering the Embedded Librarian Program to All Courses

Ann Schroeder

In January of 2004, the Iraq War was less than a year old and I was brainstorming to find a catchy name for a new library pilot. The pilot involved my setting up discussion forums in two online classes and offering library help there. The idea of embedded journalists in Iraq came to mind, and thus the embedded librarian program at the Community College of Vermont (CCV) was born.

I was not aware as I created our embedded librarian program in 2004 that the term "embedded librarian" was being used that year in an article by Barbara Dewey to include many types of library partnerships with other campus entities, including course management systems (CMS).[1] In her article she mentions integrating libraries in Blackboard and WebCT through links, tutorials, and ask-a-librarian services. However, she doesn't include the librarian taking an active part in online courses by having his or her own discussion forum, the primary focus of our program at CCV. That same year, Jamie Kearley and Lori Phillips at the University of Wyoming used the term "embedding" rather than "embedded librarian."[2] In their article, they described how they were embedding library services in online courses through links to resources and services, as well integrating information literacy instruction (ILI) through tutorials. They did not mention use of the discussion board. Two other universities, Middle Tennessee State and Framingham State, started programs that year which did use the discussion forum.[3,4] At Framingham State, Peg Snyder, the first librarian to facilitate this program, worked with two faculty members, just as I did. An "Ask a Librarian" discussion forum was included.[5] Another early library program using a discussion forum in a CMS began at the University of Rhode Island in the spring of 2005.[6]

Chances are that none of these librarians knew about each others' efforts and perhaps thought, as I did, that they had come up with the original concept of an embedded librarian in a CMS. At that time, all of us sensed that the growing contingent of online students needed to be better served by libraries right where they learned.

Although using the term "Blackboard librarian" instead of "embedded librarian," an even earlier experiment integrating the library with online classes began in 1999. Molly Dinwiddie and Linda Lilliard at Central Missouri State University wrote an article about an experiment in which a librarian partnered with a nursing professor and built a section of a Blackboard course that included resources, instructions, and contact information.[7] The librarian also communicated with the students periodically by email and could be contacted through the discussion board. Also, Shank and Dewald in

63

2003 suggested the option of "a link to a message board [in a CMS], which the librarian monitors periodically, for discussing research difficulties."[8]

Library Services at the Community College of Vermont

Providing library services at CCV has always been a challenge. The College, which currently serves approximately 3500 FTE, does not have a central campus with housing facilities. Instead, students are served in their communities by 12 learning centers, or sites, around the state, and via the Internet through online courses. Some of the sites have their own buildings but others share facilities with other enterprises. Buying books for all 12 academic locations was a heavy financial burden. Originally all sites had the same book collection, with a few

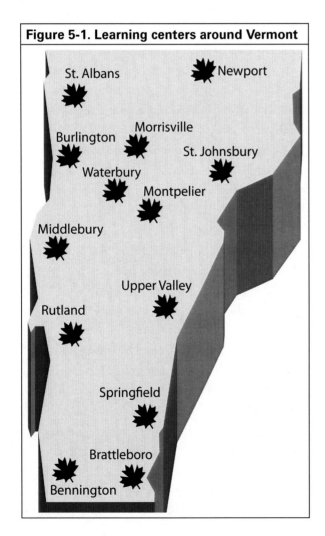

Figure 5-1. Learning centers around Vermont

St. Albans   Newport

Morrisville
Burlington
                St. Johnsbury
Waterbury
            Montpelier

Middlebury

Upper Valley

Rutland

Springfield

Brattleboro
Bennington

special collections in some of the larger sites. The media collection was housed in one site. Faculty used this collection heavily, but the book collections did not get much use. Interlibrary loan was another large expense, especially since the Library purchased no print periodicals.

Two Colleges: One Library

The Vermont State College (VSC) system consists of 5 colleges: Castleton State College, Community College of Vermont, Johnson State College, Lyndon State College, and Vermont Technical College. In 2000, the libraries of Vermont Technical College (VTC) and Community College of Vermont merged to form the Vermont Community & Technical Colleges Library. The combined entity has since been renamed Hartness Library, the name of the library on the main campus of VTC. The merger allowed for the delivery of quality library services to CCV students. The main library at VTC houses the joint physical collection for the two colleges, as well as the technical services department. CCV students can borrow materials through the online catalog and have them shipped to their home at no charge. Students at remote VTC sites have the same privilege. The VSC-wide catalog contains over 300,000 items and provides seamless borrowing from all four libraries for our students.

The CCV Hartness Library tab in Blackboard is the entry point for periodical collections, the Library catalog, and many other online resources. The tab goes to the CCV side of the joint CCV/VTC website (http://hartness.vsc.edu/ccvhome). Since CCV is a two-year college offering degrees and certificates in liberal arts, business, human services, technology, and allied health, and VTC is a four-year technical college, the content of each part of the library website has been tailored to meet the curricular needs of each college.

Among the services available to CCV students are:

- a toll-free phone number, chat, and email for reference assistance

- home delivery of books, audios, and videos
- online video tutorials, webinars, research guides, handouts, and worksheets
- access to thousands of full-text articles in more than 80 periodical databases
- eBook collections
- Information Literacy Instruction at CCV

When the embedded librarian program began in the spring semester of 2004, information literacy instruction (ILI) was offered as an option to faculty who taught face-to-face classes in all 12 CCV sites. VTC had a separate ILI program. CCV librarians and library paraprofessionals (termed library coordinators) each covered one or more sites. That semester I taught 37 sessions of ILI to three sites: Brattleboro (my home site), Springfield, and White River Junction.

There were and continue to be three class periods, morning, afternoon, and evening. Library staff members were on call to provide ILI during all three of those time periods. We created sched-

ules so we that would not be in more than one site per day, but the schedules did not always hold up. Since ILI was at the request of faculty, some students sat through as many as five ILI sessions in a semester, while other students received no instruction.

At the beginning of 2004, however, online students had no access to information literacy instruction. They could click on a Library tab in their Blackboard course to access the Library's website. On the website they learned about their two options for research help: emailing or calling a librarian using an 800 number. They also received an email from the Library at the beginning of every semester. Offering these students an array of services not connected to their specific course was not serving the library needs of these students. As Shank and Dewald explain, "...the closer the link between course assignments and library resources to help with these assignments, the greater the likelihood that students will access library information."[9]

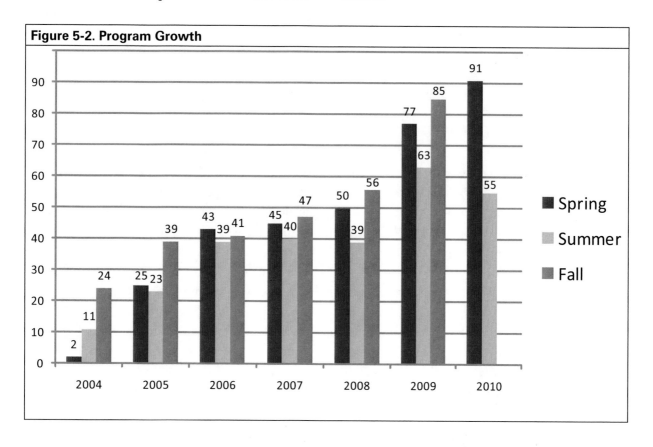

Figure 5-2. Program Growth

The Embedded Librarian Program Begins

The embedded librarian pilot at CCV began because one of the faculty members, Victoria Matthew, and I wanted to offer additional library services to her online Introduction to Psychology class. For the first iteration of the embedded librarian concept, I became a teaching assistant in Victoria's course and set up an "Ask a Librarian" discussion board. Students asked library questions as they researched topics for their mid-term and final papers. I also posted tips for their particular assignments, including threads about finding and narrowing topics, choosing and using Library databases and resources, and citing sources using the American Psychological Association's documentation style. Another Introduction to Psychology faculty member, who had modeled her course on Victoria's, signed on for this initial pilot as well.

Expanding the Program

Both faculty members and many students indicated that they appreciated the customized library support right in their main classroom, the discussion board. The quality of research papers was improved. For my part, after years of doing face-to-face ILI, it was a new and interesting challenge to convey library and research information to students I would never see. Thus, the program was advertised to all online faculty members for the following semester and that summer we served 11 courses. By fall 2004, seven library staff members served as embedded librarians in 24 courses. Three were librarians and four others were paraprofessionals.

The program grew every semester, with slight dips in the summer because fewer courses run that term. By the spring 2010 semester, 6 years after the program started, four librarians were embedded in 91 courses. 839 courses have been served since the program began and 50 courses are signed up so far for the summer semester.

Advertising and Setup of the Program

The program is marketed to faculty through emails and advertising on the Faculty Portal and the Library website. Marketing efforts include a link to a 3½-minute video about the program. Faculty members are required to use an online form to enroll. Previously we just required email requests and, while some faculty are still getting used the more formal system, it helps us better manage our increased enrollment in the program. Also, this procedure allows us to easily keep information about the course and the faculty member in one place, viewable by all librarians. As the forms come in, the courses are assigned to librarians. Faculty have the option of choosing a librarian, and that preference is honored unless the librarian already has too many courses. If a librarian is not specified, courses are assigned to librarians based on subject specialty, familiarity with the course/faculty member, or librarian preference. Approximately a week before the new semester begins, a reminder email is sent to faculty who have used the service before but who have not yet enrolled. Faculty members who do not want to continue using the service are advised to delete the "Ask a Librarian" forum and not copy it over from the previous semester. We have had problems with faculty leaving the forum up and then students asking questions when there was no librarian enrolled in the course.

Embedded Librarians are enrolled in their respective courses as teaching assistants by the librarian with some Blackboard systems manager privileges. For the first four years of the program, we had to ask someone else to enroll librarians and this led to delays when the online staff was overwhelmed with work at the beginning of the semester. Fortunately we were granted these privileges in 2008. Once the librarians are enrolled in their courses, in most cases they set up "Ask a Librarian" discussion boards. Occasionally faculty will set up the forums themselves or name the forum something different, such as Library Forum or Library Questions.

Librarian Lectures

The first librarian post typically greets the students,

describes how the service can help them, provides them with alternate ways of contacting her, and alerts them that she does not reply to questions on the weekends. As the course progresses, librarians suggest sources for the students' specific assignments, providing instructions and links to video tutorials where relevant. Naturally, we emphasize the Library's catalog and article databases in our

---

Figure 5-3. Embedded Librarian Request Form (Summer 2010)

Faculty may request that a librarian be embedded in their Blackboard course site(s) to facilitate the research process by helping students find, evaluate, and cite information.

To apply to have an embedded librarian for your Summer 2010 course(s), first review the checklist below. Then fill out the form. You may list all of your courses on one form. You will be notified before the semester begins as to whether your course has been accepted and who your librarian is.

For more information about the program, contact Ann Schroeder or (802) 254-6364.

1. Please make sure your course meets both of the following prerequisites to having an Embedded Librarian:

☐ Your course has a research component/assignment.

☐ Blackboard course pages are used as an integral part of the course, with frequent use of Bb discussion board.

✱ 2. Fill in the following:

Your Name: _____

Your Email: _____

Your Phone: _____

✱ 3. Course Information:
Course Code/Section Lookup

1. Course Name: _____

Course Code/Section: _____

2. Course Name: _____

Course Code/Section: _____

3. Course Name: _____

Course Code/Section: _____

4. Course Name: _____

Course Code/Section: _____

4. Briefly describe how you envision the embedded librarian service to be utilized by your class(es).

_____

✱ 5. Would you like to work with a specific librarian?
(Janette Shaffer, Larraby Fellows, Rebecca Roberts)

◯ Yes

◯ No

If yes, name of librarian: _____

posts, but we also discuss finding and evaluating websites, online indexes such as Google Scholar, and citation styles. Specialized websites that will help students with a particular assignment are also included. Posting about relevant sources at the right time and reminding students of deadlines is much appreciated by faculty.

Since the program has been in place for six years, we have a wealth of posts to draw on, many designed for specific courses. These posts (or mini-lectures, as we call them) are stored on librarians' personal computer drives and then moved to a shared drive if a different librarian is taking over the course. Taking on a course in a new area or one taught by a different faculty member requires several hours for the librarian to become acquainted with the assignments and create new lectures.

In summer semester 2009 we served 63 courses. For the first time, we kept track of the number of lectures we posted in each course and whether they were new or revised. The average number of librarian lectures per course was 9. Fortunately, many of the courses continue from semester to semester. Of those 9 lectures, an average of approximately one was completely new. The others were revised to reflect changes to assignments, databases, or the Library website. The average number of librarian posts per course was 14. Since 9 of those were lectures, the remaining 5 were answers to students' questions.

Answering Questions

In answering student questions, we aim for a 24-hour turnaround time, except for weekend questions. Those are all answered on Monday since none of the librarians work weekends. Students, many of whom have job and family responsibilities, do much of their work on weekends, so Monday is the busiest day for embedded librarians at CCV. Also, weekly assignments are often due on

---

Figure 5-4. Posting to students

Author: Ann Schroeder
Posted date: Thursday, July 17, 2008 12:33:32 PM EDT
Last modified date: Tuesday, July 29, 2008 12:38:54 PM EDT
Total views: 19 Your views: 3

Greetings to John's English Composition students!

I am looking forward to working with you this semester. I'll be checking this forum several times a week, but not on weekends.

I won't be reading your other discussion forums, but will check to see what your assignments are and how I can help.

Questions here (in the Library forum) are preferred because answers may be helpful to more than one student, but I can also be reached at schroedera@ccv.edu and (802) 254-6364.

Figure 5-5. Posting to students

View the Library Orientation tutorial to learn more about how the Library works:

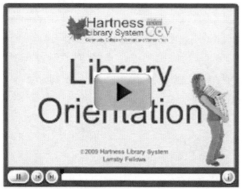

Note: videos are Adobe Flash presentations. Download the most recent version of Flash.

Here is a printable handout of Library Essentials (PDF) too.

Be sure to visit the Library by clicking the CCV Hartness Library tab above.
There you'll find more information about ordering library books, finding journal articles and general research help.

Have a great first few weeks of class,

Ann

Figure 5-6. Posting to students

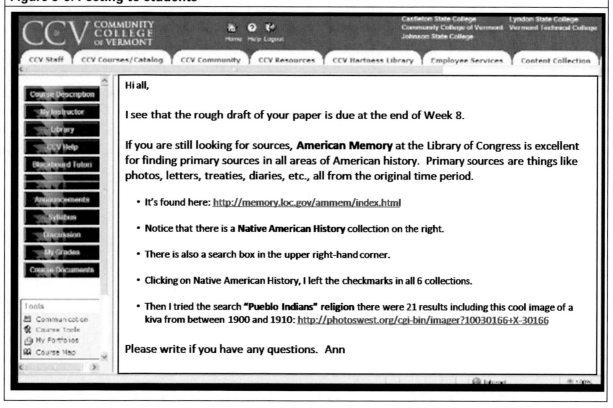

Figure 5-7. Posting from student

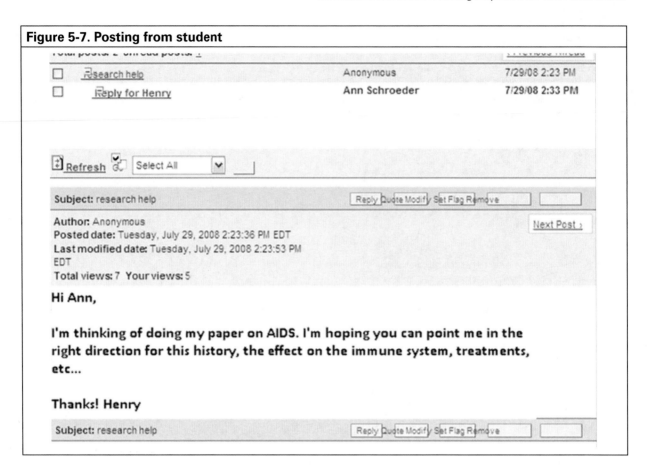

Figure 5-8. Response to student

Hi Henry,

I think for this topic I would start with our **Health & Wellness Resource Center** to get a good overview article.

Here's how:

1. Click on the **CCV Hartness Library** tab above.
2. Click on **Articles (Databases A-Z)** under FIND on the left.
3. Click on **H** in the alphabetical guide at the top.
4. Click on **Health & Wellness Resource Center & Alternative Health Module**.
5. Under DISEASES & CONDITIONS on the left, click on **More>>**.
6. Scroll down and click on **AIDS**.

You'll see that this article has sections on Causes & Symptoms, Diagnosis, Treatment, and more.

Here's a path to an online tutorial for using our article databases:

CCV Hartness Library tab > All Handouts & Tutorials > Find Articles

You will also want to try some other databases such as those mentioned in my earlier thread titled "Finding Articles for your Research Project."

There you may want to try searches like **AIDS and history, AIDS and immune system,** etc. to get at your specific questions.

Hope this helps. Ann

Monday or Tuesday. Prior to learning how to subscribe to forums in Blackboard, we only tried for a 48-hour turnaround time. Then we were manually checking courses at least three times during the workweek. We learned about forum subscription in Blackboard in 2008, and now we subscribe to all "Ask a Librarian" forums when we set them up at the beginning of the semester. This way student or faculty posts go directly into our Outlook mailboxes. This has saved a tremendous amount of time and also ensures that students' questions are answered in chronological order. Occasionally students will call or email their embedded librarian instead of posting in the discussion forum. We help students who contact us this way, of course, but it is preferable if they post in the forum so that other students can read the questions and answers. They are all doing the same assignments, after all.

The amount of time spent crafting a student response varies widely. Some of the simplest questions are procedural. They can often be answered from a collection of responses to Frequently Asked Questions compiled over multiple semesters, or with a link to a video tutorial. Questions about where to find a particular piece of information, on the other hand, can take a lot of time, just as they can in any reference situation. I've found that saving responses to students' questions can be very helpful. I have a Windows folder set up for student questions for that particular semester, using their first name and topic in the file name. That way, if a student asks an additional question, I can easily see what I wrote to him or her previously. Also, if a topic is familiar, I do not have to reinvent the wheel. In one week, for example, I had students in two different classes ask about the moon's effect on emotions.

Asking questions of their embedded librarian is the most popular way CCV students get research and reference help. Our fall 2009 reference statistics reveal that of the 839 questions we answered, 388 (or 46%) were asked in the "Ask a Librarian" discussion forums. The next most popular way of

receiving help was via chat. Two hundred and seven, or 25% of the questions arrived that way. After that, in decreasing order of popularity, the contact methods were email, in person, and phone questions. Since very few of our sites are staffed with librarians, asking questions in person is rarer than at campus-based colleges. Spring 2010 statistics reveal that a lower percentage of questions than in fall 2009 were asked through Blackboard. Of 946 reference questions, 369, or 39% were asked of embedded librarians, compared to 46% in fall. The chat percentage went down slightly, from 25% to 23.7%, but a new offline chat form we instituted that semester drew 9.6% of questions. It functions like email from our standpoint, but patrons post in a chat box area, which they seem to like.

Student Participation in the Library Discussion Forum

We also used Blackboard's Course Statistics feature to determine the number of student posts and the unique number of students who posted for the 63 courses we served in the summer 2009 semester. We found that the Course Statistics feature did not accurately calculate the number of times that each thread was viewed, so we counted those individually. This was very labor-intensive and not worth repeating. The average number of students enrolled in the courses we served was 12. Each course had an average of 7.5 student posts by an average of only 3 students. However, the number of student views of posts in the "Ask a Librarian" forum averaged 275 per course. This indicates that many students were lurkers, reading but not posting. We also found that some posts were read many more times than there were students in the course, so students clearly reread the most useful posts.

The fact that students are reading the librarians' posts is good, but we would really like to see more active participation. The average of only 3 students posting 7.5 times in each course includes courses in which every student is required to post, so in some courses, only the librarian ends up posting in the forum. This can be very frustrating for the librarian and discourages the faculty member from using the embedded librarian service again.

Encouraging Student Participation in the Library Forum

I have found that several techniques encourage students to post. If the librarian includes a photo of herself in her initial greetings post, students are more likely to reply to the post, sometimes including their own photo. Also, if students reply to any of my posts with a greeting or a comment instead of a question, I'll reply to them even though it is not a formal question. Sometimes my comment is as simple as "Nice to meet you also," but often I'll reply with information about the Library or the suggestion to read my next thread about another resource. I make a point of referring to students by name in my posts; for example: "Since Justin asked about getting copies of articles through interlibrary loan, I'm posting these tips for everyone." It really makes a difference for the whole semester if one student is brave enough to post anything, since that encourages other students to post. This is why replying to students' comments, even if the replies are not particularly informational, is a key relationship-building strategy. Occasionally faculty will post in the librarian's forum, perhaps emphasizing that a particular resource is excellent for an assignment, or just thanking the librarian. Faculty interest and participation also encourage student involvement. All of these techniques help build community.

Another way of encouraging student participation is to post "just in time," when information is needed for a project. I follow the syllabus carefully and post a week or so before a project is due, except for assignments that take several weeks or even the whole semester. In those cases I post incrementally, first about books if those are useful sources for the project, since, in our delivery system, books take a week or so to arrive at students' homes. Next I might post about finding articles in our databases

or about quality websites. Lastly I post about citation styles since most student do their documentation after writing their papers no matter how much they are encouraged to do otherwise.

Curricular Areas Served

English courses use the embedded librarian service the most. In spring semester 2010, 20 of the 91 courses with embedded librarians were English courses. Many of these are research-intensive courses and the close collaboration with a librarian is extremely helpful to both students and faculty. Of all the courses I've worked with, Introduction to Research Methods has consistently been the busiest, with at least 100 posts in the "Ask a Librarian" forum every semester.

Interestingly, the next most popular subject area where embedded librarians are requested is biology (14 of 91 courses). Some of those instructors have been with us since the first semester (summer 2004) that we opened up the program to all online instructors. Biology faculty often assign annotated bibliographies and embedded librarians post about finding, evaluating, and citing articles for these bibliographies. The next most popular curricular areas are education and psychology.

Over the six years the program has been in existence, we have served most of the curricular areas. The subject matter doesn't matter as much as whether the students have a research assignment and make frequent use of Blackboard. Early in the program we accepted interested faculty members without making sure that they used Blackboard and had a valid research assignment. This led to some desperate librarian attempts to come up with posts for courses like Tax Procedures.

Alternative Models

Over the six years of the program, we have tried some alternate models to having one librarian discussion forum. In one research-intensive course, an "Ask a Librarian" thread was added to each week's discussion. This was the most intensive work I ever did in a course and fortunately it has not been repeated. There were over 200 total posts in "my" threads. Many were responses to student questions but I also tried to highlight appropriate resources for that week's assignments. In a couple of other classes, I was added to Blackboard Groups. I had to read many posts unrelated to research which took time and also made it more likely that I would miss valid questions. Fortunately the faculty member decided that this model was too much work for him and his students.

The only alternate model that has stood the test of time is what we term the "guest lectureship." This model is used only with online classes. The librarian essentially teaches the class for one week of the semester. Two content areas in which the librarian is an expert have been the subject of lectures: Internet searching/evaluation and documentation styles. The librarian posts informative threads as usual, but she also replies to every substantive student comment, just as the faculty member does for all the other weekly discussions. The faculty member jumps in occasionally but it is really the librarian's show. English Composition has been a natural fit for the guest lectureship in citation and a Microcomputer Applications faculty member uses an embedded librarian for the one week that her course covers Internet searching.

Moving to All Virtual ILI

The two parallel options for ILI (in-class sessions for face-to-face (F2F) courses and embedded librarians for online courses) continued until the fall semester of 2008. At that point several factors led to the cessation of in-class workshops. The first was the establishment of a First Semester Seminar (FSS) course as a requirement for all incoming degree students. Information literacy foundational skills were placed in this course so that students would gain these skills early in their college careers no matter which degree they were pursuing. Prior to this, students in the same level class could have widely varying information literacy skills. Thus, li-

brary instructors were stuck in basic mode, teaching a few tools rather than real information literacy. Before the first sections of FSS courses began in the fall semester 2008, librarians worked with faculty to develop information literacy content for the course. FSS students also complete the information literacy tutorial (TILT) that we modified from the original version created by librarians at the University of Texas at Austin.

In addition to the First Semester Seminar, all students are also required to take English Composition I, plus a research and writing intensive, which can be English Composition II, Introduction to Literature, Introduction to Research Methods, or Global Issues in the Media. Information literacy skills are strengthened in these courses. Finally, prior to graduation, all students are required to take the capstone course, Seminar in Educational Inquiry. The comprehensive final paper for this course is evaluated to determine if the student has met the graduation standard in information literacy. Librarians help faculty design assignments with information literacy components for all of these courses, create instructional videos, and maintain course guides to support information literacy.

The Vermont State College Information Literacy Standards are as follows:

Upon graduation, students will be able to:
- define a research topic and the information needed
- collect and organize information, utilizing a variety of traditional and electronic sources
- evaluate the information and its sources critically
- acknowledge and document the sources needed.

In addition to the new First Semester Seminar requirement for students, another factor in the decision to eliminate library instruction for F2F classes was the College automatically turning on Blackboard components of all classes taught at

CCV. Previously these were left off for the face-to-face classes unless the faculty member selected the option to make the course available. This accessibility encouraged faculty who taught F2F classes to also use the Blackboard component of their course for posting documents and for additional discussion. The embedded librarian program was a natural fit with this new initiative.

Budget constraints were also a consideration in fall 2008. The last regular semester prior to this time, library staff taught 126 sessions of course-related library instruction. Reimbursing library staff members to drive to all 12 locations was a significant expense at a time of soaring gas prices. For example, in the fall 2007 semester, library staff traveled 5500 miles, mostly delivering instruction, and only occasionally attending meetings. A mountain ridge running vertically through the state and challenging winter weather sometimes made travel difficult. In addition, hours spent on the road were hours spent not directly serving students. A new academic dean, a new assistant library director, and a library coordinator retirement also combined to make this a time for change. Related to the latter, the library coordinator (paraprofessional) position was eliminated. The CCV library staff then consisted of three (now four) MLS-credentialed librarians.

Also, learning centers were established in every site so that students would be able to get one-on-one help for mathematics, English, and other course subjects, as well as receive basic library assistance. These sites are staffed with faculty and peer tutors, who receive ongoing library training. They also learn when to refer a student to a librarian and the various methods of librarian contact: email, phone, and chat. Chat hours were increased to 28 hours per week at this time.

The Library's focus shifted from in-class ILI to video tutorials, consults with faculty, subject guides, and an increased emphasis on the embedded librarian program. By the end of that semester, one of our librarians had created 14 video tutori-

als using Captivate. They included: Library Orientation, Faculty & Staff Guide, Learning Center Guide, Embedded Librarian Program, Find Books & Media, four Find Articles tutorials (What is a Database?, Selecting a Database, Searching a Database, Specific Articles & ILL), and five website tutorials (Searching, Evaluating, Google Scholar, Google Books, and Wikipedia). We later switched to using YouTube for our video tutorials and currently have 28 videos available on the YouTube site. In addition, we link to 23 vendor tutorials for databases.

Emphasis was placed on faculty-librarian consultations as faculty members planned their assignments. The faculty area of the Library website was enhanced to include assignment ideas, worksheets, and scavenger hunts that feature library resources. Directions for borrowing media items from the catalog, using Library databases for professional development, and creating persistent links to articles from databases were also provided. Other faculty sections include teaching tools (such as links for educational podcasts, videos, and directories), as well as background on copyright, fair use, preventing plagiarism, and CCV's information literacy program. Another section describes the embedded librarian program and includes a video tutorial and a link to the enrollment form for the program. In addition, at the time of transition to virtual information literacy instruction, librarians offered face-to-face workshops to faculty about the new plan and the new library resources. Webinars over Adobe Connect were provided for those who were unable to attend in person.

Near the end of the first semester without ILI, we subscribed to Springshare's LibGuides product and currently we have 45 subject guides. Eleven of these guides are for specific courses; the courses are chosen because they are developmental, research-intensive, have many sections offered, or are regulars in the embedded librarian program.

To help compensate for the lack of face-to-face ILI, embedded librarians were offered to every class, including hybrid and F2F courses. Many of the latter had never used Blackboard. That first semester, 16 of the 63 courses we served in the embedded librarian program were face-to-face courses, or 25%. Many of these early adopters already knew and worked with librarians in either previous face-to-face ILI or in the embedded librarian program for their online courses. A few just wanted to try the latest thing. Interestingly, the percentage has dropped, and as of spring semester 2010, only 14 of the 91 courses (15%) with embedded librarians were face-to-face courses.

Prior to the semester, we ask faculty to fill out an enrollment form that clearly states that their course must have at least one research assignment and also asks them to describe the assignment. We also ask that they make frequent use of Blackboard. We can view the online syllabus for any course to see if it has at least one research assignment, but

use of Blackboard is more difficult to assess for face-to-face classes. We've found that if students do not regularly use Blackboard, especially the discussion forums, it is not likely that they will even read any of the embedded librarian's posts or ask questions there. Another problem is lack of faculty promotion of the service. This is especially important in the case of faculty who teach F2F courses. The best faculty members remind their students about the service frequently, in assignments, announcements, and emails. As Scheuermann says "…if the professor doesn't encourage and foster engagement between the student and the librarian, it may not happen."[10]

In the fall semester of 2009, when we realized that in some cases the program was not working as well for face-to-face classes as for online courses, the librarians proposed to faculty teaching those courses that we could also email students our

Figure 5-9. Library discussion forum

Blackboard posts. On a course-by-course basis, we discussed this with faculty and set up parameters for the emails. Typically they felt that no more than one email a week from their course's librarian, or even only one every other week, was acceptable. Early evidence of this initiative has been positive; students are more engaged and ask more questions of their librarians. Another initiative to encourage students in face-to-face classes to use their librarian's services is an "Ask a Librarian" button. This link on the course menu is just a shortcut to the library discussion forum in the main discussion board. In some F2F courses, it's the only discussion forum there.

Assessment of the Program

Initially in the fall semester of 2008 when the librarians phased out F2F information literacy instruction, a few faculty expressed concern that this would not serve students well. However, in a survey done of faculty, staff, and students in fall 2009, after a year without face-to-face ILI, one survey statement was "Overall, I feel confident using the Hartness Library." 93.8% of respondents replied "Yes" to that statement. This was designed to parallel a question we asked in a survey in early 2007, when we were providing many sessions of ILI. At that time, only 68.3% replied that they were confident using the Library.

On that same survey, in order to assess faculty satisfaction with embedded librarian service, we asked faculty: "Overall, how satisfied are you with the Embedded Librarian Service?" 10.7% of the respondents said they had not used the service. Of the remaining respondents, 76% were very satisfied, 20% satisfied, and only 4% not satisfied. Our first survey of faculty satisfaction with the service took place at the end of the fall semester 2008. At that time we received 19 replies out of the 37 faculty members participating in the program. There were five questions on the survey, relating to the librarians' explanation of the program, the librarians' lectures and replies to questions, whether the

faculty member would recommend the program, and overall satisfaction. Overall satisfaction with the program averaged 4.63, with 5 being the highest. Only faculty who taught face-to-face and hybrid courses rated the program below 5. We routinely receive many unsolicited testimonials from faculty. One that nicely sums up the goal of the program was: "You have been credited by students with outstanding help and navigation through their research topics, and I will add my voice. I appreciate your willingness to help students of all levels and needs to be successful in finding what they require."

Comparing Embedded Librarian Programs

In 2007, Amy York and Jason Vance of Middle Tennessee State University and Morehead State University, respectively, distributed a survey about librarian participation in online courses through email lists. I replied to that survey, as did 158 other respondents. Their subsequent article outlined best practices for these programs.[11]

The authors recommended not becoming overextended because librarians who offer the service are usually adding it to a full plate of other duties.[12] Since CCV migrated away from face-to face ILI, the number of courses we are serving through the embedded librarian program has increased 55%. This is primarily because we no longer spend time in classes or driving between sites to offer ILI. Data from York and Vance's survey suggest that at best, librarians who responded to their survey are actively involved in no more than 10% of online courses at most institutions.[13] At CCV, for the spring 2010 semester, we were involved in 36% of online courses (77 out of 212 courses). Although most librarian respondents to the survey were embedded in only one to 10 courses a semester, I've regularly done 30 or more courses, with a personal maximum of 44 in spring semester 2010.[14] However, I manage the embedded librarian program and do not have as many other responsibilities as CCV's three other librarians do. In that same semester, they did 17, 19, and 11 courses, respectively. Some of my classes were totally quiet; I'd post tips but no one would ask questions. This is frustrating but it does cut down on the workload.

I was surprised that only 36% of the surveyed librarians posted links to specific resources and only 33% used the discussion board.[15] These two concepts are at the heart of the embedded librarian program at CCV. Unlike our program, though, 22% of respondents wrote and administered quizzes. Some of these were for information literacy courses but some were for research modules in other courses.[16]

Conclusion

A recent study of ILI at bachelor's-granting institutions in the United States found that the number of library instruction sessions was down 13.2% and the number of participants down 19.7%.[17] The John M. Budd says that "individual libraries might want to look closely at local trends in both staffing and presentations, since class presentations will be personnel intensive."[18] Certainly one of the reasons we transitioned away from class presentations was lack of adequate staffing for our 12 learning locations. However, the changes at CCV also reflect the national trend of information literacy instruction being integrated into the curriculum, rather than offered as a separate service by librarians. As Lindstrom and Shonrock say, "instead of relying on reference encounters in the library and formal library instruction, librarians are working to promote collaboration with faculty and campus units in an effort to integrate information literacy into the curriculum.[19] At CCV, librarians continue to work with faculty to support the placement of information literacy instruction in the First Semester Seminar and subsequent courses. This has proven to be much more effective than random offerings of library instruction.

Linda Lilliard suggests that when students work with an online course librarian throughout their research projects, the students develop a working relationship with one librarian.[20] This is preferable to brief reference encounters by whatever method those happen. In addition, one instructional design specialist, Elaine Chen, believes that the use of traditional methods such as lectures and handouts do not meet digital natives' needs.[21] She recommends that libraries create a Web environment where virtual research tips are provided for students to learn at their own pace. The Community College of Vermont's embedded librarian program and enhanced online presence provide students with a personal connection to a librarian as well as library resources and instruction in students' preferred online environment. This combination best serves the needs of the 21st-century learner.

Notes

1. Barbara I. Dewey, "The Embedded Librarian: Strategic Campus Collaborations," *Resource Sharing & Information Networks* 17, nos. 1–2 (2004): 5–17.

2. J. P. Kearley and L. Phillips, "Embedding Library Reference Services in Online Courses," *Internet Reference Quarterly* 9, nos. 1–2 (2004): 65–76.

3. Amy York, "The Embedded Librarian Service at MTSU," *Tennessee Libraries* (2006): 56–57.

4. "Spanning the Distance: Framingham State's Embedded Librarian Program." *Massachusetts Library Association Conference Reports*. May 8, 2008. http://mlamasslib.blogspot.com/2008/05/spanning-distance-framingham-states.html.

5. Ibid.

6. Karen M. Ramsey and Jim Kinnie. "The Embedded Librarian: Getting Out There via Technology to Help Students Where They Learn," *Library Journal* 4 (2006), http://www.libraryjournal.com/article/CA6317224.html.

7. Mollie Dinwiddie and Linda Lilliard, "At the Crossroads: Library and Classroom," Journal of Library Administration 3, nos. 1–2 (2002): 251–267.

8. John D. Shank and Nancy H. Dewald, "Establishing Our Presence in Courseware: Adding Library Services to the Virtual Classroom," Information Technology and Libraries 22, no. 1 (2003): 41.

9. Ibid.

10. "Instructor-Librarian Collaboration Can Improve Course, Make Librarians More Effective." *Distance Education Report*, 9, no. 21 (2005): 8.

11. Amy C. York and Jason M. Vance, "Taking Library Instruction into the Online Classroom: Best Practices for Embedded Librarians," *Journal of Library Administration* 49 (2009): 197–209.

12. Ibid., 204.

13. Ibid.

14. Ibid.

15. Ibid., 203.

16. Ibid., 203–204.

17. John M. Budd, "Academic Library Data from the United States: An Examination of Trends," *LIBRES* 19, no. 2 (2009): 9.

18. Ibid.

19. Joyce Lindstrom and Diana D. Shonrock, "Faculty-Librarian Collaboration to Achieve Integration of Information Literacy," *Reference & Users Services Quarterly* 4, no. 1 (2006): 18.

20. Linda L. Lilliard, "Personalized Instruction and Assistance Services for Distance Learners: Cultivating a Research Relationship," *Research Strategies* 19 (2003): 210.

21. Elaine Chen, "Empowering College Students' Research Skills via Digital Media," *Brick & Click Libraries Symposium Proceedings*, November 6, 2009: 78.

 SIX

Instruction Where and When Students Need it: Embedding Library Resources into Learning Management Systems

Emily Daly

The Need to Embed: Background and History

It has long been the role of a reference librarian to provide students with timesaving search strategies and instructional resources intended to help them conduct course-specific research. And it's certainly no secret that students expect methods for accessing these resources conveniently and efficiently—and outside the library walls. Like college students across the country, Duke University's students enjoy using library spaces for studying and working on group projects, but they want library resources and the techniques for using them at their fingertips—accessible precisely when and where they need them and, of course, fully available online.

It's not an (entirely) unreasonable demand in an age of ubiquitous wireless access, an abundance of digitized and born digital materials and increasingly seamless work environments, but it is nevertheless a demand that libraries have struggled to meet.

According to the preliminary analysis of the 2008 discussion groups conducted on seven college campuses as part of Project Information Literacy,[1] undergraduates believe the library to be frustrating and confusing, describing "findability"[2] as the "most intimidating part of course-related research." In interview sessions lead by project heads

Alison J. Head and Michael B. Eisenberg, students revealed that they were "'overwhelmed by all the choices,' 'lacked a necessary orientation to find things,' and, in general, 'always ha[d] trouble finding what [they were] looking for' (both online and in the library)."[3]

PIL respondents commented not only on the accessibility of library resources but also on their perceived effectiveness of library instruction and consultations with librarians: They find these sessions to be of little value, saying that librarians' suggested search strategies and resources may have made sense at the time of instruction but that they find them hard to recall and apply once they actually begin working on research assignments. Further, Head and Eisenberg found that when students were not able to access their desired resources or services at the moment they needed them, they were likely to find a solution on their own—typically online and involving self-taught methods.[4]

Local data, collected through Duke's 2007 LIBQUAL survey, echo Head and Eisenberg's findings and confirm librarians' suspicions that students do not take full advantage of Duke Libraries' vast resources: 80.12% of the 161 undergraduate respondents use non-library gateways daily for their information needs, while only 27.95% use library resources on a daily basis. A meager 19.25% claim to access resources through the library interface on a daily basis.[5] In fact, many students seem not even to be aware that these resources exist for their use, repeatedly telling reference and instruction librarians that they have paid for resources that they found on the so-called free web rather than accessing them through the Duke Libraries website.

Head and Eisenberg's findings, coupled with local anecdotal evidence from librarians who work with students both at the reference desk and in the classroom, confirm Duke librarians' belief that it was time to supplement their course-integrated library instruction and make a change in their delivery of discipline-specific research strategies. It was no longer sufficient for librarians merely to list their contact information and post research guides on the Libraries website and wait at the reference desk for students to request their services. The time had come for librarians to integrate these resources into students' natural work environments.

And Duke librarians were certainly not alone in their quest to move from a passive model for presenting discipline-specific information to a more active one. In their 2004 article, "Students, librarians, and subject guides: Improving a poor rate of return," Brenda Reeb and Susan Gibbons note that students' expectations have been raised by learning environments such as WebCT and Blackboard, learning management systems (LMSs) that are tailored to the specific needs of students enrolled in a given course. These very students arrive at their libraries' websites with expectations that the library will also meet their course-specific needs, and they move on to other information sources when they find that traditional library resources simply "do not impart the needed personalization or customization" to which they have grown accustomed.[6]

In an attempt to meet their students' increasingly higher expectations, University of Rochester librarians transitioned from merely hosting their subject guides, which predictably received very little traffic, to making this content available in a more course-specific context. Their CoURse Resources System, developed in-house, ensured that over two semesters, students in the approximately 450 courses (nearly one-half of all courses offered) that placed material on reserve through the Libraries website also received course-specific recommendations for library resources, including links to books, journals and databases; websites and multimedia items. While it was necessary for librarians to invest time at the start of the project, the recommendations they made for a given course were maintained from semester to semester, so the workload lessened significantly in subsequent terms. At the end of the first year, anecdotal evidence (e.g. more students were requesting librarians by name and appeared to recognize librarians from their photos on their course guides) pointed to the success of the implementation of the CoURse Resources System.

Reeb and Gibbons also speak to the importance of "well-placed access points" for these resources, believing learning management systems like Blackboard or WebCT to be ideal locations for housing support tools.[7] By directing their subject guides to students at the course level, librarians make them immediately relevant and easily accessible.

Librarians at University of North Carolina-Greensboro opted to do just that, developing a system similar to the University of Rochester's, yet integrated directly into Blackboard, their campus-wide LMS. UNC-G's Course Resources Tool, which was launched in beta in spring 2007 and then integrated into all Blackboard course sites by fall 2007, uses information about students' majors and their current class schedules to build a customized guide with resources selected by subject liaisons that are specific to users' departments, courses and course sections. Unlike the system at the University of Rochester, librarians are required to populate the Course Resources tool at the start of each semester for that term's pool of courses.

Another component of UNC-G's system is a Blackboard portal with library resources germane to students' majors. When students log into Blackboard, they see a "Library Resources for My Major" page with links to databases and websites that may prove useful for conducting research in their fields of study, as well as the contact information of their subject specialist and a chat widget that enables students to IM with a librarian. In addition to these resources, students may also easily see their class schedule, along with the resources that librarians have selected for those particular courses using the Course Resources Tool.

Traffic to the Library Resources Portal has increased steadily since its inception in fall 2008. The portal had 10,068 visitors in spring 2009, and 63% of these views represented return users. In fact, by the end of spring 2009, the Library Resources Portal had already become one of the ten most visited pages on the Library website, and this was without any formal promotion.[8]

In 2005, a project team at North Carolina State University began laying the groundwork for Course Views, yet another homegrown service that dynamically generates custom course guides for every course at NC State. Course Views, launched in fall 2008, are essentially "course-centric portals" that give users access to modules, or widgets, tailored to students' research needs in a particular course. Widgets might be generic (e.g. citation tools, catalog search) or more specific to the curriculum (e.g. history, engineering), course or even course section.

Like librarians at UNC-G, NC State's project team opted to integrate its Course Views pages into their Libraries website and, to some extent, into their LMSs, which was complicated by the fact that NC State's courses are housed in three different systems. At the time of implementation, Course Views could not be integrated into NC State's Blackboard Vista, which is the university's most heavily used LMS. Instructors have, however, requested that Course Views be linked to

their Vista course sites at an impressive rate: In fall 2008, 25% of Vista course sites featured access to Course Views.

As has been the case at the University of Rochester and UNC-G, usage data from the Course Views system indicates its success: In its first semester, it effectively created course pages for 1,368 unique courses, and these pages received an average of 1,073 clicks per week.[9]

Much like their colleagues across the country, Duke librarians were also beginning to think more about meeting students not just at their points of need but also *where they are*, which given the number of virtual and physical spaces Duke's students inhabit, is no small feat. One place that is nearly universal to the academic experience at Duke, however, is the university's learning management system, Blackboard.

Over 70% of Duke courses offered to undergraduates use a Blackboard course site in some capacity, and before fall 2007, the Libraries had little presence in it: Students' readings, "e-reserves," were available through Blackboard beginning in 2003, and a content item entitled "Ask a Librarian," which linked to a page with methods for contacting the Libraries, was placed in all course sites in spring 2007. However, Blackboard usage statistics revealed that the "Ask a Librarian" content item got very little traffic, and anecdotal evidence indicated that students simply did not notice that the Ask a Librarian menu item had been added.

Despite PIL participants' expressed frustrations with using library services and resources for course-related research, students noted that they do find value in libraries and librarians, looking especially to reference librarians as "sense-makers" and "navigational sources"[10] as they make meaning of the complex library systems on their campuses.

It was obvious to Duke librarians that students enrolled in courses with a research or writing component could benefit from increased collaboration with their "sense-makers" and that the Libraries' presence within Blackboard was insufficient and underutilized. A method for enhancing the Libraries' integration that closely resembled UNC-G's Course Resources Tool was proposed: Why not include librarians' contact information and links to instructional resources in course sites, where students may more easily find and interact with the information and, ideally, interact more frequently with librarians who specialize in areas related to their courses?

In an effort to turn this fledgling scenario into a more global reality, Duke's Associate University Librarian for Public Services charged a group of librarians and Duke's Center for Instructional Technology staff with "developing scalable methods of librarian integration in Blackboard course sites for the purpose of better supporting student research needs."

Specifically, the group, which named itself "Librarians in Blackboard," aimed to do the following:

1. Pilot the inclusion of rich library content in Blackboard sites to gauge faculty, student and librarian interest and needs

2. Explore strategies for automating the creation of course- and subject-specific content

3. Explore strategies for automating the dissemination of this content within Blackboard

4. Recommend an approach for automated creation and dissemination of this content in Duke's Blackboard system, including timeline, functional requirements and librarian and technical resource requirements

From Fledgling Scenario to Reality

In fall 2007, four librarians asked a dozen faculty in disciplines representing the humanities, social sciences and natural sciences to give them "coursebuilder access" to their individual Blackboard course sites. Every faculty member obliged, enabling librarians to edit individual course site in-

terfaces, allowing librarians to add a content item entitled "Library Links" and then populate this Blackboard "page" using a template designed by the working group. The template included a place for librarians' contact information and a note about their involvement in the course site; a section with links to general Libraries resources (stacks guides, lists of subject librarians, etc.); feeds from social bookmarking sites such as Connotea; and space for links to subject-specific databases, library resources students might find useful for particular assignments, subject guides hosted on the Libraries website, help pages for citing sources or using EndNote or RefWorks, and short animated tutorials. It was, of course, the working group's hope that these guides would extend their one-shot instruction sessions beyond the library training room, giving students the opportunity to refer later to time-saving tips and suggestions for research resources and to contact their librarians with additional questions.

The working group assessed the effectiveness of the pilot through faculty interviews and six-question surveys of students who had Library Links manually added to their course sites, as well as students who did not have access to Library Links in their course sites. All surveyed students were made aware of library resources through face-to-face library instruction, brief class visits or in the "Staff Information" sections of their Blackboard sites.

Two hundred and ten students in sixteen courses responded to the short survey that librarians posted in their course sites. Nearly 65% of students who had Library Links in their course sites indicated that they were "more likely to contact a librarian" as a result of their interaction with a librarian, while only 43% of students who did not have Library Links in their course sites indicated that they would be "more likely to contact a librarian." Approximately 60% of surveyed students indicated that they found Library Links to be "somewhat useful"; 34% found Library Links "very useful." Approximately 28% of surveyed stu-

Figure 6-1. "Library Links" Blackboard page designed using template created by Librarians in Blackboard working group

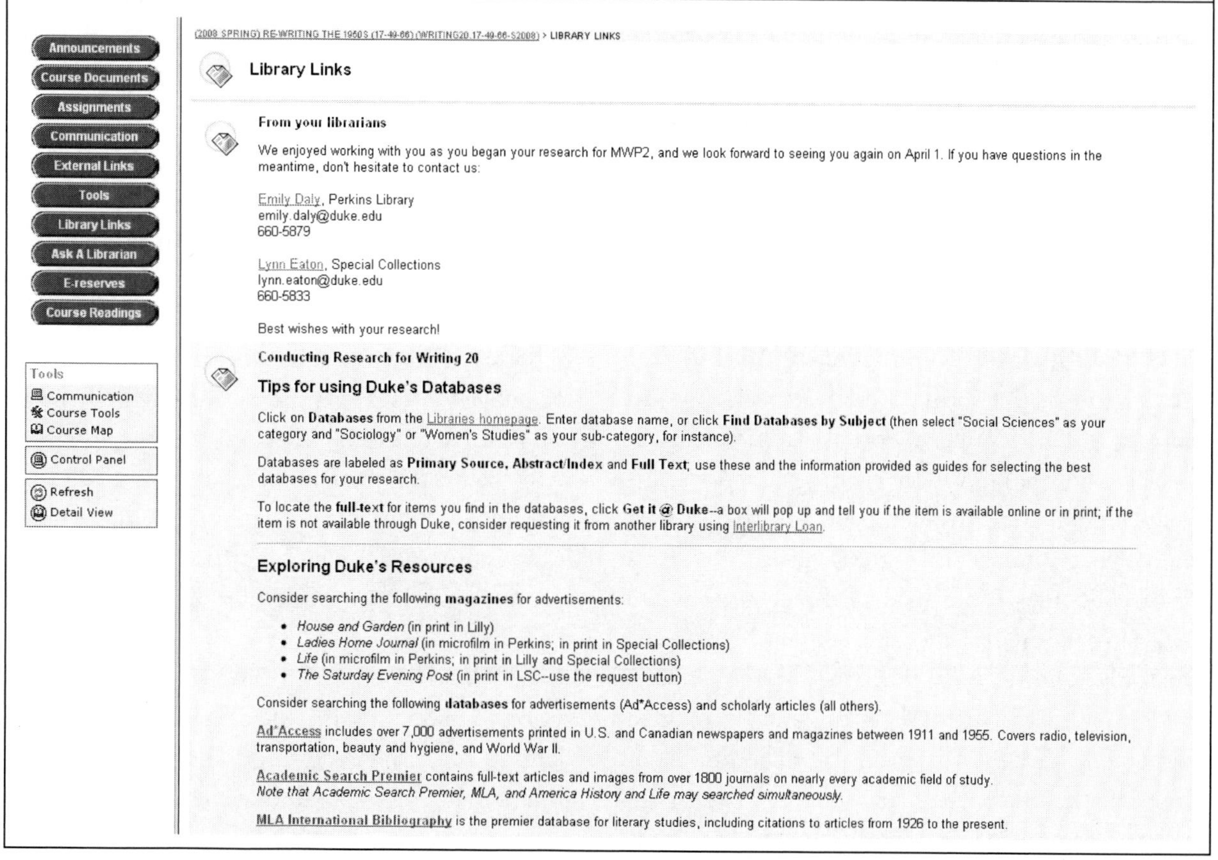

dents reported using Library Links 4–6 times over the course of the semester; 50% claimed to have used it 1–3 times.

All participating faculty provided favorable feedback and requested that Library Links be added to their course sites in the future. Several faculty members confessed that they wished they had done more to make their students aware of the resources and hoped to be able to do so the following semester. Their primary concern was not with the resources but that students were simply not accessing them.

The promising feedback from faculty and students led the working group to continue the project in spring 2008. The group shared its work and findings with several groups in the library and recruited other librarians to become course builders of Blackboard sites for faculty in their disciplines. By the end of the spring semester, 16

librarians had become coursebuilders of 56 Blackboard course sites, representing a broad range of undergraduate classes, disciplines and departments. While the group did not conduct student surveys, librarians interviewed faculty and found, once again, that they supported the project and hoped that it would continue to expand to include more courses.

Librarians benefitted from the initiative, as well: Convenient access to course syllabi and readings made it easier to plan more effective library instruction sessions, and being a part of course email lists enabled them to respond quickly to students' research needs as assignments evolved over the course of the semester. Furthermore, courseguides served as a springboard as they delivered face-to-face instruction, and the guides helped relieve the pressure they had always felt to squeeze *everything* into 50 or 75 minutes—librarians knew they could simply post resources or techniques they did not have time for in class to their Library Guides and even email students to let them know of the addition. Librarians were also beginning to see increased communication from students over the course of the semester—as the survey data indicated, students appeared to be more likely to ask follow-up questions of librarians who were part of their Blackboard course sites.

Addressing Usability and Functionality

At the end of the spring 2008 semester, a group calling itself the Subject Portals Task Force was formed and charged with creating a more user-friendly and attractive template for the Libraries' subject guides. This group, like Librarians in Blackboard, was formed in direct response to librarians' desire to alleviate students' perceived frustrations—this time, with the existing subject guides. While traffic to Duke's guides remained high, many librarians believed that undergraduates were not the ones accessing these laundry lists of web and print resources, and they wished to create tools that would be of benefit not only to experienced scholars and other librarians but also to the university's novice researchers.

Again, librarians' collective hunch that the guides they had painstakingly created were not being fully utilized was confirmed with survey data that had been collected by the Libraries' Architecture and Design Group (ADG). In order to better understand their intended audience for its web content, the ADG assessed the Duke community's usage of the Libraries website, including subject guides, through a web survey. The group then fleshed out their survey data by conducting face-to-face interviews with students and faculty.

The ADG's 10-question survey of nearly 1100 users revealed that 53% of respondents had never accessed the Libraries' subject guides and that only 3% of all respondents claimed to use subject guides "frequently." This is even more disconcerting given that the survey respondents reported heavier use

of research tools than of any other content on the Libraries site.

Duke librarians were certainly not the only ones interested in overhauling their ever-growing lists of research guides. Brenda Reeb and Susan Gibbons summarize usage statistics of web-based subject guides at the University of Rochester and other research libraries, noting that subject guides receive very low hit rates relative to the number of students they are intended to support. Reeb and Gibbons believe that students have difficulty finding subject guides and then using them effectively in large part because they are simply unfamiliar with the overall purpose of a subject guide and librarians' organization of these guides into academic disciplines and because they do not identify with or recognize the interface librarians use to design them.[11]

After consulting with librarians at peer institutions, conducting brief user interviews with undergraduates, and exploring options for enhancing functionality of and branding the hundreds of static web pages that Duke's subject librarians had created, the task force recommended that the Libraries subscribe to LibGuides, a web-based "content management and knowledge sharing system for libraries."[12] The group believed that the LibGuides interface would provide students with a highly intuitive, aesthetically appealing and uniform interface they had come to expect.

Because the LibGuides interface enabled librarians to develop fully functional, stand-alone web pages that would serve as an ideal platform for a courseguide, it seemed natural in Fall 2008, to merge Librarians in Blackboard and the Subject Portals Task Force and to transition from the Blackboard interface for Library Links to LibGuides to design pages that would serve the same purpose but with enhanced visual appeal. In addition to delivering a more consistent and eye-catching design, the LibGuides application afforded librarians the opportunity to organize their content into multiple tabs and to embed images, videos, RSS feeds to new books and journals and Google Gadgets enabling users to search library collections and databases directly from within the LibGuides interface.

Librarians continued to request coursebuilder access to Blackboard course sites and continued to add a content item manually, renaming the button "Library Guides" to mimic the LibGuides branding. The Library Guides button directed users to course-specific LibGuides that, for the first time, featured their librarians' photos alongside their contact information, as well as links to other guides and chat widgets enabling students to instant message their librarians (or the Libraries' general IM service, if their librarians were unavailable)—gone were the static Blackboard "pages" with lengthy lists of links and resources.

By the end of the fall 2008 semester, 16 librarians had developed guides for 58 course sites. And librarians were doing more than merely creating content—students were using the guides, as evidenced by the 12,737 hits that the 58 guides received between August and December (an average of 219 clicks per guide). It is worth noting that librarians' hits are included in this number. Also worth noting is that some of these hits may have come from outside Blackboard, because for the first time since the inception of the project, we were able to maintain an index page of all course guides for a given semester. LibGuides made this easy—librarians simply tagged their guides with the name of the current semester (e.g. courseguide-fall08); we then used the LibGuides-supplied URL for all content identified with the semester tag as our index to all current courseguides.

Duke undergraduates had begun to take notice of what they believed to be an improved interface for course and subject guides and, for the first time, were requesting that librarians create guides both for their academic and personal research. Like

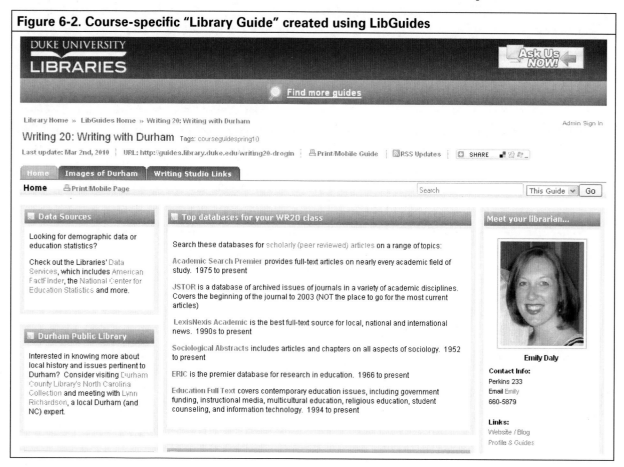

Figure 6-2. Course-specific "Library Guide" created using LibGuides

their students, faculty reported liking the new Library Guides interface, and some even claimed to see a difference in their students' work that they believed might be attributed to Library Guides, noting that the guides were particularly effective when paired with face-to-face instruction. Librarians were also interviewed: They overwhelmingly agreed that the LibGuides interface was easy to use and that the initiative helped them collaborate with faculty in more meaningful ways.

Moving Toward Automation

While the group was pleased with its efforts thus far, it had become clear after two semesters that the current process was not scalable: It was simply not realistic to expect that librarians would ever be able to integrate instructional tools into all (or even a majority) of Duke's 1,700 course sites each semester—in each of the previous semesters, librarians had been enrolled in approximately 3% of all course sites, mirroring NC State's experience with its courseguides:

> Unfortunately, the Libraries never had the resources to create and maintain custom courseguides for more than 3% of the courses offered on campus. It was clear that achieving coverage for the remaining 97% of courses would require a new approach. To achieve this goal, we needed to find a way to customize content to the course that could scale across 6,000 courses in over 150 departments on campus.[13]

The group, with the help of one of the university's Blackboard support staff, began to discuss ways to automate the inclusion of Library Guides, recognizing that while the ideal was to link a course-specific guide to every Blackboard course site, it was more realistic to attempt to link either a subject-specific LibGuide or a LibGuide with general information about accessing library resources to each of Duke's 1,700 course sites.

The process behind this automation was developed, surprisingly, with relatively little effort from just two library staff—a member of the university's Blackboard support team and one of the Libraries' web application developers. Essentially, users click on "Library Guides" in the Blackboard interface, and the following transpires: JavaScript redirects users to an on-the-fly URL with a Blackboard-defined variable (for this purpose, the variable is the subject code for the course; e.g. ARTHIST, PUBPOL). The URL points to a middleware tool; programmers chose to use Django, which is an open source "web framework that encourages rapid development," to create this tool.[14] The Django database reads the on-the-fly URL, matching the Blackboard-defined variable to the corresponding LibGuide (or other webpage) created by a subject librarian for that particular subject code. The corresponding URL is then placed in the Library Guides menu item. Because librarians have complete control over the Django database, virtually any URL—ranging from the Duke Libraries homepage to a specialized LibGuide created with the needs and assignments of a particular group of students in mind—may be pulled automatically into Blackboard. Because the system is dynamic, the page that users see when they click on Library Guides may be instantly changed at any point in the semester by simply entering a new URL in the Django database.

Of course, this functionality is worthless without content to populate the Library Guides button. Therefore, once the process was established and tested, the task force needed to determine which LibGuide (or other webpage) would be mapped to each of the 266 subject codes that correspond to the more than 1,700 course sites that are created each semester. The group looked to the expertise of the Libraries' 35 subject librarians, as well as librarians in three of Duke's professional libraries, asking that subject specialists provide one URL for each subject code falling within their areas of expertise by the start of the spring 2009 semester. Subject librarians were encouraged to develop subject-specific LibGuides (for instance, the librarian for Canadian studies created a Lib-Guide for all courses identified by the subject code "CANADIAN") but could link to non-LibGuides (more traditional subject guides using the Libraries' content management system, for instance) or even their library's homepage or index to research guides. Librarians in Duke's professional libraries opted to do this for many of the subject codes that apply to their work.

There are, of course, subject codes that simply do not correspond logically to a subject area overseen by a Duke librarian. The Blackboard sites for courses with these subject codes are linked to a general LibGuide, designed to serve as an introduction to library resources, which includes many of the instructional resources originally prescribed by the Librarians in Blackboard working group. By the start of the spring semester, 68% of the 266 subject codes had been assigned subject- or library-specific URLs; all others were directed to the generic LibGuide.

There are a number of interdisciplinary subject codes that correspond to the interests—and, therefore, LibGuides—of multiple subject specialists. Similarly, there are a number of courses at Duke that are cross-listed under two, three or even four subject codes. Each of these courses is arbitrarily assigned one subject code for the purposes of Blackboard management, and it is this subject code that determines which URL is automatically linked. Faculty members have been informed of this project and are encouraged to contact subject librarians if they feel that the LibGuide that has been mapped to their course is inappropriate (a note in Blackboard reminds faculty of this initiative and provides contact information for subject librarians so that they may have their default guide replaced, if they wish). As faculty become more fa-

Figure 6-3. Subject-specific "Library Guide" created using LibGuides

Figure 6-4. "Library Guide" created using LibGuides

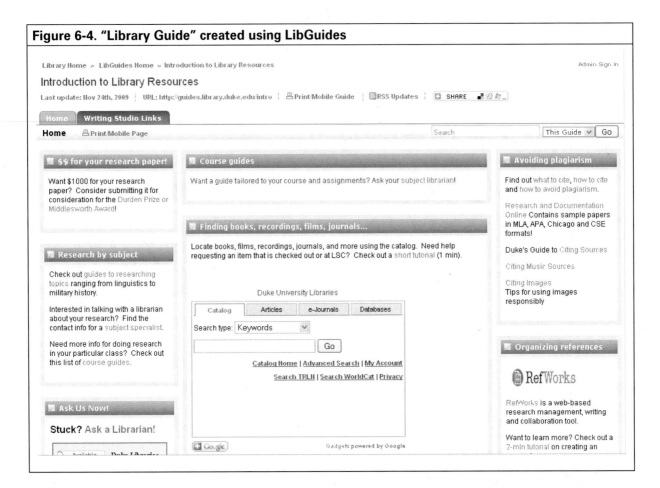

miliar with the project, librarians hope that more professors will take advantage of subject experts' willingness to modify the automatically linked guides to correspond more closely with students' research needs.

This automation may appear complex, but the staff members who worked on it repeatedly commented that it was actually fairly simple to implement. Likewise, the work for subject librarians was fairly minimal: They needed simply to provide URLs for their discipline-specific guides, many of which were already created. The pay-off validated their efforts, for many noted that the project led to enhanced communication and increased instructional opportunities with faculty and students in their departments.

It is worth noting that the current scheme enables librarians to automate content only at the subject level of a particular course (e.g. ARTHIST). It is feasible, however, to use this system to automate

content using the course number identifier (e.g. ARTHIST 49S) or even the section level identifier (e.g. ARTHIST 49S 002). This, of course, would require a much larger database with far more codes and corresponding URLs. Currently, resources are not in place to support this level of specificity, but it is a possibility that we wish to explore in future semesters.

Increased Attention to Evaluation and Usage

At the end of its first semester employing the automated system, the task force assessed the usage of both automatically and manually linked Library Guides. The group devised an extensive evaluation plan in an effort to ensure that the process the combined working groups had put into motion in the first four semesters of the project was indeed meeting the instructional and research needs of Duke's students, faculty and librarians.

Students who accessed the Library Guides menu item from within Blackboard were surveyed, and 89% of the 106 respondents reported that course-specific guides were "somewhat useful" or "very useful" for their research. Ninety percent of those surveyed believe that guides should continue to appear in Blackboard course sites.

Librarians, faculty members and the Libraries' Information Technology Services (ITS) staff were also polled: All three constituencies were pleased with both the automation that had been put into place and the improved guide interface, and ITS staff reported that the impact of the Library Guides system on their work flow was minimal.

Hits to guides were also scrutinized: There were a total of 16,379 hits to the 74 course guides created in spring 2009 (representing an average of 221 clicks per guide, a slight increase over the previous semester) and a total of 5,947 hits to the subject guides or web pages automatically linked within Blackboard. Hits to subject guides from within Blackboard represented just 14% of hits to all guides that semester, confirming librarians' hypothesis that manually linked course guides—often accompanied by face-to-face library instruction—would be more heavily utilized than the more general, automatically linked subject pages.

NC State's Course Views project team found this to be the case in their guides, as well: Clicks to a Chemical Engineering 205 page that displayed references for a research assignment were dramatically higher than the average number of clicks per course page, showing that building relationships with faculty—faculty who encourage students to use course pages by giving them reason to do so—can lead to increased usage of these types of resources.[15]

So while the automated process ensures that every Blackboard course site includes a general introduction to library resources, a subject-specific LibGuide or a professional library's webpage or list of research tools, librarians are still encouraged to foster and maintain relationships with faculty and students in their disciplines and to develop course-specific LibGuides in much the same manner that they did in the early semesters of the project. In becoming coursebuilders of Blackboard course sites and then manually linking specialized guides to the Library Guides menu item, they thereby over-write the automatically generated URL and, as before, become privy to course communication, syllabi and assignments.

While the task force disbanded in June 2009, a representative has continued to provide support and encourage these embedded librarians to maintain existing guides and create new ones each semester. Subject specialists have risen to that challenge, creating 74 guides for fall 2009 and a record-breaking 99 guides in spring 2010. These guides continue to see more traffic each semester: Fall 2009 course pages received 23,487 (317 hits per guide, on average), while those created for spring 2010 received 25,308 clicks for an average of 256 hits per guide.

And guides designed for any given semester aren't the only ones being used—students appear to continue to access guides created for previous semesters, leading librarians to believe that students must bookmark and then continue to use guides for research in subsequent semesters. For instance, a number of the guides created for the university's required writing course, Writing 20, continue to receive around 50 clicks per semester. These guides do not appear on the index page for the current semester's coursepages, and the course sites to which they were originally linked are no longer active (although students may access them for several subsequent semesters), yet they continue to see traffic.

Also on the rise since spring 2009, the first semester of automation, has been the percentage of subject codes (e.g. HISTORY, PUBPOL, ARTHIST) that direct users to subject-specific guides as opposed to the generic introductory guide. During spring 2009, 68% of the university's 266 subject codes had been assigned subject-specific URLs—just one year later, that number topped out at 98% (a handful of codes simply do not map logically to library specialists or resources).

While students use course guides more heavily than they do the subject guides linked from within Blackboard, traffic to subject guides has increased modestly over the last two semesters. Unfortunately, a substantial portion of data from fall 2009 was lost, although the information we do have indicates a slight increase in clicks to the automatically populated Library Guides button in Blackboard (these data do not include hits to guides manually added by subject librarians). In spring 2010, the Library Guides button was accessed 7,334 times, an increase over the 5,947 total hits tracked during the first semester of automation.

It was not enough, however, simply to analyze sheer numbers of visitors to librarians' thoughtfully designed subject and courses guides—we wanted to ensure that guides were as effective and intuitive to navigate as possible, prompting a small team to conduct usability testing and user interviews of the LibGuides interface early in the spring 2010 semester. Testers analyzed the results of 15 user interviews and then issued recommendations to librarians who create courseguides (e.g. "limit number of tabs across top of guide to 4-6"; "consider labeling the 'Home' tab 'Getting started' so that users do not confuse 'Home' of a particular guide with the LibGuides homepage"). They also worked with web designers in the Libraries to make system-level changes to the LibGuides interface that they believed would enhance students' experiences with these embedded resources.

Ensuring Future Success

No project is without its limitations and challenges, and the Library Guides in Blackboard initiative does indeed have room for improvement.

First and foremost, we would like to increase our marketing efforts of the Library Guides feature both to students and faculty. User interviews of 14 students and 1 staff member conducted during spring 2010, the third semester of Library Guides automation, revealed that very few users are aware of the Library Guides button in Blackboard—of our 15 interviewees, only one knew that librarians build course-specific guides (his professor had directed him to a guide created for his class). None knew that they could access course- and subject-specific guides from within Blackboard, yet they all thought that placing guides in course sites was logical and believed that students would find this feature useful. Similarly, we continue to encounter faculty who are completely unaware of the Library Guides initiative—they are, however, uniformly impressed with the concept as soon as we describe it, and many are quick to ask for course-specific guides for classes they teach.

At some point in the coming semesters, we would also like to explore the possibility of expanding our automation system to include not only subject codes, but course numbers, as well. While this will take significantly more coordination, it will provide more students with guides that are more relevant and specific to their course needs. We envision starting this on a pilot basis with one or two departments and then adding more departments once we establish proof of concept.

Of course, the value of "coursebuilder" status in Blackboard cannot be undermined: Librarians and faculty members alike have spoken to the fact that this level of access gives true meaning to "embedded librarian." As we consider moving toward comprehensive course-level automation, we must balance what we stand to lose if it is no longer necessary to make contact with faculty in order to attain coursebuilder status and then make manual changes to Blackboard—and gain access to course syllabi and communication in the meantime.

It is also essential that we continue to monitor the ever-changing landscape of online courseware at Duke. Of immediate import is the fact that the university will be migrating from Blackboard to Sakai as its campus-wide learning management system by the start of fall 2012 We are working with the task force charged with managing this shift to be sure that Library Guides is viable in the new LMS environment. Similarly, instructors are beginning to use WordPress, a free, self-hosted blogging tool, as a lightweight LMS for their courses—again, we will need to continue to work with these faculty to ensure that their students have access to the Library Guides content given that they are not using Blackboard for their courses.[16] Finally, as more and more students move from using laptops and desktops to employing smart phones and iPads for their academic work, they will understandably come to expect services like those offered through the WordPress Mobile Pack, the Blackboard iPhone app and Blackboard Mobile Learn.[17]

We must assess the effectiveness of Library Guides in the context of handheld learning and make the technical changes and adjustments to courseguide layout and content that will undoubtedly be necessary to ensure continued success.

In spite of these potential stumbling blocks, we remain optimistic that the groundwork we have laid and the relationships we have built in collaborating with Information Technology Services staff and Center for Instructional Technology staff, including Blackboard support staff, will serve us well as we continue to transcend the boundaries of the traditional one-shot instruction session in order to be available where Duke's undergraduates are and precisely when they need our expertise.

Notes

1. Alison J. Head and Michael B. Eisenberg, "Finding Context: What Today's College Students Say about Conducting Research in the Digital Age," *Project Information Literacy Progress Report*, University of Washington's Information School, http://projectinfolit.org/pdfs/PIL_ProgressReport_2_2009.pdf.

2. Head and Eisenberg look to Peter Morville's *Ambient Findability: What We Find Changes Who We Become* to define findability, noting it as the "quality of being locatable and navigable, the degree to which a particular object is easy to discover and or locate, and the degree to which a system or environment supports navigation and retrieval." Quoted in Head and Eisenberg, "Finding Context," 10.

3. Ibid.

4. Ibid., 11.

5. Association of Research Libraries (2007), *LibQUAL+ 2007 survey*, Washington, D.C.

6. Brenda Reeb and Susan Gibbons, "Students, Librarians, and Subject Guides: Improving a Poor Rate of Return," *Libraries and the Academy* 4, no. 1 (2004): 126.

7. Ibid., 127.

8. Lynda M. Kellam, Richard Cox, and Hannah Winkler, "Hacking Blackboard: Customizing Access to Library Resources Through the Blackboard Course Management System," *Journal of Web Librarianship* 3, no. 4 (2009): 349–363.

9. Jason Casden, Kim Duckett, Tito Sierra, and Joseph Ryan, "Course Views: A Scalable Approach to Providing Course-Based Access to Library Resources," *Code{4}lib Journal* 6 (2009). http://journal.code4lib.org/articles/1218.

10. Head and Eisenberg, "Finding Context," 10.

11. Reeb and Gibbons, "Students, Librarians, and Subject Guides," 123–130.

12. Springshare, Inc., *LibGuides*, http://www.springshare.com/libguides/.

13. Jason Casden and others, "Course Views," par. 4.

14. Django Software Foundation, *Django*, http://www.djangoproject.com/.

15. Jason Casden and others, "Course Views," par. 35.

16. WordPress.org, *About WordPress*, http://wordpress.org/.

17. Blackboard Inc., *Blackboard Mobile*, http://www.blackboard.com/Mobile/Mobile-Learn.aspx.

PART FOUR
Embedding in the Disciplines
& Across Them

 SEVEN

Embedded and Embodied: Dance Librarianship within the Academic Department

Christopher Miller

Dance: Bodies Moving and Interacting in Physical Space

"Ugh, I just can't find anything for this thesis proposal." The unexpected outburst of frustration and the sound of a sharp slap to a desk came from the room adjacent. I looked to the door, only recently installed, separating me from the source of the voice. It was no accident that I should be within shouting distance; my office and the collection I was hired to curate were purposefully positioned in close proximity to an existing work space tailored to meet the research and on-campus computing needs of the students of the School of Dance. I was precisely where I needed to be, strategically located to provide research assistance in a moment, at any moment, of need. Instant face-to-face access.

I crossed the room, opened the door, and peered across the computers in the next room arranged in a tidy row. The frustration matched the face, relentlessly locked into a stare-down with the monitor. The student was one of our second-year graduate students, a gifted dancer as evidenced by a recent performance. I knew the student, well enough to ask with seamless ease if I could perhaps assist with her project. "Sure."

For the next hour, we sat and talked though her "thesis document", a required component in the School of Dance, which is meant to offer the student an opportunity to seriously reflect and report

on their final MFA degree performance project, a major choreographed work. But, this is dance; it is not your standard humanities or social sciences reference exchange. The student was in the chair one moment, following along as I navigated an electronic database that I thought would be helpful. And, then, she was up out of her chair the next, illustrating a thought with a quick gesture and some movement from the work she was making. If the dots were not always connecting, it was not for the absence of focus on the part of the student. The vocabulary was not only rich, it often transcended spoken language and transferred into movement. This, I thought, is what I am here to do.

This event was neither isolated nor unique but rather a natural part of my daily routine. And the exchange above, even at the time that it was happening, was understood by us both to be a beginning and not a one-off. I crossed paths with this student at least a few times a week, and we continued to converse about her project. Updates to my running journal were just as likely to be the result of a passing conversation in the hall or something new I saw in a rehearsal as they were to be direct actions from a follow-up reference interview. And, in the end, I look forward to a fantastic performance of her new work just as much as reading her thesis.

If I face any criticism here from the community of academic librarians, it must be that I lead a charmed life, which I cannot deny. Yet, in closely considering my own possible contribution to the wealth of exchange on the evolution of embedded librarianship, I assume no better illustration than the story above for the two major points that I hope to convey in this chapter. First, I extend the argument for successful librarian participation in the academic enterprise to the furthest frontier possible: residence within the academic department. Second, I establish a measure of resistance to the notion that setting up shop in the virtual world is a clear path to providing the best possible service as information professionals in the digital age. Allowing that specific circumstances provide no other option than a virtual presence, I insist that not only do we continue to have access to our user community in the physical world but that we should continue to do all that we can to give those exchanges preferential treatment.

And, could there be any better context in which to remind the library community that knowledge and its exchange loses much when it is disembodied, than to view my arguments from the perspective of a dance collection? Shall we dance?

The Cross-Cultural Dance Resources Collection at Arizona State University

In the fall of 2008, Cross-Cultural Dance Resources (CCDR, an organization of dance scholars and practitioners whose scholarly contributions focus primarily on the fields of dance ethnography, ethnochoreology, and ethnomusicology and by extension into the allied disciplines of anthropology, sociology, and religious studies) gifted its Collection directly to the Herberger Institute School of Dance at Arizona State University. Ultimately, relocating the Collection to the School of Dance (as opposed to a central university library) was highly desirable to the Board of CCDR as it promised greater access to the Collection among its primary audience.

The CCDR Collection documents the knowledge embodied within us all and stands as a monu-

ment to the study of dance in cultural context. Its uniqueness is only further enhanced by virtue of its hybridity: equal parts library, archives, and museum (with hundreds of objects of material culture, including: costumes, musical instruments, and dolls). The gift was accompanied by a monetary endowment to support the CCDR Collection in its new location, including funding for a trained curator/librarian. The positive consequence of the arrangement is that the School of Dance enjoys the support of and direct access to a librarian now embedded within the department.

Defining What it Means to be "Embedded"

I do not wish to re-present here the eloquent explorations of the "embedded" model of librarianship published in the past decade. Suffice it to note that the investigation continues here in other chapters of the present publication, and that I have found most rewarding the evolving thoughts of David Shumaker in his finely crafted *The Embedded Librarian* blog,[1] as well as his work with Tyler.[2] Added to these are a thoughtful and recent review composed by Kesselman and Watstein.[3] With the growing availability of publications on the matter, I am comfortable to assume that the readership is already knowledgeable of the topic.

I do, however, wish to challenge the somewhat hyperbolic assertion that has been forwarded by Barbara Dewey, that the origin of the term "embedded" comes to librarianship from the practice of embedding journalists among military units during the war with Iraq.[4] While certainly borrowed, the term also has been made new in use among librarians. Perhaps if those journalists had relied on soldiers carrying helmet-mounted cameras, or if more librarians were on the front lines of classrooms, the metaphor could be more potent.

As it is now, the model of the embedded librarian is more often a virtual one, where Blackboard (or comparable course management software) provides the space in which the librarian interacts with students, allowing for an instruction session or two. The "menu item" model plays prominently,[5-8] while prolonged class attendance and participation in course construction by the librarian is the exception, at least in the academic setting.[9-11] The special libraries model,[12] on the other hand, naturally follows a more integrated role for the librarian, one I will argue that the academic community should better emulate. Accepting "embedded" on its own terms at least necessitates a discussion of physical presence to the extent that it plays a role in what we do and how we do it as librarians.

Past Experience

As an academic librarian, I am experienced with the predominantly virtual model of embedded librarianship. When I was first hired at Arizona State University in 2004, it was to the position of Southeast Asian Studies Bibliographer in the Collection Development (later Collections and Scholarly Communication) Office of ASU Libraries. The position was similar to those in other academic institutions that hosted both an Area Studies (geographic region) focus among an interdisciplinary faculty cohort of humanists and social scientists as well as a large vernacular collection to support the research of that faculty, their students, and foreign language instruction. The expectation of the librarian in such a position is that he will work across disciplinary boundaries and that some language expertise is essential. In general terms, I believe, it is also safe to assume that the area studies librarian enjoys a very close collegiality, beyond the typical subject liaison librarian, with the faculty that she serves.

For a brief period, Arizona State University supported the composition of Learning Communities among incoming freshmen who elected to join ranks in a precomposed semester of set courses and curriculum designed on a theme. Built on a strong literacy focus with writing instruction closely tied to seminar courses led by the faculty, each Learning Community was also assigned an "embedded" librarian. The expectation of the librarian was to extend past the single instruction session into a more participatory role. Of course, I eagerly agreed to serve as librarian to a Learning Community developed by the Southeast Asia studies faculty at ASU.

I will be the first to admit that what I possessed in enthusiasm for both the subject matter and specific opportunity, I sorely lacked in execution. The tools available and general trajectory of action will be well known to librarians who have sought to be embedded. I was welcomed into the classroom as often as I could attend; I was given instructor status both in the virtual space and by introduction to the students; I developed clean connections from our Blackboard site to electronic library resources; I provided multiple information literacy instruction sessions; and I maintained a blog that traced quality web-based resources directly linked to course content. In essence, I believed that I was in a situation that could not fail. A group of students had selected Southeast Asia as a topic of interest and dedicated an entire semester of their university experience to it; and, we were meeting them at least halfway by moving a large part of their educational experience to the online environment.

But, in the role of librarian to the Learning Community, I was continually frustrated by a sense of ongoing disconnectedness. While a handful of students responded well to the ways in which information access had been constructed around the course load, sadly most remained disengaged. And, as I reflected on the experience later, I often wondered if my reliance on both the digital environment and the assumed generational preference for online and asynchronous exchange was far too heavy. Though they were encouraged to visit my office or ask for help during classes, I only saw one or two students beyond the one required bibliographic meeting they each separately attended with me in person.

I do not want to paint a completely negative picture of the Learning Community model for the embedded librarian. There were certainly triumphs and more than a few well-written final papers. And, these were undergraduate freshman, only just finding their footing in the university setting. But, if I were to be asked if I thought that healthy research skills had been secured among their personal tools for academic success, I would have to say no. If anything, I may have reinforced a few bad habits, not least of which was that we were willing as instructors to be disembodied from the learning process. Given the opportunity to start anew, I was certain that I would have approached the Learning Community differently, and I would have leveraged online tools in a different way. But how?

A Different Sense of Embeddedness in the School of Dance

With the arrival of the Cross-Cultural Dance Resources (CCDR) Collection in the Herberger Institute School of Dance at ASU, an unexpected pathway opened to me. Invited into the ranks of an academic department, I was offered an opportunity that I honestly had not previously imagined. And while there was no doubt that it was a move I wanted to make professionally, it did take a certain amount of time for the reality of the positive and negative outcomes of this change to sink in. I will take a moment in the passages below to elaborate on both the advantages and challenges of being an academic librarian embedded within a department to provide some insight into such a structural arrangement. Though all of my observations are necessarily tied to my own direct experience, I believe that they are in many ways generalizable to the overall conversation regarding embedded librarianship. Despite that my current situation is unusual, the reflections offer observations from the periphery for discourse and perhaps some inspiration for new models to those who seek them.

Some advantages of being embedded within an academic department, to be further investigated below, are:

- the department is invested in a collection and a librarian

- the embedded librarian is completely integrated into the department and its processes
- the embedded librarian is a departmental colleague
- the embedded librarian has greater input into curriculum elements that have a direct impact on information literacy
- the embedded librarian is conversant in the cycle of knowledge production and specialized vocabularies in the given academic field
- the embedded librarian has the opportunity to influence information management within the department
- the embedded librarian serves as a liaison ("translator") with the central campus library and its representatives
- the embedded librarian participates in donor development, grant writing, and other funding opportunities
- the embedded librarian benefits from the inter-departmental connections, often strategic relationships, developed across campus by the home department
- students within the department perceive the librarian as having a more pronounced role in their educational experience; the embedded librarian is a motivated mentor

Some challenges of being embedded within an academic department, to be further investigated below, are:

- The professional review and evaluation process requires the establishment of a new set of standards within the department
- The embedded librarian is professionally isolated from peers
- The embedded librarian loses influence and input within the central campus library or information center, as well as the advantages of its infrastructure
- The embedded librarian must create sup-

port for a collection or library in a non-traditional location

Advantages to Being an Embedded Librarian within the Academic Department

First and foremost, if the department administration and faculty have invested in the idea of bringing an embedded librarian into the fold, with or without a departmental collection present, then an advantage is already built into the experience. While I will explore actual arguments for creating this position within the department later, we start here with the assumption that the decision has already been made in the positive. If the embedded librarian is in the department, then someone else has acknowledged that the new challenges facing today's university students warrant greater access to an information professional among the department's tools for academic success. Greater still if this librarian is also attached to a departmental collection, for reasons that I will explore later in an argument for such collections.

Once hired into the department, the embedded librarian is incorporated into the department and its own internal processes. This is perhaps the point of closest articulation to the existent corporate or special librarian model, in which the librarian is given the proverbial place at the table. In the academic experience, the potential for the embedded librarian's influence over departmental affairs could certainly vary widely and will even have much to do with the nature of the discipline or field of inquiry represented within the department. At the least, the embedded librarian is offered the opportunity to directly present the benefits of their toolset to the department and administration, not only in the official sanctums of departmental meetings but in the more informal settings of committee meetings or simply the passing hallway conversation. While much of the standard embedded library liaison community continues to aim for the goal of a nested Blackboard menu of library

resource links and one or two instruction sessions (with exceptions being just that, exceptional), that model becomes the baseline for the librarian embedded within the department. The path to increasing librarian participation is less a maze and more a straight line between points.

Part and parcel with the above are the improved opportunities that the departmental embedded librarian has to establish a collegial relationship with the administration and faculty housed in the department. You may have caught the words "one of our second-year graduate students" in the story that opened this chapter. There is that intangible feeling of familial ties that create the collective identity of an academic community or campus unit. And to be a vibrant participant within that community will most often lead to a mutual respect among peers within the unit. In a healthy academic setting there is, at the very least, the acknowledgement among departmental colleagues that the common interest drives a concern for each other's work. If the unit is thriving, as I believe the School of Dance at ASU to be, there are not only tangible examples of support and vested interest in the work of colleagues but open offers to participate, critique, contribute, and more.

This is not to say that I, personally, did not enjoy a great deal of respect and professional courtesy from the faculty aggregated into the Program for Southeast Asian Studies at ASU. In fact, nothing could be further from the truth. During my tenure in ASU Libraries, I was invited by those faculty members to help plan conferences, publications, and exhibits. I received strong support for my own research, and I worked on many projects with select faculty, including information literacy sessions for their courses at all academic levels. But, I remained based within the campus unit of the Libraries, and was therefore disconnected in ways that I felt were important and unfortunate. These were not the result of personal decisions by the faculty or me but a simple matter of infrastructure. The Southeast

Asia faculty themselves were further divided into other academic departments.

My experience in the School of Dance has been significantly different. Many of the advantages will be quite obvious. I participate in departmental meetings and am therefore informed on most significant matters relating to the enterprise of the School of Dance. So, I begin with a pulse for the School that I did not previously have as a traditional academic librarian. Then, the benefits extend even further. Not only do I have access to discussion and debate regarding the School's curriculum, I have the opportunity and invitation to contribute to the conversation as an embedded information professional. And, since the exchange is happening within the space of the department, the mood is at once relaxed but more direct. I am not someone from an outside unit peering into the internal processes of another. We are all part of the School of Dance, and that is a powerful connection when direct communication may determine tangible results in the classroom. The faculty, I believe, are much more direct about what they think works, and I feel even greater comfort in offering the services and tools that I think will make a difference in the classroom and the student experience.

When the Director of the School of Dance last composed a schedule for a daylong departmental retreat, he posted an email asking if I thought a two-hour window would be enough for a library and research resources presentation. I wasn't really the star, to be honest; the Cross-Cultural Dance Resources Collection was soon to re-open in its new space in the School of Dance, and there was much to tell the faculty about CCDR. But, this didn't dispel the excitement for me. I was being given the opportunity to address the faculty on all matters relating to information, within the department and beyond. And it turned into a fortuitous event. Not only did the faculty receive a thorough introduction to this new and valuable resource available to them within the School of Dance, I learned a great deal about growing disconnects

to the ways in which the School of Dance faculty accessed information in general, not to mention passed on that knowledge to their students. Like many academic libraries of its size and facing well-known budgetary challenges, ASU Libraries had distributed responsibility for a range of disciplines to a dwindling number of librarians. The School of Dance and ASU Libraries had grown accustomed to a shared silence. I immediately saw an opportunity to bridge a burgeoning divide and to be of service to my new colleagues.

But what tools does the embedded librarian have to foster a better information access conversation within an academic department? First and foremost, whether by training or experience, the librarian embedded in the department is assumed to be conversant in the modes of inquiry and exchange inherent to the discipline represented by the department. This ensures not only the invaluable respect of the faculty but a familiarity with the core literature that facilitates an exchange about the subtleties, periphery, and explorations in the discipline that push boundaries, all necessary to playing a vital role as the embedded librarian. In my case, it was my graduate training and fieldwork in ethnomusicology that best corresponded to the curation needs of the CCDR Collection. But, it was my conservatory training, performance experience with dancers, and research into connections between music and dance in Java that better prepared me for interaction with the faculty of School of Dance. Paired with training in library science and previous experience as an academic librarian, I was perfectly positioned to act as "translator" in an effort to revitalize exchange between the School of Dance and ASU Libraries. While the CCDR Collection offers much to the faculty, ASU Libraries remains the primary hub for traditional information resource support.

The librarian embedded in the department further benefits from direct access to, and if willing, participation in the production of knowledge within the field represented by the department.

There are opportunities on this front from the very local to well beyond, and they are, as far as I can see, limited only by the ingenuity of the embedded librarian. And while the librarian is well within a good career trajectory to simply participate in the scholarly community (e.g. paper presentations and publication avenues), creative opportunities likely abound.

In the case of the "dance library" as a point of preservation and access to dance culture, I have developed the sense as a direct result of my interaction with the School of Dance faculty that much territory is left to explore. By way of example, I will cite the *e-kiNETx* concept that I have been developing with key faculty and the administration. The idea behind *e-kiNETx,* or Embodied Knowledge Integration in Networked Experiences, is that the dance collection is so much more than an archive of the repertoire and its history. It may be, when strategically engaged, a regenerative resource that not only provides a point of access and preservation but an opportunity to create new work. The dance collection, if maintained in an open environment of creative exchange and organized with a vocabulary of movement, naturally lends itself as a complex entity capable of participating in the act of creation. We, in the School of Dance, anticipate pushing this concept to its furthest limits on many fronts. But, the most exciting is that we aspire to create a means by which a dance scholar or performer may access dance information through the vocabulary that is best known to that user: movement. What better discipline than dance to contribute to movement-based query in the future?

Distant goals aside, I would offer an upcoming project as a more tangible example of potential fruits of direct participation in knowledge production. In the coming year, the School of Dance will host German choreographer Thomas Lehmen for a residency that will span the academic year. Lehmen's work as a choreographer is drenched in engagement with text, making him a perfect participant for the project that I have proposed. Hav-

ing visited recently, we agreed that I would archive his creative process (essentially, the artist himself). And the project will be inclusive of every aspect of his work at ASU that we can manage to capture; from composition to rehearsal; from inspiration to conversation. As a result, I am in the position to offer the CCDR Collection as a hub, not only of existent content in dance research but as a nexus and repository of new inquiry. Knowing Lehmen, he'll have a few tricks up his sleeve for me, and I hope I can even muster a few for him. What is promised to us both is an inspirational experience that I am not certain we would have been afforded were it not for my place in the School of Dance.

Another benefit of being embedded within the department are the strategic relationships that belonging to the academic unit facilitate. Certainly, the campus library is not without such intersections, but in my experience they are somewhat distant, as removed as the library is from discipline-specific engagement. Whether we are discussing the cultivation of docents and donors or the development of grants and foundation support, the academic unit is a more dependable location of focus. Faculty and former faculty, after all, endeavor to keep gifts and financial support as close to home as possible. Directly following the re-opening of the CCDR Collection in its new home at ASU School of Dance, I received no fewer than six offers of donations on the spot, and the ability to cultivate similar offers will continue to expand. Faculty have approached with grant applications that now contain a component focused on information resources support. And, I have had the full support of the department in submitting my own grant applications for digital projects and to further expand infrastructure for the collection. At the end of the day, the faculty and administration are pouring their energy and support into their own unit and directly into the Collection.

Here, I arrive at a final thought on the advantages of being embedded within the academic department, but it is by no means an insignificant point. There remains the act of teaching and the instructional enterprise. The opportunity to develop meaningful exchanges and to act as a mentor to students across all academic levels may be the single most significant advantage to the embedded librarian. When housed within the academic department, the embedded librarian has the added benefit of not only the departmental connections shared with the faculty but also an identity of some authority in the eyes of the student. If cultivated carefully, a sound relationship with the student enables the librarian embedded in the department to act as a trusted mentor.

Within the School of Dance at ASU, I have just recently had the opportunity to co-teach a course on dance ethnology. I mention it here, because I am aware that embedded librarians have cited such endeavors as an important step in expanding the influence of librarians in information literacy programs. I am less enthusiastic about this notion for a few reasons. First, I am increasingly comfortable with the avenues I have available to me as a member of the department with regard to curriculum. In essence, I suspect that embedded librarians as co-instructors hope to leverage some influence over information literacy components by their roles in the classroom, which I am beginning to find unnecessary. Secondly, I am conflicted in the subtle shift that happens in the transition from librarian to instructor. And, it may very well be that the act of giving grades is central to that discomfort. But, restated, I am equipped for a different approach to evaluation than a faculty member. And, I believe my skills are best applied in a role that does not cross over (at least not permanently) into the realm of the teaching faculty. I also believe, for the reasons I have cited above, that I am able to achieve the effects desired by a greater presence in the classroom through different means.

This Interruption Brought to you by the Internet

Before I launch into the challenges faced by the librarian embedded within the department, I want to address the elephant in the corner: the internet and digital environment. It is apropos of its essence, distraction of distractions, and the beloved resource(s) that we love to hate that we love. If I'm taking you in circles, then good. Is it an advantage or a challenge? Is it good or is it bad? Will we as librarians survive it? I would not know where to begin, really. And that is perfect given the medium up for discussion.

I do not aspire to provide any substantial analysis of how the internet and embedded librarianship intersect, only to say that the overlap is significant. And I, for one, find myself somewhat alarmed that the transition of our content from the physical to the digital (good) has also seemingly resulted in the need to transition ourselves in the same direction (bad, I think). And, having only just recently guided fifteen upper undergraduate students through a major paper, I am more convinced than ever that we as librarians are enabling a shift in research skills in our reactions and adaptations to the digital age. I want to be careful here to ensure the readership that I am neither a Luddite nor curmudgeon, because I am as tech-happy a librarian as I could possibly be. Yet, I do believe that there is cause for concern and the opportunity, especially in the embedded model of librarianship, to effect positive change. And by change, I do not herald resistance to new digital directions as much as I caution for reflective thought of how it changes us.

Access to our resources now resides in what Cory Doctorow has called an "ecosystem of interruption technologies."[13] And while we may all be thankful for the incredible growth in accessibility we have experienced, one cannot deny that we are seeing other shifts as well. The fifteen undergraduate papers I read at the end of the past semester were like none I have ever composed myself or read before. And I speak here not of quality of thought and argument, because that remained in natural ranges, but I am speaking of mechanics and construction. And the best analogy that comes to my mind is the very disjointed and distracted way I (and many people I know) have begun to read as a result of the internet. In fact, I would not be altogether surprised if more than a few of those fifteen authors have never read a large piece of fiction from cover to cover in their lives.

Nicholas Carr, in an engaging investigation of this possible phenomenon, describes his evolving reading habits like this:

> Whether I'm online or not, my mind now expects to take information the way the Net distributes it: in a swiftly moving stream of particles. Once I was a scuba diver in the sea of words. Now I zip along the surface like a guy on a Jet Ski.[14]

As information professionals, embedded or not, we are facing an increasingly distracted student body, and a notable shift away from reading habits that include a measure of isolated reflection. And let us not let ourselves or the faculty we serve off the hook so easily. Just recently, at a vibrant digital humanities conference, I realized very early on that there weren't a single pair of hands without a connection to the internet. And with a good percentage of those eyes staring down into their TweetDecks, questions from adjacent rooms (or far-off places) were traveling in and out of the room at lightning pace. In every way, this was an invigorating and exciting conference for all involved. But, there was not much in the way of quiet reflection or deep analysis of the ideas and exchanges presented. I wondered if those would ever come.

In the case of our students, there appears little doubt that the medium is changing the way we think and engage with information. But, are we going to find ways, as I clearly think that we should, to reintroduce opportunities for deep consideration and quiet contemplation as the waves of available information ebb and flow beneath our Jet Skis? Unlike our faculty, our newest students are coming from the first of generations that read no other way and will therefore be free of the burden of nostalgia for reading contemplatively.

I will say this, both for the argument in favor of embedding librarians within the department and as a follow-up to the story that began the chapter. The act of physically sharing a space and a conversation is possessed of societal norms that we remain hesitant to break. En masse, such as in the conference mentioned above, a group may abandon those norms if agreement seems implied. But, within the confines of the face-to-face interview with the librarian, there remains some hope left for the contemplative dialogue. As a librarian, I am still embodied in my work, and among practitioners of dance no less. I accept that this too may pass, but I hope not.

Challenges to Being an Embedded Librarian within the Academic Department

In the end, all significant challenges that I have encountered personally in my embedded experience filter down into variations of isolation from other library and information professionals. None of these, I believe, are deal-breakers for the librarian that endeavors to establish departmental positions. And they pale in comparison to the benefits, in my very humble opinion. But, these challenges should be noted for their importance and acknowledged through appropriate action.

The evaluation and review process remains a cornerstone of the academic infrastructure and the single most important indicator for one's career trajectory. As librarians, we are best evaluated by our peers and colleagues in the library profession. While faculty input into the promotion process for academic librarians is far from unusual, the fact remains that those voices remain secondary to peers in the profession. And, with all honesty, the head of an academic department may possess some measure of appreciation for the librarian embedded within the department without much ability to judge and quantify his contribution. I am a librarian interested in dance that does not necessarily work for a dancer familiar with the details of librarianship. If anything, this model sets up an interesting reversal wherein a fellow librarian on campus may be called in as a secondary evaluator in support of the direct supervisor, which stands as a viable solution to the problem as the librarian is well-situated to advise knowledgeably. In the day-to-day, I have to market the work that I do to the administration of the School of Dance, which I find quite healthy in the end.

The isolation from the central campus library is a different challenge. Removed from committees, the acquisitions process, and without an avenue to input on campus-wide information strategies, the librarian embedded within the department faces some adjustment to a different role. It is surprisingly easy to simply lose touch. But, the tools available to counteract such isolation are plentiful. Libraries naturally seek out campus connections, and the same may be said of individual librarians. Social networking offers an open avenue as much as a quick meeting at the coffee stand. In the past semester, I mounted an exhibit of CCDR Collection resources in the vestibule of ASU Libraries' main branch.

While some academic departments are traditionally home to large collections (music and law libraries are obvious examples) and an embedded librarian, most are not. And by that measure, any collection and librarian embedded within the academic department will face some level of scrutiny. And, I do not despair in this. A librarian should be able to skillfully articulate the benefit of his presence and that of the collection. Any such challenge presents an opportunity. Not only does a critique focus the embedded librarian on the work at hand, it challenges the librarian to build support both within and outside of the academic unit. Recently, the ASU School of Dance successfully petitioned on the strengths of the CCDR Collection and *e-ki-NETx* concept to become just the tenth core member of the Dance Heritage Coalition, a national organization of major dance collections committed to working collaboratively to ensure ongoing access and preservation of our dance culture.

Outro: Whither the Embedded Librarian within the Department?

In this chapter I have clearly advocated for the presence of an embedded librarian within the academic department, and as a result the potential reorganization of traditional campus information access structures. The assumption that increasingly digital access to information necessitates the disembodiment of the library and information professional appears ill-conceived and disjunct from the perspective of my own personal experiences as a librarian embedded in the Herberger Institute School of Dance at Arizona State University, where my physical presence has encouraged increased exchange. In essence, the librarian embedded within the department leads naturally to greater accessibility of resources offered both within the department and through the central campus library as access decentralizes. Further, the librarian offers to renew discourse within the department regarding resources and foster contemplative consideration of information among an engaged student base.

If an interpretation of this chapter is that I am suggesting an exodus of subject librarians from the central campus library into academic departments, I can at the least agree to let that reading stand with some caveats. I acknowledge that I am in a unique position in the ASU School of Dance, one that would be difficult to create directly from a traditional academic librarian position. Essentially, my job had to be created to exist. And to readers that decry the arguments I have made in the chapter as an impossibility given their own current situations, I offer the challenge to apply as much of my experience as is possible to a re-conception of traditional subject librarian roles:

- Establish a strong presence in the academic departments with which you liaise. This need not be limited to a desk, a chair, and recurring office hours within the department (though those would be a great start). Ask to attend faculty meetings, and extend a Blackboard presence into recurring classroom participation. Make attempts to not only attend faculty presentations but also presentations of student work, papers, showings, and performances. In fact, a vested interest in the students and their success is what has been the biggest change for me in my move to the School of Dance at ASU.

- Seek out conversations.
- Look for events beyond traditional department affairs and the opportunity to establish a personal presence.
- Forgo an ALA or ACRL meeting to attend an annual conference hosted by a scholarly community focused on a specific discipline. Offer to serve on a committee or participate in publications.

In looking toward our future as librarians and the role that we will play in the academic enterprise, I do think it is important to ask the question: If provided the opportunity to house an information professional among its community of stakeholders, would the academic department see the benefits and act? The ASU School of Dance said yes, and we have embarked on a compelling journey as a result.

Notes

1. David Shumaker, "The Embedded Librarian," http://embeddedlibrarian.wordpress.com/
2. David Shumaker and Laura Ann Tyler, "Embedded Library Services: Initial Inquiry Into Practices For Their Development, Management, and Delivery," Contributed Paper, Special Libraries Association Annual Conference, 2007.
3. Martin A. Kesselman and Sarah Barbara Watstein, "Creating Opportunities: Embedded Librarians," *Journal of Library Administration* 49 (2009), 383–400.
4. Barbara I. Dewey, "The Embedded Librarian: Strategic Campus Collaborations. *Resource Sharing & Information Networks* 17 (2004), 5–17.
5. Victoria Matthew and Ann Schroeder, "The Embedded Librarian Program: Faculty and Librarians Partner to Provide Personalized Library Assistance in Online Courses," *Educause Quarterly* 29 (2006), 61–65.
6. Karen M. Ramsey and Jim Kinnie, "The Embedded Librarian," *Library Journal* 131 (2006), 34–35.
7. Rachel Owens, "Where the Students Are: The Embedded Librarian Project at Daytona Beach College," *Florida Libraries* 51 (2008), 8–10.
8. Emily Daly, Emily, "Embedding Library Resources into Learning Management Systems: A Way to Reach Duke Undergrads at Their Points of Need. *College & Research Libraries News* 71 (2010), 208–212.
9. Michael R. Hearn, "Embedding a Librarian in the Classroom: an Intensive Information Literacy Model," *Reference Services Review* 33 (2005), 219–227.
10. Susan Sharpless Smith and Lynn Sutton, "Embedded Librarians," *College & Research Libraries News* 69 (2008), 71–85.
11. Russell A. Hall, "The Embedded Librarian in a Freshman Speech Class," *College & Research Libraries News* 69 (2008), 28–30.
12. Shumaker and Tyler, 2007
13. Cory Doctorow, Cory, "Writing in the Age of Distraction," *Locus (2009)*. http://www.locusmag.com/Features/2009/01/cory-doctorow-writing-in-age-of.html
14. Nicholas Carr, *The Shallows: What the Internet is Doing to Our Brains* (New York: W. W. Norton & Company, 2010).

 EIGHT

Collaboration in Speech Communication: A Case Study in Faculty-Librarian Collaboration to Teach Undergraduates to Write a Literature Review

Kate Gronemyer and Natalie Dollar

Saying that challenges create opportunities sounds clichéd, but that is certainly what happened in this case study in collaboration. Speech Communication professor Dr. Natalie Dollar and instruction librarian Kate Gronemyer matched strengths to take on the task of teaching non-major upper-division undergraduates to write a literature review. Kate, a brand-new librarian and Natalie, an experienced professor who won an award for her teaching, used both online and in-class instruction to help students move from the earliest stages of topic exploration through their final edits. Our unique campus, home to three institutions, creates unusual barriers, but those barriers also created an opportunity for a collaborative teaching experience that was valuable not only to the students but to the teachers as well.

The Setting: Cascades Campus

The Cascades Campus, a branch campus of Oregon State University (OSU), started in 2001 when the Oregon University System selected Oregon State University to serve the growing Central Oregon region. Co-located with Central Oregon Community College (COCC,) OSU-Cascades offers upper-division bachelor's and master's-level coursework, while COCC offers lower division classes. Described as "Oregon's Transfer University," its students arrive with varied backgrounds, many transferring directly from COCC but many others transferring from other community colleges and four-year institutions from around Oregon and the rest of the country. Still others enroll to complete degrees started years ago. This wide range of backgrounds means a student body with a wide range of experiences and preparation, a reality in many institutions of higher education but one that is particularly acute on a campus where every student is a transfer student.

Students at OSU-Cascades choose between 11 majors along with a selection of minors that can be used to either focus or diversify degrees. Interestingly, about one third of Cascades students pursue a bachelor's degree from the University of Oregon (UO), which offers four of the available majors. Students can enroll in courses from OSU, UO and COCC in the same term, on the same campus. As such, OSU-Cascades is a campus unlike all others in Oregon. The partnerships among COCC, OSU, and UO offer students a unique college experience while also presenting some challenging situations for faculty.

In some ways, the small, interdepartmental nature of Cascades makes it an ideal place for collaboration of all kinds. Librarians are regular faculty members and Cascades is treated much like a department (though all Cascades faculty members are also members of their "home" department on the main campus.) This arrangement results in intangible benefits like hallway conversations that arise naturally when working in a relatively small physical space. Equally important, however, are the tangible benefits; when the library is not a separate department and faculty members are part of one body, collaborative teaching produces fewer concerns about FTE or other time and money issues that sometimes result when departments are pitted against one another for limited resources.

This is not to say that Cascades is free of the types of structural or cultural issues that sometimes complicate higher education. As might be expected, three institutions do not work together entirely without complications. The collaboration at the heart of this case study was created in response to one such complication and ultimately undone by another.

Teaching Context: Multiple Institutions, Varied Backgrounds

Though the Cascades Campus is a branch of Oregon State University, some majors at the campus, as noted above, are provided by another of the state's public universities, the University of Oregon. This partnership has been a part of the campus since it began, the result of a fierce competition between the two schools to win the rights to begin a new campus in the fast-growing region. While OSU provides student services, including library services, students earn their degree from the institution responsible for their chosen major. Students are allowed to select classes offered by either school but the classes must fit their program requirements and the students must meet their academic residency requirement, caveats that mean this cross-registration happens only rarely. Additionally, the UO offers four credit classes while OSU's classes are generally three credits. Of course an additional credit translates to more work and longer time in class each week, but the added credit also proved

appealing to students. These differences between the programs mean few UO students enroll in the OSU classes even when they could be used to fill a UO requirement. With this in mind, and faculty's belief that there is adequate course material to warrant an extra hour per week, the Liberal Studies program began adding a required one-credit independent study to some three-credit classes. It was this adjustment in response to a local situation that led to the addition of an information literacy-focused credit to COMM 318, Advanced Interpersonal Communication.

The OSU-Cascades major with the second highest concentration of students is the Liberal Studies major, a multidisciplinary degree overseen by OSU's College of Liberal Arts and headed up by professors of Speech Communication, Political Science, English, and Art History. Students who choose a Liberal Studies major must organize their coursework around a theme, either one that is pre-developed like one advised by Natalie, *Communication, Identity, and Place*, or one that the student develops with the guidance of his or her faculty advisor. While a student can opt for a Speech Communication minor, there is no option for a Speech Communication major. This means that even in a 300-level Communication course many students will have little-to-no familiarity with Communication literature. Furthermore, as non-majors these students are unlikely to need a strong theoretical grounding in Communication literature as they go forward with their studies.

For Natalie, the experience converting upper division speech communication courses for students majoring in Liberal Studies rather than Speech Communication was a difficult challenge that manifested itself in several ways. Students pursuing a Speech Communication major on the Corvallis campus are required to complete four pre-requisites before enrolling in upper division courses. The students enrolling in Cascades' Advanced Interpersonal Communication course had completed varying numbers of lower division communication courses taken from different institutions. At Cascades, though the course is listed as "advanced," the students' varied backgrounds meant many were encountering the language and literature of interpersonal communication for the first time. Without the fundamentals, it became clear that an additional hour per week would be valuable to assist these students, particularly with regard to assignments involving library research.

Teaching only upper division courses proved to have challenges beyond just working with students who had varied disciplinary knowledge. The process of implementing the Liberal Studies major in coordination with our partners, COCC and UO, took more time than anticipated, and while students were meeting the course requirements to begin upper-division work, many were initially coming in unprepared to meet upper-division expectations for writing and research. Working with the Joint Curriculum Council (a group including members from all three institutions,) Liberal Studies faculty discussed content in pre-requisites, major and minor requirements with regard to the associate degrees being offered by COCC, and related issues. In time we would develop relationships with COCC faculty that allowed us to address students' preparedness. In the meantime, it became clear to some Liberal Studies faculty that we needed assistance helping these students make the transfer from community college to the university. One place that was well positioned to help was the library. Though the COCC and Cascades Campus communities are served by the same physical library, as students make the transition to the university they also gain access to the university's electronic resources. As Cascades' instruction librarian, one of Kate's important roles is to help students make that transition.

Finally, the changing university library landscape creates a potentially challenging disconnect between students' and disciplinary faculty's research processes. Because faculty are, as Leckie notes, familiar with the research happening in

their disciplines, they are often less dependent on searching the literature when developing a "research idea."[1] This challenge is only intensified when students are working with the literatures of multiple disciplines. In Speech Communication courses, Natalie discovered that Kate's outsider perspective and searching expertise helped her and her students situate their communication literature review assignment in their particular Liberal Studies focus, particularly those themes with limited communication coursework, or within their non-Liberal Studies majors like Tourism & Outdoor Leadership, Business, Natural Resources, or Human Development and Family Science.

The Class: Collaboration in Action

Once we agreed to co-teach the course, we began to meet to discuss assignments, class schedule, teaching schedule and our expectations. We went through the existing COMM 318 syllabus identifying dates for assignment milestones and discussion boards that worked with the other obligations of the course like readings and tests as well as with the research process. We were fortunate enough to co-teach the course fall terms 2005 and 2006. In 2005 we had fifteen students and in 2006 we had 10 students.

As a 4-credit course, Advanced Interpersonal Communication with Independent Study, met twice a week for 1 hour and 50 minutes for ten weeks. Of this time four classes—about 8 hours—were dedicated specifically to discussion and exercises regarding the literature review assignment. Although the assignment was not limited to these time slots, students knew in advance that these particular class periods would be dedicated solely to it. We spaced these literature review days across the term to facilitate students' focus on the process of writing a literature review. Though Kate led the class discussions and exercises on these days, Natalie was always present to contextualize the assignment, make suggestions for students struggling with language or content difficulties, and to add her perspective as an expert researcher. On other days, the topic of the assignment was integrated into the particular content discussion. As such, we blurred the lines between the Independent Study credit and the course credits with the goal of helping students see these as two interdependent parts of the whole rather than separate learning experiences.

Though much of the first day of class was dedicated, as would be expected, to introducing the topic at hand, the syllabus, and the professor's expectations, we also took the opportunity on the first day to introduce the students to our co-teaching arrangement. This was reinforced by the inclusion of Kate's name and contact information in the syllabus. Additionally, we introduced the literature review assignment (Figure 8-1) on the first day of class. This helped to emphasize the expectation that this project was not something that was only important on the day it was to be turned in or even solely on the days it was the topic of class, but something we would be talking about and working on throughout the quarter. The project itself was course content. Finally, we took the time to introduce the students to a major component of the independent study, an online discussion designed to help students both stay on track and reflect on their research process. These discussions formed the backbone of the process work we were expecting of the students.

For many students, this assignment was not only the first time they had been asked to write a literature review but their first encounter with the term. Choosing to assign a literature review rather than a research paper was not simply a semantic choice. There are few (if any) places outside of the classroom where anyone is ever asked to write a research paper. For many scholars, research is their work, the process through which they create new knowledge through analysis, gathering data or testing of hypotheses. For undergraduate students, research too often means gathering a few citations to use in support of an already-decided thesis state-

ment.[2] While this is not to paint the task as without value, many students assume the purpose of a research paper is to report what is known about a particular topic or, perhaps, to make and support a particular argument decided in advance. They frequently do not understand where their own voice comes in, particularly when they are, as novices, writing for an expert audience, the professor.[3] Asking students to write a literature review breaks them out of this habit of cherry-picking information in an effort to prove a particular point, and instead they discover what scholars know about a particular topic and put that information together in a way that addresses their unique question.

Figure 8-1. The assignment

Each of you is to develop a research question that focuses on an interpersonal communication topic for which there exists a substantial body of scholarly literature. Your task is to write a literature review that answers your research question, demonstrating your understanding of the history of the topic and providing an account of what scholars know about your subject. In addition, your literature review should provide an assessment of the value of this knowledge and a discussion of where the research should be directed at this point in time. Remember, as Hart says, "A key element that makes for a good literature review is integration...making connections between the ideas, theories and experiences." (p. 8)

Because we wanted students to focus on the process of gathering, learning from, and synthesizing information rather than solely on the product at the end, a critical part of this assignment was to participate in discussions about their process. We chose to use the discussion board feature of our university's course management software, Blackboard, because it was already available and familiar to students. Since Kate had no official role in the class she was not added to the course Blackboard space automatically; instead Natalie requested that the campus Blackboard administrator add Kate as a "course builder," a role that gave her the ability to add content including the discussion board and external links to library resources as well as to email students but not the ability to access students' grades. Once added, however, Kate had no difficulties with permissions or other settings in the course management software.

Using an online discussion board had several benefits. It allowed us to devote more time to discussion than was available in the face-to-face class. It gave more introspective students a chance to participate more equally in the discussion than if they were asked to contribute only in class.[4] It created an automatic record of the discussion helpful for students looking back on the process and to the professors who wanted to grade fairly and to provide constructive feedback on students' process. Students were not, however, expected to be motivated to participate in the discussion solely out of interest in their own learning; asking them to devote time and energy to the process of gathering, learning from, and synthesizing literature but awarding points based only on the finished product seemed to send the wrong message. The first time we taught the class, we used the discussion board we required four initial posts plus two responses. The second time, we improved the questions we asked but reduced the requirement to three initial posts and two responses.

Requiring and assessing students' participation in online discussion is recommended to encourage participation whether the platform for the discussion is a listserv, a blog, or, as was used in this project, a CMS discussion board.[5] Writing a strong post or a careful response is (and should be) a thoughtful and time-consuming effort. Few students are motivated to pursue in-depth discussions outside of regular class time on their own, particularly in a course that brings together students from different majors who are likely to think of the course as a discrete unit rather than a building block for future courses. Additionally, students tend to put effort into the tasks that are shown, by virtue of point assignment, to be of value. Rec-

ognizing this we set up required discussion topics with due dates for both initial posts and responses to one another's posts. Students were also given specific guidelines for post content including requirements for their responses (see Figure 8-2); this was an effort to get students to move beyond simply responding to one another with a "good job!" The downside to specific requirements, of course, is that students rarely go beyond the requirements. Few posted more than the two responses required by the guidelines.

Figure 8-2. Requirements for students' Blackboard discussion board posts

An original post must include the following:
- examples from your research, properly credited
- evidence that you have thought about your post
- evidence that you are progressing through the research process

A response to a post must include the following:
- an accurate re-statement of the idea to which you're responding
- the reason you chose to respond to that particular idea
- the question, criticism, suggestion, etc. you have for the original poster

---

Though these students are not communication majors, there is no doubt that interpersonal communication is relevant to them in both their personal and their professional futures. Given this, students were encouraged to use a personal and/or professional interest as a starting point for selecting their topics. While this is a fairly standard way to try to engage students in scholarly writing, the thread of interpersonal communication meant this was not artificial for most. Literature review topics included many seemingly personal topics like communication in blended families or at the dinner table, questions about letter writing and online dating, and the relationship of depression to communication between married couples. Others looked at topics relevant to their current or desired careers, choosing to investigate questions focused on communication in classrooms, in business and organizational settings, and in outdoor leadership.

Class discussion and the students' first reading assignment, the first two chapters of their course text, *Bridges not Walls: A book about interpersonal communication*, helped to give them an overview of the kinds of questions interpersonal communication tries to investigate.[6] Natalie also provided examples of both broad topics (like "communication boundary management" or "relational maintenance") and of research questions (like "what is communication apprehension and how does it affect individuals' success in the workplace?") to help students begin to interact with the language they would need to successfully investigate a question from an interpersonal communication perspective. The first discussion board question asked them to explore their potential literature review topic(s), including why they found the topic interesting, how they thought it might be related to interpersonal communication, what they already knew about the topic and what they knew they didn't know.

On the days the discussion board topics were introduced, we also planned some kind of in-class discussion and, if possible, a related in-class activity. The first literature review session looked most like a typical information literacy instruction: the class learned to use a particular database in a hands-on computer classroom. In a normal "one-shot" instruction setting Kate always encourages instructors to schedule her visit later in the quarter rather than the first or second week, as few students will have begun to think about their topics at that point, but in this class our time in the computer lab was intentionally scheduled during the second week. Because this would be only one of several chances to work with the students, we wanted them to use their early searches to help define their topics, learning what was in the literature before defining their topics too narrowly.

Because most students had used at least EBSCO's Academic Search Premier, our institution's broad multidisciplinary database, the computer lab session mostly focused on learning to use the Communication Institute for Online Scholarship's (CIOS) ComAbstracts database, a new and relatively difficult interface for them. Students were encouraged to seek out the language of the literature (with Natalie's guidance for the kinds of terms they might use.) Knowing that the librarian would remain involved all quarter helped remove the perception that this was the one time they would be searching. Both Natalie and Kate talked about our own personal processes of searching and how we keep track of what we find. Additionally, the class had to cover how the students could get the full text of the articles they found.

At the time, ComAbstracts did not work with the library's link resolver. Some articles were available full-text through a proprietary download system that students had to install. Some were available through electronic subscriptions from other publishers. Others were available in print at our main campus library and could be ordered through the library's catalog. This was particularly confusing after reinforcing that the articles themselves could not be found in the catalog. Finally, of course, some articles needed to be ordered through the inter-library loan system. The "getting" part of searching the literature, something that has thankfully been simplified in the years since, is something that could have easily taken an entire 50-minute instruction session. Because the classes were fairly small and we had nearly two hours we were also able to provide plenty of time for students to begin exploring on their own.

Our next literature review-focused class was scheduled late enough that students could be expected to have the articles they selected, including any that needed to be ordered. This is when we could begin to talk about the ways they might organize their literature. In the first year we showed students a model from Hart's book *Doing a Literature Review.*[7] This model had commentary in the margins about how and why the review was organized the way it was, but it was not about a communication topic and students struggled to separate the structure of the document, the useful part for their needs, from the content which was not related to the class topic. The book was aimed at graduate-level students conducting comprehensive literature reviews and we realized the example seemed to overwhelm and confuse many students. In the second year we sought out a short review from the communication literature and included it as a class reading.[8] This, combined with a synthesis exercise we detail below, seemed to give students a model they could more easily understand. Knowing that students had at least a preliminary collection of literature with which to work, we used the professional literature review they had read to demonstrate concept mapping and then gave them time to practice on their own. This was intended not only to help them understand what they were finding in the literature, but to see that there were likely multiple ways it could be organized.

Unsurprisingly, students struggled with the difficult task of synthesis. In our second year of collaboration we came up with an in-class exercise drawn from an article published in Business Communication Quarterly that helped students understand what it meant to synthesize the literature they found.[9] We provided them with a series of article abstracts all focused on a particular topic. We asked them to read through the abstracts looking for common themes and then to work in groups to write a one-to-two paragraph "mini-review" of the abstracts. Working in groups with these manageable chunks of relatively accessible information gave students the opportunity to practice organizing information and helped them to understand how to make broad statements by citing multiple sources that make the same claim as well as how to incorporate sources that make diverging claims. Group work was projected and students shared their attempts at synthesis. Because they were all working with the same original sources, groups were able to critique others' work and to learn from what they did well. The papers written by the students that participated in this exercise showed considerably more effective attempts at synthesis than the papers from the year before.

The second discussion during the first quarter asked students to talk about their search strategies. Though students were able to discuss where and how they searched, most had not yet had a chance to read the articles and were not really able to critically assess their success at that point. We dropped this question the second time we taught the class and revised what had been the third discussion: asking students to share how (not if) they had refined their topics as they explored the literature they found and learned more about interpersonal communication. This change meant the students had a much better sense of what they had found so far; something that helped them frame their searching in a more meaningful way. In the second iteration of the course the second discussion came around mid-term and while most students' responses showed clear progress, many were also feeling confused and overwhelmed.

Asking students to reflect on the process at that point not only gave us a sense of where they were in the process; it also helped them to see they were making progress. One student began her response by observing that "[a]fter reading through my initial post, I discovered that I have actually made some progress, despite my feelings of confusion and frustration." Even students who began by claiming they had not changed their topics went on to describe how what they had learned so far was helping them narrow and direct their research question. Asking students to reflect on their progress at this point gave us an opportunity to discuss what Kuhlthau calls "the dip" of confidence, reassuring students that feeling more confused and overwhelmed than they did when they started was actually a normal part of the research process.[10]

In 2005 a family emergency put the class behind schedule and the final discussion board, one that asked students to talk about the original research they might design as a follow up to their literature review, was replaced by one asking students to post a detailed outline because many were still struggling with synthesizing what they had found. In the second year, more confident that students were on track, we posed the original final discussion question to them, asking them to describe a new research question that might follow from their literature review. This question was, of course, difficult for the students to answer. In some ways we were asking them to think like graduate students who had taken a research methods class and were familiar with formulating research questions.

As the first quarter of this collaborative project drew to a close, it became apparent that neither the standard library student evaluation form nor the campus-wide student evaluation of teaching (SET) would help us evaluate the effectiveness of our focus on process. With an eye towards improving the process for the next year, Kate created an evaluation form (Appendix A) that attempted to examine students' perception of the usefulness of the process. Rather than focus on students' satisfaction with the process, we were interested in their perceptions of what was helpful and what additional help they would have wanted. Students were not overwhelmingly positive about the discussions, though it was evident that focusing on process made them begin researching earlier and work more continually on the project, something several admitted they would not have otherwise done. The value we placed on process was clearly a new expectation for many students and some perhaps preferred their normal strategy of waiting to prioritize a project until it was due.

As one student noted, "if I hadn't done the discussions it would have dropped my paper an entire grade." While it is clear from this comment that the student understood that we valued the discussions, it is not clear that he or she understood why the final product was not the final arbiter of the grade. Also, students did not necessarily find the feedback they were required to provide one another particularly helpful, which is probably an accurate assessment. Because students struggled to make sense of their own work, it was likely unrealistic to ask them to give substantial commentary on others' projects. Asking students to comment on one another's work did serve other important purposes however, including making sure they were familiar with others' topics, which helped build the sense that this was a class effort rather than something to be produced alone the night before it was due. It also ensured they were reading one another's posts, providing an audience for writing the posts beyond simply the professor and the librarian.

In addition to the changes to the discussion board questions discussed above, Natalie also made some significant changes to both the Advanced Interpersonal Communication course content and to the literature review assignment the second time we offered the class. Tests were reduced from three to two, and a draft literature review assignment was added. Though we reduced the discussion board assignments from four to three, the points awarded for students' Blackboard participation was increased, thus increasing the total value of the literature review assignment. We also focused more specifically on in-class exercises—like the synthesis exercise described above—to help make sure students had the skills and understood the concepts necessary to complete the assignment requirements. The second time we co-taught the course was also the first time that both instructors provided written feedback on papers. Working together and using a set of clearly articulated assessment criteria let Natalie focus her feedback on writing style, use of course materials, synthesis of research materials with course materials, and insight produced while Kate focused her comments on students' use of sources and citation along with the overall clarity and coherency of the paper.

Things that Worked

The Association of College and Research Libraries (ACRL) states unequivocally that "[c]ollaboration between teaching faculty and librarians is fundamental to information literacy."[11] While the three factors ACRL identifies as critical to successful collaboration—carefully defined roles, comprehensive planning and shared leadership—certainly played a role in our successful collaboration, a true commitment to shared leadership and a willingness to adjust our comprehensive plan as needed meant that carefully defined roles were perhaps less important in our case. We undoubtedly recognized one another's strengths and areas of expertise, but we also, particularly in the classroom, left room for these roles to develop and overlap as well.

Just as our varied backgrounds meant we both had a lot to teach students in the class, we also discovered we had much to learn from one another. Though our co-teaching arrangement was not designed with our own peer learning in mind, it was certainly a valuable outcome. Much credit for this goes to Natalie's supportive classroom climate. As an experienced classroom instructor her ability to balance her own authority while maintaining rigorous class discussions to which students feel comfortable contributing is a result not only of confidence gained over her years of teaching but also of an intentional move away from a traditional classroom climate. Though students often need to be encouraged to challenge the traditional student role of listening during lecture and rarely questioning their instructor, when the professor and the students both "let go" of these roles there is far more opportunity for engagement in the process of learning, something clearly evident in the lively and meaningful discussions that take place in Natalie's classes. This environment is one that is not only stimulating for students but also welcoming to a co-instructor.

For Kate, a novice instruction librarian and relatively inexperienced teacher, the opportunity to observe a master teacher at work both in and out of the classroom provided not only an entree to the class but also a valuable mentoring experience. For Natalie, the opportunity to see the way a librarian approaches information literacy instruction has continued to have an impact on the way she teaches and talks to students about their research. This modeling of the ways a librarian helps novice students negotiate the gaps in their knowledge in order to do research using the tools designed for and the literature written for an expert audience served as perhaps the ultimate "train the trainer" program (or, perhaps more accurately, a show the trainer program.) Additionally, with both of us present and contributing to the students' information literacy instruction the students received a consistent message about our expectations for their research and writing. Natalie's willingness to share some authority with Kate meant students knew they could ask either of us for assistance and many students continued to contact Kate when they needed research assistance with other courses as they progressed through their studies.

Things We Would Improve if (When) We Collaborate Again

The hope that students would truly engage with their topics and with one another in the discussion board environment was not totally in vain, but was not fully realized. While students did, for the most part, meet the requirement to respond to one another, they did not participate in any spontaneous discussion or participate in any back-and-forth exchanges resembling conversation. This reluctance to fully engage was likely caused by a number of factors: students also met regularly face to face, they did not all share a common major or discipline, and they had no external motivation to go beyond the required number of posts. If we ask students to participate in online discussions in the future we will likely experiment both with assignment requirements and with the tools we ask them to use in an effort to overcome this reluctance.

Though Kate had used discussion boards as a student, the boards were a new pedagogical tool for both of us. With any new teaching technique it often takes a few attempts before learning how it can be used in a way that best helps students meet the learning outcomes of the course or the assignment. While several sources suggest instructor participation in discussion boards is important to model ideal responses and to push students' thinking, attempts by Kate to join in the discussion resulted in resounding silence. Perhaps this is a result of overly prescriptive discussion requirements making students unwilling to participate if it didn't "count." Perhaps Natalie responding as the professor would have made more of an impact. Perhaps the responses needed to be different in some way to have the desired effect. These are all possibilities we could attempt to investigate when we have the opportunity to collaborate again.

Final Thoughts

While the ACRL lists three factors critical to successful collaboration between teaching faculty and librarians, this collaboration was felled by a fourth factor that was beyond our control: institutional politics. Ideally we would have four years of collaborative teaching to analyze and a plan to make even more improvements to the course the next time it is taught. Unfortunately, two years of successful collaborative instruction was no match for structural changes within the College. Despite the local challenges that led to Natalie's adaptation of COMM 318, OSU's Speech Communication department, Natalie's home department, asked her to cease adding the 1-credit co-requisite

as it was inconsistent with their implementation of the Speech Communication curriculum. A new collaboration, however, is under development; Cascades recently brought the American Studies degree from Corvallis to Bend and is converting American Studies courses to four credits. Natalie will teach a 300-level course titled "Women and Rock 'n' Roll, Work and American Society," and Natalie and Kate are already at work figuring out the best way to incorporate information literacy into the course. The specifics of the class will be very different: there will be no literature review assignment and likely no Blackboard discussion. What will remain the same, however, is our strong collaborative relationship and the benefits our different perspectives have for not only our students, but our own practice as well.

It is always easy, particularly with case studies, to find all the reasons why an example from one setting will not translate to another. There were many things about this collaboration that would be difficult to replicate. Few professors are willing, let alone able, to add an additional required credit to an upper-division class, especially to help develop students' information literacy. Many librarians would be hard-pressed to find enough time and institutional support for such an in-depth collaboration. We would encourage librarians to seek out the parts of our experience that are useful and possible and adapt them to fit your own situation whether it is using your campus course management software to connect with students, adapting the synthesis exercise described above, or simply passing this chapter along to interested disciplinary faculty. Perhaps a door will open.

Appendix A: Student feedback form

Please share your feelings about the Blackboard discussion component of COMM402 (Independent Study). Your input will be used to improve future classes. Your input is anonymous and will not affect your grade in any way.

Creating the initial Blackboard posts was a good use of my time.

Strongly disagree	Disagree	Disagree Somewhat	Neutral	Agree somewhat	Agree	Strongly agree
1	2	3	4	5	6	7

My classmates' response(s) to my posts were useful to me.

Strongly disagree	Disagree	Disagree Somewhat	Neutral	Agree somewhat	Agree	Strongly agree
1	2	3	4	5	6	7

Responding to my classmates' posts was useful to me.

Strongly disagree	Disagree	Disagree Somewhat	Neutral	Agree somewhat	Agree	Strongly agree
1	2	3	4	5	6	7

Participating in the Blackboard discussion helped me write a better literature review than I would have without the discussion.

Strongly disagree	Disagree	Disagree Somewhat	Neutral	Agree somewhat	Agree	Strongly agree
1	2	3	4	5	6	7

Discussing the research topics in class would be more useful than discussing them on Blackboard.

Strongly disagree	Disagree	Disagree Somewhat	Neutral	Agree somewhat	Agree	Strongly agree
1	2	3	4	5	6	7

I would like to use Blackboard to help with the research process again.

Strongly disagree	Disagree	Disagree Somewhat	Neutral	Agree somewhat	Agree	Strongly agree
1	2	3	4	5	6	7

The next time I have a research project I will use some of the things I learned while doing my literature review research.

Strongly disagree	Disagree	Disagree Somewhat	Neutral	Agree somewhat	Agree	Strongly agree
1	2	3	4	5	6	7

I already knew how to do most of the things the librarian was teaching the class.

Strongly disagree	Disagree	Disagree Somewhat	Neutral	Agree somewhat	Agree	Strongly agree
1	2	3	4	5	6	7

Your participation in the Blackboard discussion is worth x% of your grade for the independent study credit

The discussion should have been worth more than x% of my grade.

Strongly disagree	Disagree	Disagree Somewhat	Neutral	Agree somewhat	Agree	Strongly agree
1	2	3	4	5	6	7

The discussion should have been worth less than x% of my grade.

Strongly disagree	Disagree	Disagree Somewhat	Neutral	Agree somewhat	Agree	Strongly agree
1	2	3	4	5	6	7

What was the most useful thing you learned about the research process?

What was the most difficult part of the research process?

Do you have any additional comments or suggestions?

Thanks for your input!

Notes

1. Gloria J. Leckie, "Desperately Seeking Citations: Uncovering Faculty Assumptions about the Undergraduate Research Process," *Journal of Academic Librarianship* 22 (May 1996): 202..

2. Robert A. Schwegler and Linda K. Shamoon, "The Aims and Process of the Research Paper," College English 44 (December 1982): 817–824.; Jennie Nelson, "Reading Classrooms as Text: Exploring Student Writers' Interpretive Practices," *College Composition and Communication* 46 (October 1995): 411–429.

3. Barbara Read, Becky Francis, and Jocelyn Robson, "'Playing Safe': Undergraduate Essay Writing and the Presentation of the Student 'Voice'" *British Journal of Sociology of Education* 22 (September 2001): 387–399.

4. Prashant Bordia, "Face-to-Face Versus Computer-Mediated Communication: A Synthesis of the Experimental Literature," *The Journal of Business Communication* 34 (January 1997): 99–120.

5. Samia Khan, "Listservs in the College Science Classroom: Evaluating Participation and 'Richness' in Computer-Mediated Discourse," *Journal of Technology and Teacher Education* 13 (April 2005): 325–351.; Anne-Marie Deitering and Shaun Huston, "Weblogs and the Middle Space for Learning," *Academic Exchange Quarterly* 8 (Winter 2004) 272–276.; Nancy Harrison and Carole Bergen, "Some Design Strategies for Developing an Online Course," *Educational Technology* 40 (Jan-Feb 2000): 57–60.

6. John Stewart, ed., *Bridges Not Walls: A Book About Interpersonal Communication* (New York: McGraw-Hill, 2002).

7. Chris Hart, *Doing a Literature Review: Releasing the Social Science Research Imagination.* (Thousand Oaks, CA: Sage, 1998).

8. Ian Hutchby, "Children's Talk and Social Competence," *Children & Society* 19 (January 2005): 66–73.

9. Ted Zorn and Nittaya Campbell, "Improving the Writing of Literature Reviews Through a Literature Integration Exercise," *Business Communication Quarterly* 69 (June 2006): 172–183.

10. Carol Collier Kuhlthau, *Seeking Meaning: A Process Approach to Library and Information Services.* (Westport, CT: Libraries Unlimited, 2004)., p. 207.

11. Association of College and Research Libraries, "Collaboration." Online. Available from: http://www.ala.org/ala/mgrps/divs/acrl/issues/infolit/resources/collaboration/collaboration.cfm (June 7, 2010)

12. Andrew Topper, "Facilitating Student Interactions Through Discursive Moves: An Instructor's Experience Teaching Online Graduate Courses in Educational Technology," *The Quarterly Review of Distance Education* 6 (2005): 55–67.; Mary M. Christopher, Julie A. Thomas, and Mary K. Tallent-Runnels, "Raising the Bar: Encouraging High Level Thinking in Online Discussion Forums," *Roeper Review* 26 (Spring 2004): 166–171.

NINE

A Tale of Three Disciplines: Embedding Librarians and Outcomes-based Information Literacy Competency in Business, Biology, and Communication

Baseema Banoo Krkoska, Camille Andrews, and Jim Morris-Knower

This is the tale of how three librarians worked to embed themselves and an information literacy curriculum into classes in three different academic departments at a large research university. Before we get to that narrative of high stakes and intrigue, however, we'd like to briefly review what has been said about embedded librarianship in the professional literature.

In discussions of embedded librarianship and integrating information literacy into the curriculum, librarians have often focused on collaborating with disciplinary faculty and departments.[1] The importance of tailoring information literacy to the disciplines has been recognized in efforts such as the ACRL Instruction Section's Information Literacy in the Disciplines. There is a broad literature on the integration of information literacy into the life sciences, and to a lesser extent, business and communication. Librarian-faculty collaboration to integrate information literacy in the sciences, particularly biology, has taken numerous forms: supplemental workshops, presentations to faculty and other groups and meetings with departmental faculty and extracurricular groups;[2] inclusion of library information in a lab manual;[3] co-creation of assignments and group projects completed in conjunction with in-person library sessions;[4] use of online methods such as tutorials;[5] blended learn-

ing approaches that combine both face-to-face and online instruction;[6] and teaching of full-credit courses that are aligned with various disciplines.[7]

In other areas, such as business and communication, examples of a similar range of approaches can be found: providing single or multiple session face-to-face instruction and online support;[8] creating course-integrated assignments;[9] and providing full curricular integration by attending classes and project meetings, scheduling research consultations, grading assignments, and working with faculty to align information literacy standards with their department objectives.[10]

At Cornell's Mann Library, we[11] have worked to extend the instruction and liaison program and embed information literacy in three different disciplines at Cornell: biology, business and communication. In each area, we have tried a mix of most of the approaches mentioned above (except for full credit classes); this is the story of the evolution of our efforts, their success and failures, and our future directions, as well as valuable lessons learned in collaborating with faculty.

The Context

Cornell University is a large, distributed research-intensive university with over 20,000 students, nearly 14,000 of whom are undergraduate students. Mann Library serves the College of Agriculture and Life Sciences (CALS) and the College of Human Ecology (CHE). In CALS, the biology, business (or applied economics and management, as it is known), and communication departments serve a large number of undergraduates throughout the university. The undergraduate business and biological sciences majors are two of the largest on campus, conferring 14% and 12% of total undergraduate degrees respectively in 2009. Only Engineering confers a higher number of degrees (18%), and that advantage disappears if agriculture (13% of degrees conferred) is included in the total of biology students, raising it to 27% of degrees conferred in the life sciences.[12] Even beyond those students majoring in the disciplines, the introductory courses in these disciplines are all large popular gateway courses of several hundred students for grounding in biology, business and marketing, and speech presentation skills for non-majors. As such, we feel that it is important that we embed information literacy into these key majors and important gateway areas.

Baseema's Story—the Undergraduate Business Program

Since 2007, the business information competency program at Mann library has become comprehensive and well integrated into the Applied Economic & Management (AEM) curriculum. AEM is one of the largest undergraduate programs at Cornell University with nearly 700 business majors. Information competency skills are embedded into several courses throughout a student's career. The embedded librarianship program was my single most important priority when I assumed the position of business librarian in 2007. During my interview for the position, I proposed a model for embedded librarianship, then implemented the model to move from one-shot instruction towards an embedded instruction program.

If we view information literacy as an inverted pyramid (see Figure 9-1), the "information com-

petency" stage takes the greatest time investment, while introductory steps are crucial but take the least amount of effort. It is possible to move a single course upwards through increasingly more complex activities and it is also possible that several courses may be targeted depending on a variety of factors, such as faculty engagement, the nature of the assignment and practical constraints of time and financial resources.

Introductory Steps: The introductory phase includes important liaison work such as face time and presentations in faculty meetings, attending orientation sessions, sending introductory emails targeting key opinion leaders in the department, and arranging one-on-one meetings.[13] This step was absolutely crucial as both the embedded librarianship philosophy and my position were new to the undergraduate business faculty.

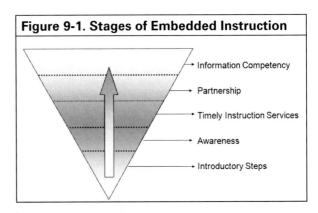

Figure 9-1. Stages of Embedded Instruction

- Information Competency
- Partnership
- Timely Instruction Services
- Awareness
- Introductory Steps

Awareness: The ratio of business librarian to students is quite often unfavorable at most institutions, where often a single librarian is attempting to reach hundreds, sometimes thousands of students in large schools such as College of Agriculture and Life Sciences at Cornell University. An inter-disciplinary approach allows students from all majors to take introductory business courses, with class enrollment exceeding 500 students. The web is the one of the most effective mechanism available to reach the Net generation; according to the Pew Internet and American Life Project, 93% of those between 18-29 years of age use the Internet.[14] During the awareness phase, I created the brand *"Business @ Mann"* (affectionately called businessmann, which may be slightly gender biased but is easily remembered). This new resource has become a one-stop shop for AEM students, including access to subject and course guides, an online tutorial for first-year business students, and instructional videos (or screencasts) showing how to use key business resources and perform common tasks.

The website at http://business.mannlib.cornell.edu is embedded within the main navigation of the AEM department website for both prospective and current students to discover the resource. The website is heavily utilized in instruction and blog posts come up rather high in Cornell domain search results. These tools helped generate awareness about Mann's Bloomberg services and other business databases as well as promoted new library services such as text a librarian.

Timely Instruction Services: The one-shot model still has a strong place in our implementation strategy. The Introduction to Business Management course requires students in a large enrollment course to complete a company research project which most students encounter for the first time at Cornell. I make a presentation on how to locate, interpret, and synthesize company financial data and news for their projects to a class of 500 students every year. After this one-shot session, the students can meet with librarians during designated office hours and chat on Meebo in the late evenings (8–10 p.m.). The Meebo chat proved to be the timeliest channel for students to utilize librarians' expertise from the comfort of their computers at a time when they are most likely to be working on the project.[15] This instruction program is orchestrated over three weeks towards the end of the Fall and Spring semester. In 2009, we answered 300 reference questions within three weeks and 60% of these questions came through Meebo chat. This model of support is also employed in entrepreneurship courses in the curriculum. Students of entrepreneurship often write unique business plans

and one-shot instruction often does not meet their needs.

Partnerships: Bloomberg services at Mann library are an example of a successful collaboration between university offices, the department, the library and industry. Due to ongoing budget cuts, my challenge was to ensure that Bloomberg services continue at Mann library. This challenge provided an impetus to collaborate with the development office at Cornell to reach out to alumni who actually use the tool in their workplace. I was fortunate to work with a visionary library director, a dedicated faculty member who teaches advanced finance courses (fixed income securities and technology & financial markets), and an effective development officer at Cornell. Part of the development strategy was stepping out of the boundaries of academic libraries and visiting investment banking firms on Wall Street to learn how the Bloomberg service is utilized on the trading floor. I interviewed finance professionals in New York City to understand access and use of information at the workplace. I met and interviewed 11 analysts, sales persons or traders with experience ranging from 6 months to 30 years in the fixed income sector. This effort convinced our donor that Mann is committed to support the resource and our quest to keep Bloomberg services running successfully came to fruition.

Students of the upper level finance courses are now graduating with sophisticated knowledge of financial technologies and gaining a competitive edge in interviews. Outcomes are embedded deeply in the course leading to completion of the Bloomberg certification process and a portfolio contest at the end of the course requiring students to apply their Bloomberg knowledge in a simulated investment environment.

Information Competency: The introductory Marketing course is also a large enrollment course on campus, and we worked with the professor to integrate marketing intelligence into this large introductory class. Over the course of the fall semester, students complete five online Marketing Intelligent Quotient (MIQ) for-credit exercises which aim to introduce students to the depth and breadth of marketing research resources and help student acquire skills in locating and using marketing research information on a variety of topics such as environmental scanning, consumer behavior, branding, pricing and distribution channels.

MIQs are a series of exercises with increasing levels of difficulty over the course of the semester. These exercises introduce and then reinforce search strategies. In the first two MIQs, step by step instructions are provided for every question. In the latter three exercises, hints were provided only for questions that introduced new strategies. For reinforcing questions, students were expected to draw upon their learning in previous MIQs to search and retrieve marketing information with minimal instruction. Over 90% of the students completed the earlier assignments. As the level of difficulty increased, it was encouraging that 80% of the students completed the later exercises successfully and received 5 points toward their semester average.

Self-reported feedback indicated that many students found it relevant to the course work. When asked to indicate the extent to which MIQs increased their familiarity with the breadth and availability of marketing resources on a scale of 1 (not at all) to 5 (to a great extent), 78% of the respondents rated the MIQ exercises as 3 or above. Similarly, when asked to indicate their confidence level (1=not confident at all and 5= highly confident) in being prepared to use marketing research databases at another time during their career, 84% of students rated the MIQ exercises as 3 and above. Students also described MIQs as "useful and educational," and "doing a superb job demonstrating relevant marketing databases."

Outcomes are also measured when students apply their skills in another end-of-semester for-credit assignment called Marketing Derby, an exercise requiring students to present a creative marketing plan and use marketing research resources to sup-

port their idea. Administering online exercises to over 500 students is challenging and we utilize the assessment tools available through Blackboard to deliver the exercises.

Future goals: In spite of the progress, there is much left to do and many lessons learned. In the introductory business management course, we need to work on reducing the labor intensity of Meebo chat, even though it is a timely service designed to meet user needs. The course lends itself to being moved up in the Stages of Embedded Instruction pyramid towards the integrated information competency phase such that students learn how to conduct company research over the course of the semester instead of packing it into the last two weeks.

For the marketing course, we are not yet satisfied with measurement of outcomes. In the future, it would be ideal to measure students' learning before and after the MIQs are administered. Also, a large number of students perceived it as "busy work" as they did not implement this knowledge until the end of the semester.

Overall, the experience of embedding information competency into the business curriculum has proven to be successful, with both the faculty and the students supporting the goal wholeheartedly. As I move on to a new position within the library managing international programs, it was rewarding to hear from a faculty that the program was "responsible for an important innovation in the faculty's thinking." For the library, there is no better outcome.

Camille's Story—The Evolution of Mann's Biology Instruction

The biological sciences at Cornell have a long history within Mann's instruction program. In this context, I will show the evolution from paper-based workbooks to online tutorials and on a larger scale, from single assignments to integration at the curricular level.

Traditionally, all Cornell students majoring in biology, as well as all pre-med and pre-vet and other life sciences majors, were required to take BioG 1101-1104, a two semester sequence of paired lecture and lab. This formed the foundation of students' introduction to the complex web of biology courses at Cornell and drew not only from the College of Agriculture and Life Sciences, which Mann serves, but also the College of Arts and Sciences and other colleges on campus.

Typically, Mann has provided instruction only for the BioG 1103 first semester laboratory course and some smaller first-year biology seminars. In our earliest biology instruction for BioG 1103, we gave the several hundred students in the class a paper worksheet with a walking tour of the library that had them stop at marked points in the library and note certain services or ask questions. In addition, students were given an exercise that gave them step-by-step instructions on finding particular articles in BIOSIS, then our main biology database. Finally, students had to find a print book in the library on a particular subject, locate the book, and indicate whether or not Cornell owned it, what the call number was and what floor it was on. Naturally, with over 600 students, these exercises created a great deal of chaos in the library every fall, with lost students wandering the stacks, multiple people requesting the same materials, and loads of questions at the reference desk about the same exercises. We also found that the BIOSIS exercises, even though split into three different example articles, still did not prevent plagiarism as students could simply find others who had their exercise and exchange answers. Finally, the cookie cutter nature of the exercise emphasized familiarization with the physical structure of the library and its classification systems and mechanistic focus on databases as tools. The exercise did little to introduce students to the kind of critical thinking or information literacy concepts they needed to complete further classes.

To mitigate this, by 2002 the tutorial was changed to a step-by-step paper-based assignment with greater emphasis on information literacy concepts and active learning . Students were given examples of searching in BIOSIS but were asked to use topics of their own devising and generate their own concepts, keywords and search strategies to find primary literature articles for a poster they would have to complete for a later lab exercise, tying it more firmly into the curriculum and to an authentic task. The walking tour was dropped in favor of a simple map and brief instructions about the library's services in the students' lab manuals. As the class was so large, again no in-person instruction was added; however, the TAs for the class had a session with the librarian at the beginning of the semester to go over the tutorial and answer any questions. This formula worked much better than the former exercise; however, as the size of the class continued to grow, administering the paper tutorial to over six hundred students became more and more unwieldy and both the librarian and the course instructors hoped to make the assignment even more relevant and engaging to the students

When I became instruction coordinator in 2006, one of my tasks was to find another way to deliver first semester biology instruction. Around this time, Cornell University Library was expanding its information literacy efforts into a system-wide coordinated effort that eventually became the Cornell Undergraduate Information Competency Initiative (CUICI; http://www.infocomp.library.cornell.edu). As co-director of the CUICI, I thought that the BioG 1103 course would be the perfect test case for a redesigned online tutorial.

In the summer of 2008, CUICI held its first week-long information competency "institute," designed to help faculty improve their students' ability to find and process information. Working with the instructors of BioG 1103, Laurel Hester and Kuei-Chiu Chen, at the first institute, we put the same tutorial online with some minor but important changes. Most importantly, the tutorial was transferred to a wiki (https://confluence.cornell.edu/display/restbio/Home) with the help of a summer library school intern from Syracuse University.

We chose the Confluence wiki platform for its ease of updating for both librarians and faculty; at that point, the rest of our website was in CommonSpot, a Cold Fusion-based Content Management System that required building special templates for tutorial pages and training to update.

In addition, putting the tutorial online allowed us to expand it to address more conceptual issues, such as the differences between primary and secondary literature. We also added elements such as multimedia and automatic feedback quizzes that our research had indicated would make the tutorial more engaging for students with varied learning styles.[16] Multimedia screencasts showed the students step-by-step how to find, access, evaluate and cite their articles, while optional multiple-choice quizzes allowed the students to test and get instant feedback on their understanding of the concepts before they completed the free choice exercises they would submit for their assignment.

In designing the tutorial, we tried to take a more modular approach and specifically designed it so that examples could be plugged in and removed at will, making later updating easier. We also changed our example database to the Web of Knowledge platform (featuring several life sciences databases including BIOSIS) and dropped the catalog searching portion, as we were still having the problem of six hundred students searching for books in the library with little success. The librarians also expanded their participation in the assignment by editing and adding to the library material already present in the lab manual, adjusting the existing assessments to include rubrics with more about the literature search tutorial, and ultimately displaying the best posters as judged through peer review (which were also printed at Mann) in the library lobby.

The first revision of the tutorial assignment was fairly well received, though some students complained about its length and were confused about opening multiple windows to fill out the final exercise. In a second iteration, we streamlined

and updated the tutorial to reflect changes to the library website and databases. It was a first step in greater involvement in the biology curriculum, and we were pleased with the results.

Those results were made clear in a Fall 2008 survey of students in the classes that had been modified in the previous summer's institute, which also included classes in English, Food Science, Communication, Music, Information Science, and Crop and Soil Science/International Agriculture and Rural Development among others. 86% of the 167 respondents in the survey came from the BioG 1103 class, and the students were indirectly assessed on their perceptions of their information literacy skills and the change in those skills after the courses. In the report compiled by Cornell Information Technologies, the evaluator, Kim Nicholson, reported:

> For each question, students self-reported an improvement for each area. Specifically students were asked to rate different research skills on a Likert scale (Excellent, Very Good, Good, Fair, Poor). Prior to their Information Literacy course, the majority of respondents rated themselves "Good" on all skills except one (distinguishing scholarly information from unreliable which they rated themselves "VG"). After their Information Literacy course, the majority of respondents rated themselves "Very Good" on all research skills. However, when asked directly if their research practices changed, respondents were split (44% "Yes" and 56% "no") with[a] similar phenomenon on questions: Did your type of resources change (46% "Yes", 54% "No") and Did your view of research change (24% "Yes," 76% "No"). But data from open comment fields suggest students do attribute change in their behavior to what they learned as part of information literacy assignments, in particular, Using Library Databases More Often.

In addition, seventy-two respondents submitted free text comments indicating that they felt that their research practices had improved. "I attribute this change to more experience with and more practice in research," said one student in a representative comment. Others said "I use the library databases much more often now," "I use databases for reliable sources to use rather than general search engines [and] used more effective, specific search terms," and that "my thought processes became clearer." Students also commented that, "It was fun," "Library staff are extremely helpful," and "It was a cool experience that made me want to look into doing undergraduate research at Cornell."[17]

The second institute was held in the summer of 2009 and the classes, which included an additional biology course (BioG 1105), were implemented in Fall 2009. We achieved similar results in the Fall 2009 survey, in which just over half of our respondents came from both the BioG 1103 and 1105 classes. Outcomes-based assessment of the assignment was limited, consisting of a grade for completion and some evaluation for quality, which was done by teaching assistants. In the rubrics for their lab reports, students were assessed on inclusion of cited references in the proper APA format as a component of their final grade, but due to staffing issues, this rubric item was not examined separately. A more in-depth assessment is planned for future classes.

The CUICI also provided a vehicle for expanding our initial work on the tutorial and strengthened our partnership with the biology department. In the second institute we were fortunate enough to have the participation of Darlene Campbell, an instructor for the BioG 1105 auto-tutorial course (similar to BioG 1103 except that approximately two hundred students work on the course material in an individualized, self-paced environment with fewer lectures and more study sessions with TAs). Using the first tutorial on primary literature as a base, I worked with the instructor to change the examples to fit that course's curriculum. In addition, we added two other modules: one on the scientific method and background research, and another created for an academic technology department course on reading scientific literature. In this iteration, we worked on better articulation of learning outcomes for all the tutorials. We explicitly started with the ACRL standards, in particular those for science and technology.[18] For example, we explicitly stated the outcome "Explores general information sources to increase familiarity with current knowledge of the topic," from Standard One of the Information Literacy Standards for Science and Technology/Engineering, then had the students search the library catalog for a book or other background resource on their subject, identify relevant subject headings, and report their search strategy and whether or not the library had the resource.

In addition, we incorporated material from other universities and moved from the wiki (which was not ideal as a web delivery platform, particularly since we were not using its collaborative features) to a tutorial creation software called SoftChalk, which made the tutorial much easier to produce, used a cleaner interface, and integrated the media and assessment in a much tighter package. Collaboration with Cornell Information Technologies' Faculty Support Services was essential, not only for the addition of a scientific article dissection tutorial, but also for identifying and deploying the tutorial with SoftChalk.

In the institute and in other areas, we also moved from integration in a single course in the life sciences to a departmental-wide outreach effort. At approximately the same time as the first and second institute in 2008-9, the most sweeping change in the biology curriculum in decades was beginning. The dean had charged a task force with the job of "assess[ing] our current curriculum and overall program in Undergraduate Biology, benchmarking it against our major competitors and making strategic recommendations for its continuing excellence."[19] One of the heads of the biology curriculum implementation team, Ronald Hoy, an award-winning teacher and a strong advocate for information literacy in the sciences, took part in the second institute in partnership with our then-bioinformatics librarian, Medha Devare, in order to help re-envision the BioG 1103 course.

Just as the library was shifting information literacy instruction to a more conceptual approach, the introductory biology laboratory was changing to emphasize basic scientific concepts and critical thinking. In collaboration with the current instructors, Laurel Hester, Kuei-Chiu Chen, and Ron Hoy, our bioinformatics librarian offered input on the new investigative biology lab that will serve as a foundational course for all biology majors. This effort has led to greater collaboration between members of the biology department and the library on communication around the changing biology curriculum, as well as on grant writing. In addition, in the 2010 summer institute, we have begun a deeper partnership with a biological and environmental engineering faculty member, which also includes staff and librarians from the College of Engineering.

Our work has not stopped with the biology courses and initiatives mentioned above. We have also had some effect on the broader life sciences. These include our integration into most of the small first-year seminars in life science, which often have a focus on writing and reading scientific literature; our work with the director of undergraduate studies in food science and her upper-level microbiology lab; and the crop and soil sciences/international agriculture course co-taught by our bioinformatics librarian. Medha not only taught many of the class sessions, but also graded assignments, helped build the course wiki and educate students on its use, and added comments to weekly reading posts.

Lessons Learned
Learn to speak the language of the discipline or at least understand your disciplinary faculty's particular goals and concerns.

I do not have a science background so it was especially important for me not only to listen to what faculty said about the specifics of the course, but also to ask questions about how they understood their discipline and what it meant to them to teach students to "think like scientists." Their explanations clarified my understanding of their goals and helped me translate them into the language of the ACRL standards. I do not expect to become a subject expert (nor do faculty expect me to), but at a basic level, understanding the approach of scientists to their discipline and training others in it is extremely useful, particularly in lower-level courses. In many ways, working on the first-year laboratory course was ideal for me as a non-subject specialist, because talking to faculty about their expectations of students (who would also be novices in the field) educated me about their implicit knowledge and allowed me to ask some of the same "dumb" questions that students would. Our bioinformatics librarian, Medha Devare, has a Ph.D. in crop and soil sciences. She was invaluable, not only in the more advanced life sciences courses, but also in speaking to faculty on a curricular level. As someone trained in the discipline, she has a deep, intuitive grasp of the subject matter and the ways in which people trained in the field approach it, as well as the authority of her educational and field experience. However, even without that background, a librarian who makes the effort to probe a bit and speak to faculty in language that they will hear can accomplish a lot.

Clarify roles and responsibilities and collaborate!
As recommended by Pritchard,[20] I made it clear that my role was as a subject matter expert in information literacy and the resources available to the students and tutorial coordinator. My suggested changes to the citation style and database used and to the information literacy concepts addressed were well-received by the faculty. In other areas, such as the actual scientific curriculum and examples, technology, and assessment, collabora-

tion with the faculty and others was key. Without that team effort, integration into the curriculum wouldn't have been possible. The library can also serve a unique role as neutral mediator and connector between various areas and members of the university during a curriculum revision.

From course to curricular integration: start small and build scalable tools.

When moving from thinking about individual courses to an entire program, one of the first steps was figuring out the fit between courses and the information competency materials we had already created. With a biological sciences program that spans multiple colleges, departments and faculty members, looking at the whole would have been too daunting, especially since the curriculum was a moving target due to curriculum revision. We were fortunate to build on existing strong relationships with instructors in the departments, leverage those to test pilot the first tutorial and then work with other similar courses to add additional modules. In the end we hope to build a suite of online modules and assignments that can then be integrated into to the new core biology courses that are being created, as well as other life sciences courses, in a systematic and developmental fashion.

Jim's Story—Communication 2010: Oral Communication

According to those who have been around long enough to know these things, Mann Library has taught some form of library research for what is now called Communication 2010: Oral Communication for at least thirty years. Offered through the Department of Communication in the College of Agriculture and Life Sciences, Comm 201 is a large (200–250) lecture class in which students research and present four speeches to their class for a grade.

Like most library research classes, Mann's instruction for Comm 2010 has traditionally been a one-shot session done in a single lecture class (twice, really—once for each section) early in the semester. The librarian has 45 minutes to stand up in front of 125 students and show them everything from searching the Cornell library catalog for books about oral communication to using databases like ABI/Inform and Factiva to find magazine articles on topics ranging from changes in the American family to bioterrorism. These classes are typically aided by PowerPoint presentations with database screen shots and librarian contact information.

Both the Comm 201 faculty and the librarians teaching these workshops have long been frustrated with the results of these one-time library research presentations. The faculty continue to see their students citing Google and Wikipedia almost exclusively as their information sources, picking overused topics like drunk driving, and seldom narrowing their topics effectively. And the librarians can all too easily gauge the disinterestedness of the students in the auditorium by the texting and newspaper reading going on during the library sessions and by the almost complete lack of any contact for research help, despite repeated invitations to ask .

But what to do about this frustration? Well, change does not, as they say, happen overnight, and this is the story of how the library instruction for this course evolved over the past several years and how librarians and faculty, working together, took the chances that made this change happen.

In June of 2008, I was invited to participate in the Cornell Undergraduate Information Competency Initiative (CUICI), an inaugural weeklong program designed to help Cornell faculty improve undergraduate research and information literacy skills in their classes. Part of the plan at the Institute was to partner participating faculty members with Cornell librarians who, as a team, would work on overhauling the library research component of their classes. I was partnered (embedded, really) with Comm 2010 instructor Kathy Bergen, an outgoing and open-minded lecturer in the Communications Department; our task was to address her biggest complaints about the Comm 2010 class, especially students' lack of understanding of how to narrow down their topics and the need to use credible sources beyond what was easily found via Google and Wikipedia.

Frankly, I was a little nervous about this whole partnership. While I had taught many library workshops in my ten-plus years as a librarian at Cornell, I knew little formally about information competency standards and had little experience with the subject of Communication. When I was partnered with Kathy, though, I was also fortunate to be able to work with Camille who, as instruction coordinator at Mann, had taught the Comm workshops for several years and had much more knowledge of the theory of information competency.

In the fall of '08, Camille and I co-taught the Comm 2010 lectures. Working with Kathy, we agreed that we would slowly start implementing some of the things we'd talked about over the summer, rather than dramatically overhauling the whole course. We decided to try using clickers to incorporate some interactivity in the classes. So instead of just showing the class how to use Lexis-Nexis or Statistical Abstracts to find information for their speeches, we asked the class to use their clickers to answer questions, such as what was the first successful commercially cloned animal (a dog named Booger) and which of five listed states had not voted Democratic in a presidential election since 1964 (Alaska). We then demonstrated how to find the answers using the library databases.

After the class, Kathy told us that she appreciated our "creative innovations" and noted that students generally seemed more engaged in the lectures. She also emailed us the students comments she received about the session, which were pretty evenly split between those expressing some variation on "A waste of time; I've heard this lecture so many times!" to "Liked the lecture. Clickers are a nice touch!" Clearly we were making some (slow) progress.

Over the next year and a half, we followed the strategy of slowly implementing a few changes that we thought would address some of the problems with the class. We learned as we went along. For the Spring 2009 sessions, for example, we switched the delivery mechanism to Libguides, the system of easy-to-create web guides which was new to Cornell at that point. Although the sessions were still one shots to large groups in a lecture hall, we now presented the class material in the more visually engaging and better organized format that Libguides offers.

Libguides also allowed us to try a pre-assignment that required the students to complete an online exercise on narrowing down the topic of separation of church and state for a 5-7 minute speech. Then, during the sessions, we used their answers as a departure point for a series of clicker questions similar to the ones we did in the fall 2008 class.

The results, like our clicker experiment the previous semester, were mixed. The Libguide did organize the class materials better and the pre-assignment did get the students to think about picking and narrowing a topic before the class. After a couple of clicker questions at the start, though, the rest of the class devolved into the classic one-shot demo format and students seemed to tune out. And Libguides, while excellent for organizing class information, proved less successful in administering the exercise.

Picking a topic and narrowing it down continued to be a major issue for the class. Kathy had told us after the fall 08 lectures that while the clickers were great for making things more lively and participatory, she thought it would be better if the library lectures were more specifically tied to one specific topic and showed the steps involved in researching and focusing a speech topic. By Fall 2009, I was teaching the Comm 201 research sessions solo, and Kathy and I decided I would use the topic of social contagion, which had been recently profiled in the *New York Times Magazine*.[21] I ditched the clickers and made a conscious effort to keep the presentation of each resource brief and lively, walking through the process of narrowing down the social contagion topic using the class Libguide step by step.

This brief and focused one-shot format was an improvement over some of the earlier sessions—fewer students seemed to be texting or napping in class, and Kathy said the comments afterwards were the best she had heard for these sessions. Beyond these comments, though, there was no formal assessment of what the students knew and did not know, and what they had learned in terms of information competency. At that same time, Communications was under pressure (some pedagogical, some budgetary) from the University and the College to have information competency and assessment become central parts of all classes.

Kathy told me shortly after the Fall 2009 sessions that she had decided to completely overhaul the structure of Comm 201 to comply with those mandates. "We would like a comprehensive plan with much input from the library on how to best educate our students in research competency," she told us. Most important was a change from the two large lectures to nine smaller sections led by Kathy and student TAs. We met as a group several times over the fall, and the plan that came out of these meetings combined the most successful results from the workshops given over the three semesters with our goal of incorporating specific elements of the ACRL information competency standards into our workshops and assessing the effectiveness of what we were teaching.

We aimed to accomplish the following: make the experience for students more engaging and participatory than is usually possible in the large lecture, one-shot format; introduce the various information sources for their speeches (statistics, demographics and psychographics, journal and magazine articles, polls, etc.) in a step-by-step fashion that demonstrated not only where to find information, but how to choose fresh topics and narrow them down to a focused presentation; and, if pos-

sible, increase my visibility as the class's embedded librarian so that students would know me and feel comfortable contacting me with any questions.

What we came up with was a set of two different multimedia tutorials (one for informative speeches and one for persuasive) that incorporated a combination of Blackboard, Libguides, and YouTube-embedded videos and screencasts. The class's new structure of nine sections precluded my one-shot in-class lectures twice each semester, but Kathy was concerned that I might be lost as a "presence" for the class to know as "their librarian." We decided to use Camtasia screencast software to create a series of short (under 3 minutes each) web videos in which I narrate the steps involved in doing everything from using CQ Researcher to locate a topic to searching Polling the Nations for polling data. Once all the videos were created, I uploaded them to YouTube, and then easily embedded them into Libguides.

We also decided to use Blackboard, which the students already used for all their courses, as our assessment tool. Blackboard can be used to administer quizzes, which allowed us to create graded assignments that measure the students' mastery of the basic library research concepts highlighted in the workshops, while at the same time provided the incentive for the students to complete the assignment. Another advantage was that students could answer as many questions as they had time for in one sitting, then save their work and return later to complete the assignment. Each question in Blackboard linked to the appropriate page in the Libguide, where we put the video and links to the databases and other resources highlighted in those videos. When they were done watching the videos, the students returned to Blackboard to answer the question.

From my perspective, the biggest challenge was not the technology involved in screencast creation (they took about five hours each to create, but production sped up as I mastered the techniques) but rather crafting tutorial questions that matched specific information competency standards and designing a grading rubric so the undergraduate teaching assistants could grade the assignments. It was very helpful to be on a team with Camille and Bassema, who know a lot about outcomes (the information competency piece) and assessments (the rubric).

Working as a team, the three of us translated the ACRL Information Literacy Competency Standards for Higher Education into a working set of outcomes that we felt the students could tackle for this assignment and that could be effectively assessed using a rubric. We created ten questions in all, each of which corresponded to an ACRL standard and each of which was measurable using the rubric Camille designed. Thus, for the ACRL performance indicator stating that the information-literate student "identifies key concepts and terms that describe the information need," we created a screencast about identifying keywords and locating a popular article in Academic Search Premier, along with a question in Blackboard asking the students to list at least two keywords used to locate a popular article. When these online quizzes were completed, the TAs could consult the rubric to determine whether the student met the standard by completing the entire task.

The results of this experiment were overwhelmingly positive. Kathy told us that the class discussions and the speeches that semester were some of the best she had ever had in her many years teaching the class. There were some technical problems with the tutorials, and students registered a few complaints about the Blackboard technology—mainly its quirkiness on a Mac—and some difficulty accessing Academic Search Premier and Refworks from off campus.

The best confirmation that this new system was working, and that we had successfully crossed from one shot to embedded information competency, was reading the students' end-of-the-semester comments on the tutorial. The responses, unlike the mixed reviews we received immediately after the Fall 2008 lectures, were almost entirely positive. Again and again, students noted that the assignment opened their eyes to valuable databases and resources like Mintel and Refworks, that they did not know existed, and that they especially appreciated the section on the credibility checklist for documenting the worthiness of websites. Even the few "negative" reviews grudgingly acknowledged that the students got something out of the experience, even though they didn't really enjoy the task. Said one,

> Although the tutorials weren't my favorite assignments, they opened my eyes to resources I did not know existed. Overall, they made me a better prepared, more credible speaker. In hindsight, the Mann Library Tutorials were not the highlights of the course, but served as an excellent alternative to simply listening to the professor lecture in class.

This was a distinct improvement over the earlier "this is a waste of my time" comments.

There were two other clear benchmarks of the effectiveness of this new method of delivering information competency skills. First, the class statistics showed that use of the class Libguide jumped from 1172 hits in Fall 2009 to 7900 in the Spring 2010 semester. Second, the number of requests for help by students in the class went from exactly zero in the Fall 2009 semester to twenty-eight different questions the following semester.

I recognize that a major part of these increased statistics is connected to this assignment being graded, and I am comfortable with that. The bottom line is that the students watched the video tutorials, completed the assignments that tested their mastery of basic information competency performance indicators, and felt free to contact the embedded librarian to help them with this task. We as librarians could not ask for much more.

One final note on the benefits of being embedded in the Communication Department: For the past two years, Camille and I have been invited by Kathy to be guest judges for the department's annual speaking contest, which is held in May of each year and features speeches by five top students vying for a $600 top prize. These were the best of the best, and it proved to be a lot of fun (and hard work) deciding who should win the top prizes. It is also another great way to deepen our embeddedness in the class—especially now that we do not offer a lecture session in person. An added benefit at this year's Spring 2010 contest was seeing the tangible results of the new tutorial system: all five speeches were copiously researched and supported by the sort of credible sources, like Mintel and the CDC, that we had pushed in the tutorials. Students are all still using Wikipedia and Google, but it seems like they are learning to extend their research beyond those resources. These are small, but important, steps on the road to creating information competent students and citizens.

Future Directions

Our next step in all departmental areas—biology, business and communication—is further curricular integration. Cornell is scheduled for reaccreditation in 2011 by the Middle States Commission on Higher Education and the self-study process leading up to this has led to the naming of information literacy as university-wide learning outcome.[22] This has aided our efforts to embed the library and information literacy into departmental curricula not only in biology but also in business and communication. In the Communication department, our deeper involvement in COMM 2010 led to work with the COMM 2820 Research methods course. In the spring of 2010, we began preliminary curriculum mapping efforts in Communication based on this work.

In her article, "Effective Librarian and Discipline Faculty Collaboration Models for Integrating Information Literacy into the Fabric of an Academic Institution," Stephanie Sterling Brasley notes:

> The University of Illinois at Urbana-Champaign defines curriculum mapping as a way of examining a program of study and the courses within that program in order to "understand curriculum structures and relationships; gain insight on how students experience the discipline; increase awareness of curricular content; identify common or 'gateway' courses that students are required or choose to take; and reveal opportunities for library integration."[23] Bullard and Holden view curriculum mapping as "the systematic analysis of the content of the courses in a curriculum [and] a communication tool for introducing collaborative opportunities to faculty with the least amount of compromise to the vision of their course."[24] This is a particularly beneficial approach for information literacy development, as both classroom faculty and librarians then possess mutual understanding of its placement and timing within the department's curriculum. Additionally, the curriculum mapping process affords insight into the overall curricular and instructional objectives of a department.[25] Information gleaned from this tool is vital to producing a shared vision and goals among collaborators.[26]

For the two courses in Communication, COMM 2010 and COMM 2820—both required courses—I indicated the courses we were working on given learning outcomes using a modification of the concept mapping process and tools advocated by Megan Fitzgibbons in her presentation "Connecting the Dots: Alignment of Information Literacy Instruction to Course Learning Outcomes Through Concept Mapping" presented at EDUCAUSE Annual 2009.[27] Using the CMap mindmapping tool, I diagrammed the ACRL Information literacy Competency Standards for Higher Education and then used a color-coded key to indicate which outcomes were addressed in the assignments for each course. This made it easier for me and others to see which outcomes were being addressed and which still need to be incorporated in previous or later classes in the major. This preliminary information competency curriculum map was also recently included in the Communication department's retreat on accreditation and assessment and helped serve as a model for larger departmental efforts to address outcomes-based learning.

Conclusions

So what is the take away from this story of three librarians embedding themselves in large lecture classes in a research university? Well, it would probably be fair to say that we embedded librarians are certainly *not* to be confused with embedded journalists, who join up with a military unit in order to better tell the story of a war and the soldiers who fight in it. The risks involved for embedded librarians are far fewer, and the stakes certainly are not as high. Nor are we out to tell anyone's story. The real difference, however, is that unlike journalists, who would never think to tell the brass how to fight their war, we do so with the hope that course leaders will indeed learn something from us—that instructors and course designers will change their strategies as they make their classes more respon-

sive to the idea of creating information competent students.

This is also a tale of change, adaptation and opportunity. While we have worked closely with these three departments for a long time, it has only been in the last few years that we have extended the relationship to something that would truly be considered embedded, or perhaps more properly, integrated. What Camille learned through her experience embedding in the biology curriculum is true for all course-based instruction that librarians offer faculty—we have moved, and must continue to move, from single assignments to integration at the curricular level.

The Internet has changed the way students get information as well as the way we teach, and the era of the one-shot library instruction workshop is almost over. Faculty members are by necessity becoming more receptive to the idea of integrating information competency into their classes, and many recognize the benefits to be gained by partnering with librarians to achieve this. At the same time, technologies like Blackboard, Meebo, Libguides, Camtasia and YouTube are giving us the opportunity to engage students where they live—online, 24/7—in ways that avoid most of the pitfalls of the one shot lecture while also creating outcome-based tutorials that can demonstrate the students' mastery of information competency. There is no better outcome for the library than to have faculty and students acknowledge that the information competency package librarians provide makes their teaching and research better.

Notes

1. Stephanie Sterling Brasley, "Effective Librarian and Discipline Faculty Collaboration Models for Integrating Information Literacy into the Fabric of an Academic Institution," *New Directions for Teaching & Learning* 2008, no. 114 (Summer2008, 2008), 71–88, http://search.ebscohost.com/login.aspx?direct=true&db=aph&AN=32750177&site=ehost-live.

2. Peggy A. Pritchard, "The Embedded Science Librarian: Partner in Curriculum Design and Delivery," *Journal of Library Administration* 50, no. 4 (2010), 373, http://www.informaworld.com/10.1080/01930821003667054 (accessed May 04, 2010).

3. Ignacio J. Ferrer-Vinent and Christy A. Carello, "Embedded Library Instruction in a First-Year Biology Laboratory Course," *Science & Technology Libraries* 28, no. 4 (2008), 325, http://www.informaworld.com/10.1080/01942620802202352 (accessed June 06, 2010).

4. Kathrine Aydelott, "Using the ACRL Information Literacy Competency Standards for Science and Engineering/Technology to Develop a Modular Critical-Thinking-Based Information Literacy Tutorial," *Science & Technology Libraries* 27, no. 4

(2007), 19-42.; Ferrer-Vinent and Carello, *Embedded Library Instruction in a First-Year Biology Laboratory Course*, 325.; Pritchard, *The Embedded Science Librarian: Partner in Curriculum Design and Delivery*, 373.

5. Aydelott, *Using the ACRL Information Literacy Competency Standards for Science and Engineering/Technology to Develop a Modular Critical-Thinking-Based Information Literacy Tutorial*, 19–42.; Jeanine Marie Scaramozzino, "An Undergraduate Science Information Literacy Tutorial in a Web 2.0 World," *Issues in Science & Technology Librarianship* (2008).; Pritchard, *The Embedded Science Librarian: Partner in Curriculum Design and Delivery*, 373.

6. Kathleen M. Gehring and Deborah A. Eastman, "Information Fluency for Undergraduate Biology Majors: Applications of Inquiry-Based Learning in a Developmental Biology Course," *CBE Life Sci Educ* 7, no. 1 (03/01, 2008), 54–63, http://www.lifescied.org/cgi/content/abstract/7/1/54.; Jeanine M. Scaramozzino, "Integrating STEM Information Competencies into an Undergraduate Curriculum," *Journal of Library Administration* 50, no. 4 (2010), 315, http://www.informaworld.com/10.1080/01930821003666981 (accessed May 04, 2010).

7. Cynthia A. Raquepau and Louise M. Richards, "Investigating the Environment: Teaching and Learning with Undergraduates in the Sciences," *Reference Services Review* 30, no. 4 (2002), 319, http://proquest.umi.com/pqdweb?did=281929161&Fmt=7&clientId=8424&RQT=309&VName=PQD.

8. Chad F. Boeninger, "Blogs, Wiki, and IM: Communication Tools for Subject Specialists," http://www.higheredblogcon.com/index.php/blogs-wikis-and-im-communication-tools-for-subject-specialists/ (accessed June/1, 2010).; Jennifer S. A. Leigh, Cynthia Gibbon and Janelle Wertzberger, "They Click! Information Literacy and Undergraduates in an Introduction to Management Class," in *Teaching Information Literacy Skills to Social Sciences Students and Practitioners: A Casebook of Applications*, eds. Douglas Cook and Natasha Cooper (Chicago, IL: Association of College and Research Libraries, 2006), 175-185.; Vaughan Judd, Betty Tims and Lucy Farrow, "Evaluation and Assessment of a Library Instruction Component of an Introduction to Business Course: A Continuous Process," *Reference Services Review* 32, no. 3 (2004), 274–283, http://vnweb.hwwilsonweb.com/hw/jumpstart.jhtml?recid=0bc05f7a67b1790e807bdb2b310ae7cec2a829183c61ca0764d2fff0907e246eeb5da8d61aaded58&fmt=C; The author of this article has chosen the following Web sites: http://www.idea.ksu.edu/papers/ldea_Paper_32.pdf http://www.cit.cornell.edu/campus/teach/grad/gtdw/portfolio. html http://www.merriam-webster.com.

9. Ann M. Fiegen, Bennett Cherry and Kathleen Watson, "Reflections on Collaboration: Learning Outcomes and Information Literacy Assessment in the Business Curriculum. at California State University, San Marcos," *Reference Services Review* 30, no. 4 (2002), 307-318, http://www.ala.org/acrl/nili/ilit1st.html http://www.csusm.edu/acrl/il/toolkit/standards.html.; Judd, Tims and Farrow, *Evaluation and Assessment of a Library Instruction Component of an Introduction to Business Course: A Continuous Process*, 274–283.

10. Russell A. Hall, "The "Embedded" Librarian in a Freshman Speech Class: Information Literacy Instruction in Action," *College & Research Libraries News* 69, no. 1 (January, 2008), 28–30, http://vnweb.hwwilsonweb.com/hw/jumpstart.jhtml?recid=0bc05f7a67b1790e807bdb2b310ae7cea6d884e65251e2e03e675bf6f967deed707bfae197e3ad5b&fmt=C.; Steven C. Koehn and Janet McNeil Hurlbert, "A Communication Capstone Project: A Developmental Model for Undergraduate Research Skills Training," in *Teaching Information Literacy Skills to Social Sciences Students and Practitioners: A Casebook of Applications*, eds. Douglas Cook and Natasha Cooper (Chicago, IL: Association of College and Research Libraries, 2006), 47–54.

11. Camille Andrews, former instruction coordinator and current learning technologies and assessment librarian; Baseema Banoo Krkosa, former instruction/reference coordinator and liaison to Applied Economics and Management and current International Projects librarian; and Jim Morris-Knower, public relations and outreach librarian and liaison to the Communication department.

12. Cornell University, "Common Data Set. Degrees Conferred July 1, 2008–June 30, 2009," http://dpb.cornell.edu/F_Common_Data_Set.htm (accessed June/1, 2010).

13. David Shumaker, "Who Let the Librarians Out? Embedded Librarianship and the Library Manager," *Reference & User Services Quarterly* 48, no. 3 (Spring, 2009), 239–42, 257, http://vnweb.hwwilsonweb.com/hw/jumpstart.jhtml?recid=0bc05f7a67b1790e807bdb2b310ae7cef5003a8d5f33972f4f8bc53a4d7bead264813146b4b59729&fmt=C.

14. Lee Rainie, "Internet, Broadband, and Cell Phone Statistics," Pew Internet and American Life Project, http://www.pewinternet.org/Reports/2010/Internet-broadband-and-cell-phone-statistics.aspx (accessed June/1, 2010).

15. Rachel Singer Gordon and Michael Stephens, "Embedding a Librarian in Your Web Site using Meebo," *Computers in Libraries* 27, no. 8 (September, 2007), 44–45, http://vnweb.hwwilsonweb.com/hw/jumpstart.jhtml?recid=0bc05f7a67b1790e807bdb2b310ae7cedfc79adf2efcace0cb4c95b06e8d32e4db818da5fb141e4b&fmt=C.; Lori Northrup, ""MeeboMe!" for Embedded Chat Reference: Patron-Initiated Encounters without Downloads Or Accounts," *College & Undergraduate Libraries* 15, no. 3 (2008), 357–363, http://vnweb.hwwilsonweb.com/hw/jumpstart.jhtml?recid=0bc05f7a67b1790e807bdb2b310ae7cea6d884e65251e2e0d9f9521a28f62b5f83ea4709957b300f&fmt=C; The author of this article has chosen the following Web sites: http://communication.howstuffworks.com/instant-messaging.htm http://www.pewinternet.org/pdfs/PIP_Instantmessage_Report.pd f http://www.readwriteweb.com/archives/10_chat_widgets.php.

16. Nancy H. Dewald, "Web-Based Library Instruction: What is Good Pedagogy?" *Information Technology & Libraries* 18, no. 1 (03, 1999), 26, http://search.ebscohost.com/login.aspx?direct=true&db=aph&AN=1743932&site=ehost-live.

17. Kim Nicholson, "Cornell Undergraduate Information Competency Initiative Report. Fall 2008." 2008).

18. ALA/ACRL/STS Task Force on Information Literacy for Science and Technology, "Information Literacy Standards for Science and Engineering/Technology," http://www.ala.org/ala/mgrps/divs/acrl/standards/infolitscitech.cfm (accessed June, 2010).

19. Susan Henry, "Charge to the Undergraduate Biology Task Force," http://www.cals.cornell.edu/cals/faculty-staff/task-forces/undergraduate-biology/task-force-charge.cfm (accessed June/1, 2010).

20. Pritchard, *The Embedded Science Librarian: Partner in Curriculum Design and Delivery*, 373.

21. C. Thompson, "Is Happiness Catching?" *New York Times Magazine* (Sep 13, 2009), 28, http://proquest.umi.com/pqdweb?did=1870066671&Fmt=7&clientId=8424&RQT=309&VName=PQD.

22. Cornell University, "Learning Outcomes at Cornell," http://www.cornell.edu/provost/assessment/learning_outcomes.cfm (accessed June/1, 2010).

23. University of Illinois, Urbana-Champaign, University Library, " Curriculum Mapping " *Sine Nomine 2*, http://www.library.uiuc.edu/administration/services/news/issue2.html

24. K. A. Bullard and D. H. Holden, "Hitting a Moving Target: Curriculum Mapping, Information Literacy and Academe" Published for the University Library, Eastern Michigan University, by LOEX Press, 2008).

25. L. D. Lampert, "Searching for Respect: Academic Librarians' Role in Curriculum Development," in *Proven Strategies for Building an Information Literacy Program*, eds. S. C. Curzon and L. D. Lampert (New York: Neal-Schuman, 2007).

26. Brasley, *Effective Librarian and Discipline Faculty Collaboration Models for Integrating Information Literacy into the Fabric of an Academic Institution*, 71–88.

27. Megan Fitzgibbons, "Connecting the Dots: Alignment of Information Literacy Instruction to Course Learning Outcomes through Concept Mapping" (Denver, CO, 2009, 2009), http://www.educause.edu/E09+Hybrid/EDUCAUSE2009F-acetoFaceConferen/ConnectingtheDotsAlignmentofIn/175844 (accessed June 8, 2010).

Bibliography

ALA/ACRL/STS Task Force on Information Literacy for Science and Technology. "Information Literacy Standards for Science and Engineering/Technology." http://www.ala.org/ala/mgrps/divs/acrl/standards/infolitscitech.cfm (accessed June, 2010).

Aydelott, Kathrine. "Using the ACRL Information Literacy Competency Standards for Science and Engineering/Technology to Develop a Modular Critical-Thinking-Based Information Literacy Tutorial." *Science & Technology Libraries* 27, no. 4 (2007): 19–42.

Boeninger, Chad F. "Blogs, Wiki, and IM: Communication Tools for Subject Specialists." http://www.higheredblogcon.com/index.php/blogs-wikis-and-im-communication-tools-for-subject-specialists/ (accessed June/1, 2010).

Brasley, Stephanie Sterling. "Effective Librarian and Discipline Faculty Collaboration Models for Integrating Information Literacy into the Fabric of an Academic Institution." *New Directions for Teaching & Learning* 2008, no. 114 (Summer2008, 2008): 71–88.

Bullard, K. A. and D. H. Holden. "Hitting a Moving Target: Curriculum Mapping, Information Literacy and Academe."Published for the University Library, Eastern Michigan University, by LOEX Press, 2008.

Cornell University. "Common Data Set. Degrees Conferred July 1, 2008–June 30, 2009." http://dpb.cornell.edu/F_Common_Data_Set.htm (accessed June/1, 2010).

———. "Learning Outcomes at Cornell." http://www.cornell.edu/provost/assessment/learning_outcomes.cfm (accessed June/1, 2010).

Dewald, Nancy H. "Web-Based Library Instruction: What is Good Pedagogy?" *Information Technology & Libraries* 18, no. 1 (03, 1999): 26.

Ferrer-Vinent, Ignacio J. and Christy A. Carello. "Embedded Library Instruction in a First-Year Biology Laboratory Course." *Science & Technology Libraries* 28, no. 4 (2008): 325.

Fiegen, Ann M., Bennett Cherry, and Kathleen Watson. "Reflections on Collaboration: Learning Outcomes and Information Literacy Assessment in the Business Curriculum. at California State University, San Marcos." *Reference Services Review* 30, no. 4 (2002): 307–318.

Fitzgibbons, Megan. "Connecting the Dots: Alignment of Information Literacy Instruction to Course Learning Outcomes through Concept Mapping." Denver, CO, 2009, 2009, http://www.educause.edu/E09+Hybrid/EDUCAUSE2009FacetoFace-Conferen/ConnectingtheDotsAlignmentofIn/175844 (accessed June 8, 2010).

Gehring, Kathleen M. and Deborah A. Eastman. "Information Fluency for Undergraduate Biology Majors: Applications of Inquiry-Based Learning in a Developmental Biology Course." *CBE Life Sci Educ* 7, no. 1 (03/01, 2008): 54–63.

Gordon, Rachel Singer and Michael Stephens. "Embedding a Librarian in Your Web Site using Meebo." *Computers in Libraries* 27, no. 8 (September, 2007): 44–45.

Hall, Russell A. "The "Embedded" Librarian in a Freshman Speech Class: Information Literacy Instruction in Action." *College & Research Libraries News* 69, no. 1 (January, 2008): 28–30.

Henry, Susan. "Charge to the Undergraduate Biology Task Force." http://www.cals.cornell.edu/cals/faculty-staff/task-forces/undergraduate-biology/task-force-charge.cfm (accessed June/1, 2010).

Judd, Vaughan, Betty Tims, and Lucy Farrow. "Evaluation and Assessment of a Library Instruction Component of an Introduction to Business Course: A Continuous Process." *Reference Services Review* 32, no. 3 (2004): 274–283.

Koehn, Steven C. and Janet McNeil Hurlbert. "A Communication Capstone Project: A Developmental Model for Undergraduate Research Skills Training." In *Teaching Information Literacy Skills to Social Sciences Students and Practitioners: A Casebook of*

Applications, edited by Douglas Cook and Natasha Cooper, 47–54. Chicago, IL: Association of College and Research Libraries, 2006.

Lampert, L. D. "Searching for Respect: Academic Librarians' Role in Curriculum Development." In *Proven Strategies for Building an Information Literacy Program*, edited by S. C. Curzon and L. D. Lampert. New York: Neal-Schuman, 2007.

Leigh, Jennifer S. A., Cynthia Gibbon, and Janelle Wertzberger. "They Click! Information Literacy and Undergraduates in an Introduction to Management Class." In *Teaching Information Literacy Skills to Social Sciences Students and Practitioners: A Casebook of Applications*, edited by Douglas Cook and Natasha Cooper, 175–185. Chicago, IL: Association of College and Research Libraries, 2006.

Nicholson, Kim. "Cornell Undergraduate Information Competency Initiative Report. Fall 2008.".

Northrup, Lori. ""MeeboMe!" for Embedded Chat Reference: Patron-Initiated Encounters without Downloads Or Accounts." *College & Undergraduate Libraries* 15, no. 3 (2008): 357–363.

Pritchard, Peggy A. "The Embedded Science Librarian: Partner in Curriculum Design and Delivery." *Journal of Library Administration* 50, no. 4 (2010): 373.

Rainie, Lee. "Internet, Broadband, and Cell Phone Statistics." Pew Internet and American Life Project. http://www.pewinternet.org/Reports/2010/Internet-broadband-and-cell-phone-statistics.aspx (accessed June/1, 2010).

Raquepau, Cynthia A. and Louise M. Richards. "Investigating the Environment: Teaching and Learning with Undergraduates in the Sciences." *Reference Services Review* 30, no. 4 (2002): 319.

Scaramozzino, Jeanine M. "Integrating STEM Information Competencies into an Undergraduate Curriculum." *Journal of Library Administration* 50, no. 4 (2010): 315.

Scaramozzino, Jeanine Marie. "An Undergraduate Science Information Literacy Tutorial in a Web 2.0 World." *Issues in Science & Technology Librarianship* (2008).

Shumaker, David. "Who Let the Librarians Out? Embedded Librarianship and the Library Manager." *Reference & User Services Quarterly* 48, no. 3 (Spring, 2009): 239–42, 257.

Thompson, C. "Is Happiness Catching?" *New York Times Magazine* (Sep 13, 2009): 28.

University of Illinois, Urbana-Champaign, University Library. " Curriculum Mapping " *Sine Nomine* 2, (May 1, 2003, : January 2010, http://www.library.uiuc.edu/administration/services/news/issue2.html.

 TEN

One University, Two Approaches: The Regis Experience with Embedded Librarianship

Paul Betty and Martin Garnar

Introduction

In this chapter, we'll examine the work of embedded librarianship as performed by librarians at Regis University, a Jesuit institution in Denver, CO. Regis University is comprised of three colleges: Regis College (RC) serving traditional college students, the Rueckert-Hartman College for Health Professions (RHCHP) serving both traditional and non-traditional students enrolled in accelerated courses and degree programs, and the College of Professional Studies (CPS) serving non-traditional students enrolled in accelerated courses and degree programs. Currently, librarians in the Distance Services and Reference departments are using embedding practices to target students and faculty in RC and CPS. We will explore the origins of these embedded efforts, the techniques used, and the challenges in offering these services, while noting similarities and differences in practice among the Regis librarians.

Online Embedded Librarianship at Regis

The Distance Services department in the Regis University Library has been engaged in embedded librarianship for several years. Development of online embedded library services at Regis University for distance students can best be described as gradual, organic, and somewhat ad-hoc. The success

and longevity of online embedded library services so far has largely been dependent upon the establishment and retention of effective work relationships and sustained collaboration between the Distance Services department of the Regis University Library and the Distance Learning department in CPS. Oddly enough, initiation of online embedded library services did not arise from formal assessments or strategic planning initiatives. Rather, it has simply been understood by the librarians involved as necessary and appropriate in fulfilling the library's mission.

CPS offers 35 accelerated undergraduate and graduate degree programs in the humanities, social sciences, and sciences targeted at non-traditional adult students.[1] In addition to the degree offerings, the university also offers a variety of undergraduate and graduate academic certificates of completion. Courses are offered at the main university campus, six satellite campuses in Colorado, a campus in Las Vegas, NV, and online. Of the 14,841 students enrolled at Regis (Fall 2009), 10,055 are taking courses and completing degrees in CPS.[2] Within CPS, the Distance Learning Department holds responsibility for developing and administering all online courses and the ground based courses offered at locations other than the main campus.

The two librarians in the library's Distance Services department serve as the primary liaisons for students, faculty, and staff in CPS. The extensive online course offerings and a global student population are a boon for the university, but do present their own set of challenges. The sheer volume of students and courses in CPS means that the practice of online embedded librarianship at Regis must be selective and finite. Effective collaboration between departments is a must for success, since no single department possesses the subject expertise or administrative rights within the course management system to go it alone. How well the librarians in the Distance Services department become embedded and contribute to the overall distance student experience at Regis University is largely the result of persistent effort, adoption of new technologies, and timely collaboration with faculty and staff in CPS.

Making Roots: Being Embedded in the Course Design Process

With the above in mind, understanding the shape and nature of embedded library services at Regis University requires a better understanding of how CPS develops and administers online courses so as to elucidate the "entry points" for embedded library services. CPS uses an enterprise model for course development, which is characterized by, "centralized administration and oversight, collaborative course design, courses standardized across sections and instructors, and faculty assessment and training in methods appropriate to online environments."[3] When the enterprise model is applied to online courses, collaboration is most commonly understood to occur between affiliate faculty who act as subject experts and instructional designers, but the door is open for collaboration with, "other experts in the course design process (e.g., web developers, graphic artists, video experts, library faculty and staff, and service learning staff)."[4] In addition to its value in the enterprise model works by David Kennedy and Tim Duffy,[5] and Kay Johnson

and Elaine Magusin[6] affirm the important place of collaboration in the course design process.

Given the degree to which collaboration is emphasized in the enterprise model, one would think that librarians would naturally be involved from the very beginning of the course design process. In our own experiences, this is not always the case. Exploring why this is opens a number of possible explanations. For example, turnover among instructional design staff and affiliate faculty poses a number of challenges. Simply maintaining continuity among individual collaborators is a challenge as faculty and instructional designers move between institutions. Similarly, as affiliate faculty and instructional designers move between institutions, they often bring with them practices associated with their former employer as well as preferences for certain resources and academic materials that may not be available at their current institution. Even worse are new affiliate faculty members or instructional designers who remain ignorant of the library's online resources and services. So, one of the first challenges associated with online embedded librarianship at Regis is simply creating an awareness of available library services and resources among faculty and instructional designers.

In the enterprise model of course development, the failure to integrate library services and resources from the start of the design process can have lasting negative consequences. The model's emphasis on standardized content leaves little room for customization and alteration after the initial design process. Affiliate faculty members are handed fully developed curricula and syllabi, and more often than not, are restricted or discouraged from making revisions or modifications to the course content.[7] Nor is it necessarily the responsibility of the affiliate faculty members teaching the course to make continual changes and updates, as it is generally understood by all parties involved that they are hired and paid to facilitate the course, not design it. However, following this model of development can easily lead faculty and students to the illusion that the newly finished (re) designed course is complete and inscrutable. This is particularly problematic as the course content ages, and if erroneous library content was added during the development process without prior consultation with library faculty and staff. Dead links, references to retired or no longer existing services, incorrect hours and contact information, and assignments utilizing dated library materials can easily create a negative impression about the library among students and faculty. Successful embedded librarianship in the online learning environment means more than just participating in the course on a repeated basis. It also means being an integral member of the course administration team.

As a participant in the collaborative design process associated with the enterprise model, embedded librarians should aspire to "own" the library content found in the course. Ownership means the librarian assumes responsibility for creating relevant library content related to the course as well as updating it as necessary. In terms of online learning, librarians should seek administrative access to course management systems (CMS) if possible, allowing them to author and update content in a timely manner. However, due largely to organizational cultures and institutional bureaucracies we understand that not all embedded librarians have this option at their disposal, and this is true for librarians at Regis. When approaching instructional designers, administrators, or faculty during the course design process, we have found it beneficial to emphasize the fact that we are willing to act as co-creators and assume responsibility for updating and delivering relevant library content to the instructional designer who retains administrative control. One way or another, our goal is to have embedded librarians responsible for creation and management of library content as it appears in online courses and syllabi.

Macro or Micro: Which Way to Go?

Embedded librarians who participate in the course design process will have better control over delin-

eating their level of participation in the course. Two basic levels of participation have been identified by Susan Gibbons: micro and macro.[8] In summary, macro level participation occurs when librarians deliver information and content via the course management system or other web pages, but do not actively participate in the course. At Regis, this most often occurs by placing links and library information on pages within the CMS or by creating separate research guides that are linked from the CMS. In the macro level approach, content is made readily accessible, but interaction with a librarian requires students or faculty members to initiate contact.

Micro level participation occurs when the librarian actively engages students and faculty using the discussion forum or chat features found in the CMS. The micro approach is proactive. Librarians initiate discussion of research topics and search strategies with students and push relevant materials and services. At Regis, we are engaged in both macro and micro level embedded librarianship, and Gibbons notes pros and cons to both approaches. Embedded librarians who are integrated into the course design process and "own" library content in the CMS may find satisfaction with a macro approach, but Gibbons admits that, "the digital world has created an expectation of customization and personalization that increases with each new class of students. When it comes to library resources, students naturally expect more than a mere link to the library Web site. They are expecting librarians to push course appropriate library resources to them through the CMS."[9]

Getting a Foot Inside the Door: Securing Librarian Participation in the Course Discussion Forum

There is evidence in the education literature that further supports the micro approach. Nancy Dewald notes that library instruction "is best received when it is course-related, and specifically assignment related. Students are most receptive to library instruction when they can see its immediate benefit to their course work or to an assignment that they face."[10] Creating static content, void of interaction, which engages the learner to the level Dewald suggests is difficult to craft. Furthermore, when compared to students who complete online, self-paced, independent study courses, students who receive interactive instruction in their online classes show a greater development and application of critical thinking.[11] If we apply social learning theory to embedded librarianship, the need for interaction becomes essential for knowledge building, "because cognition is not considered an individual process, learning and knowing are shaped by the kinds of interactions a student has with others, and the context within which these interactions occur."[12] In addition, interactions in discussion forums and course chat rooms between online students and librarians can create a general awareness among the student population of online library services. While this last fact might seem self-evident, our own experiences suggest students often enter online degree programs under the assumption that online library services are limited or not available.

While there is strong support in the academic literature that interaction is necessary for effective learning in online courses, the fact remains that librarian interaction with students is not built into every online course at Regis University. Instead, specific courses that include research assignments or projects are targeted by the Distance Services department. This is due in large part to the extensive (and ever growing) online course and degree programs offered at the university. The Distance Services department consists of two full time librarians, and as such, we must be selective otherwise we risk extending ourselves beyond our capacity to perform effective work. We have enjoyed varying degrees of success working with faculty and instructional designers in creating stand-alone "macro" library content for inclusion in the course management systems and course syllabi. However,

these efforts are done with the understanding that, minus contact and interaction with the library, the learner is less likely to gain a full comprehension of online library services and resources, gain and employ critical thinking skills, and become increasingly information literate.

Even with macro level library content present and visible in the CMS, securing librarian participation in online courses at Regis University often requires soliciting instructors individually before the start of each session, inquiring if they would like a librarian to join the discussion forum in the course management system for a defined period of time. The success of this approach relies primarily on the development of positive work relationships between affiliate faculty and librarians. The challenges to this approach are several. New affiliate faculty members teaching online, just like new online students, are often unaware of online library services and resources. As noted earlier, instructors who have taught at other institutions bring preferences for certain resources that may not be available through the library, leaving instructors with feelings that the library does not have anything of value to offer. Increasingly, we have noted a trend in which online instructors themselves will rely on free web sites that are of questionable accuracy and authority. Even more problematic are instructors who take upon themselves the responsibility of providing library instruction and inadvertently direct students to dated library materials and links. Just like students, online instructors need to be educated about new online resources and services in a timely manner.

To help ensure that affiliate faculty members are aware of online library services and resources, the library offers a ten-day workshop delivered using the course management software.[13] During the course of the workshop, faculty members receive instruction about performing effective searches using library databases, differences between Web search engines and subscription databases, and how to develop information literacy assignments and activities. The workshop provides a venue for CPS faculty and librarians in the Distance Services department to build working relationships. Faculty members who have completed the workshop are more likely to seek out, or accept when offered, librarian participation in the online courses they are facilitating.

Zen and the Art of Online Embedded Librarianship at Regis University

Once a librarian's participation in the online course is secured, the work of micro level embedded librarianship begins. Before the start of each session, the librarian and instructor come to an agreement about the length and method of the librarian's participation. Afterwards, faculty members who have included a librarian's participation in previous courses generally feel secure in what will be delivered by the librarian, but this does need clarification when working with instructors for the first time. The majority of online courses offered by CPS are eight week accelerated courses. In an eight week course, we typically join the course discussion forum for a single week, usually during the first three weeks of the course, and particularly during the week when the research assignment or course project is first introduced. Participation in the discussion forum is asynchronous, meaning discussions occur over the course of the week as posts are submitted at the convenience of the author. Asynchronous discussion forums are commonly used in many course management systems and the literature points to a number of best practices for librarians engaging students in this arena.

Recent studies support the adoption of active learning in online courses as a means to generate high levels of student achievement.[14] In the discussion forum of the course management system, active learning is supported by the librarian's use of hypertext, which invites students to navigate between online resources. Replies to student queries and general instruction on the use of library resources and services can be formatted in a man-

ner that engages students in self-paced exploration, requiring them to complete a task or series or steps, replicate a database search, or revise search strategies rather than providing direct links to answers or search results. As students progress through the research process, links to handouts and tutorials can be provided to assist the student at the time of need. This has generally been our baseline model of interaction with students. Once the student posts an introduction or research question, we will reply with search suggestions and links to handouts and tutorials, prompting the student to be an active learner.

Tone is as equally important when using asynchronous instruction as when communicating face-to-face. Vanessa Paz Dennen and Kristina Wieland noted in their research that online classes "that had a peer-like, consistent facilitative instructor and discussion anchored around questions and shared artifacts were more likely to engage in discussion leading to the negotiation of knowledge and understanding."[15] Our own experiences suggest that adult students are more likely to view librarians as peers, as fellow professionals who happen to possess skills and knowledge beneficial to their needs, while instructors remain authority figures whose words are to be understood as definitive and final. At Regis University, this perception of librarians as peers among adult students can in part be attributed to the tone and language used when posting in the discussion forum. Rather than demand use of specific materials or techniques, we gently push resources or services, often selling the fact that the student can save time or effort by consulting the suggested resource or utilizing a specific service. In utilizing this approach, we position ourselves as collaborators, like a co-worker with years of experience under the same employer and who possesses a solid understanding of the organizational culture of the company.

As a whole the Regis University library works to support different learning styles. The impact of learning style on educational outcomes for online and distance students has been noted in research by John Battalio,[16] Celeste Walls,[17] and Mahnaz Moallem[18] and others. In practice, this means we frequently augment the text-based instruction offered in the discussion forum via the use of interactive audio-visual tutorials, PDF handouts, and screenshots. In course management systems that emphasize or mandate the use of discussion forums, embedded librarians should remain alert for students who express difficulty in comprehending written instructions. When faced with replies in the discussion forum that suggest this, the embedded librarian should offer alternate forms of instruction utilizing visual aids, audio, or synchronous communication. Synchronous communication via phone, chat, instant messaging, VOIP, or web conferencing software can be advantageous in helping assist students at the point of need, but at Regis, its use comes with certain limitations. Since students taking courses online can be located across the globe and operate on different schedules, the use of synchronous communication cannot be required of students, only offered as optional. In practice this means student attendance cannot be required for any web conferences or chat sessions offering additional library instruction. Faced with this limitation to participation, we tend to favor software or platforms that provide a record(ing) of the synchronous session that can be made available afterwards.

Enrollment in online CPS courses is generally capped between fifteen and twenty students, but most courses have at least ten or more students. During each eight week session, it is not uncommon for each librarian in the Distance Services department to be embedded in multiple courses and sections at any one time, especially since the demand for library instruction favors the first few weeks of each eight week period. In this scenario, writing posts and replies to each student in each section can easily consume an entire day. Imagine writing forty to fifty personal email replies that include research topic specific search instructions

and links to relevant handouts and tutorials, and you gain a sense of how intensive online embedded librarianship can become. To mitigate pressure related to time and availability, we use a number of templates and "canned messages" that address widely used services and resources. These templates can be posted as general messages to the entire class or modified to address specific student research topics and questions. However, as students and librarians become more engaged in discussion, at some point the instruction provided will need to be customized to the individual's needs. Templates and canned messages will only go so far, and in many cases, lead to follow-up questions or discussion that is unique and unscripted.

Similarly, the literature suggests that while the overall number of reference transactions has decreased at many academic libraries, the complexity of the questions has increased. The impact of this trend on embedded librarianship is one of several valuable points covering workflow and time management summarized by Erica Bennet and Jenni Simning[19] at Capella University. They note "the greatest challenge for continuing the embedded librarian model is to find a less labor-intensive means of serving distance learning students, while still maintaining the same level of personalization that is so critical for embedded librarianship."[20] Based on our own experiences, this conclusion can certainly be applied to the Regis Library and our own embedded librarianship efforts. As we continue to gain access to more students, faculty members, and courses, we are now at a point where we risk being victims of our own success and unable to meet the demand.

A cursory review of the literature suggests that most attention, efforts, and research related to embedded librarianship among academic librarians are occurring in online courses, and so far our discussion has mimicked this trend. However, we believe the practice of embedded librarianship is not dependent on any single model of delivery for library instruction, and it is at this point that we turn our attention to embedded library practices used in traditional face-to-face instruction. While similarities exist between the two arenas of practice, librarians embedded in the traditional 'brick and mortar' classrooms also face unique challenges, some of which we hope to elucidate in the remainder of this chapter.

And Now for Something Completely Different: Embedding in the Regis College Honors Program

As explained in the introduction, Regis University is comprised of three colleges. While CPS is the largest college at Regis, Regis College (RC) is the oldest, dating back to the university's founding in 1877. RC offers a liberal arts curriculum in the Jesuit tradition to 1,400 traditional college-age students on the university's main campus in northwest Denver.[21] Unlike CPS, which offers a combination of online and ground-based courses, most RC courses are offered in a face-to-face classroom setting. Also unlike CPS, where incoming students have a range of previous college experience and are therefore not good targets for universal requirements at the start of their programs, all first-year RC students are required to take a writing seminar in their first semester. This requirement was a factor in deciding where to locate the embedding efforts in RC. Finally, while there are two Distance Services librarians involved in embedding efforts in CPS, there's just one reference librarian experimenting with embedding in RC. Before discussing that experiment, I will tell you what prompted me to think about using this approach to improve research skills.

My interest in embedded librarianship stems from attending a presentation by the University of Wyoming's Cass Kvenild and Kaijsa Calkins, editors of the book in hand, at the Colorado Association of Libraries' annual conference in 2008. I was inspired by their experiences and began to think about the possibilities at Regis University. As my primary liaison responsibilities are with

RC, I knew I was looking at embedding myself in a traditional classroom experience and began to think of the best targets for this project. My first thought was the first-year writing seminar, as it has long been the first (and sometimes only) entry point for library research in the curriculum. As the library's liaison to the RC Core & Curriculum Committee, I was involved in the multiyear effort to revise the core curriculum and worked with my College colleagues to craft language that reflected the library's role as part of the curriculum. Those with experience on academic committees will understand what it took to get the last word added to this sentence: "These small seminars develop competencies in writing, speaking, critical thinking and research."[22] Protocols for the first-year writing seminars explicitly recommend library instruction as part of the fall semester experience.

Even before the adoption of the new core curriculum in 2008, the library played a regular role in the first-year writing seminars, which had existed in a similar form under the previous curriculum. Through years of promoting the importance of library instruction at the beginning of a student's college career, we now can boast a near 100% participation rate for the first-year writing seminars in the library's information competence program, which calls for two integrated library sessions in the fall semester of the first year as well as advanced sessions connected to the majors in later years. The information competence program was adopted by the library in 2008 and was implemented in the fall of 2009 in conjunction with the new RC core curriculum. The program calls for a thirty-minute physical orientation and introduction to library services at the beginning of the sixteen-week semester and a seventy-five-minute hands-on research session later in the semester closer to when a research paper has been assigned. Most sections are also provided with customized web-based research guides on the LibGuides platform to use throughout the semester. In some ways, the LibGuides are designed to mimic the "macro" level of participation discussed above, though any communication with librarians must be initiated by students through the chat or e-mail options on each LibGuide. As will be discussed below, the "macro" level of participation is the only realistic ongoing option for these courses.

The writing seminars are taught by faculty from across RC and have a range of themes that reflects the diverse expertise of the faculty, such as a biologist's offering of "Plagues and People" to a sociologist's class on "Writing for Change." As a result, the appropriate subject specialists on the library faculty teach some of the library instruction sessions, including three sections reserved for nursing students, thus reducing some of the demands on my time as the primary liaison for RC. However, of the nineteen regular (non-nursing) sections offered in the fall of 2009, I still taught a total of twenty-eight sessions for fifteen of the sections. To make matters more difficult, the seminars are normally scheduled in a special slot that meets for an extended session three times a week, so a majority of sections are competing for the same forty-eight possible options for library instruction sessions. As no one wants an introduction to the library in the last month of classes, the effective number of timeslots is smaller. Factor in that we have just one classroom dedicated for library instruction and it is clear that scheduling the basic sessions is a major challenge. It also makes it impossible to consider embedding in one of those sections, as that would preclude my teaching the basic classes for the other sections due to time conflicts. Therefore, though the positive impact of having an embedded librarian in a first-year class is well documented (Hearn,[23] Manus,[24] Hall[25]), embedding in a first-year seminar was simply not an option for me. I had to find somewhere else to go.

A Perfect Match: The Honors Thesis Research Seminar

Reflecting on the University of Wyoming presentation, I wanted to follow Kaijsa's example of attending every class, but I also thought it would be worth exploring a connection with a course that met less frequently. I also knew that scheduling pressures in the fall meant a prudent choice would be a course offered in the spring. Following Hall's advice of capitalizing on an existing faculty relationship,[26] I approached the director of the RC honors program and proposed embedding myself in the honors thesis research seminar, which is offered every spring. This class is for those honors students choosing to write a thesis in their senior year and is designed to help them develop a research proposal by the end of their junior year. Not surprisingly, the honors students tend to be fairly proficient at parts of the research process, but both the honors director and I agreed that the group as a whole could benefit from more library support during the thesis experience. Knowing that I would be available to all students working on a thesis, I felt this was a more equitable use of my time than selecting just one of nineteen sections from the writing seminars.

In any given year, the course has between twelve and fifteen students split into two sections to accommodate the honors students' predictably busy schedules. I had a long tradition of meeting with both sections in a hands-on research session consisting mainly of one-on-one consultations bookended by general comments about research strategies and library support for thesis writers, so library involvement in the course was not new. I was also a known quantity to the honors students, as I regularly teach the library sessions for the first-year honors writing seminars. Another attractive aspect to this class was the frequency of meetings: as a one-credit course, the class meets once a week and often has a few weeks between meetings to allow the students time to develop various parts of the research proposal. Thus, the classroom time commitment was limited to nine meetings per section for a total of 22.5 hours during the semester. After a very brief discussion, the honors program director (also the professor for the class) readily agreed to an embedding experiment in the spring of 2010. By mutual consent, we agreed my initial role should focus on being an in-class resource, and exploration of a co-instructor role with grading responsibilities should wait for future semesters.

Despite the intention to attend every session, scheduling conflicts prevented my attendance during the first few weeks. My embedding began with the traditional library instruction sessions. At the start of those sessions, the professor gave my usual introduction and also went on to say that I'd be joining the class for the rest of the semester. The students looked intrigued, and there was an immediate impact on the conversations we had during the one-on-one consultations. Instead of suggesting that students contact me if they had any ongoing questions, I could say that we'd touch base at the next class session to check on their progress. Compared to previous years, I found that the students were much more likely to contact me after the instruction sessions for research consultations.

The class sessions may be most comparable to what Hall experienced, as there was a project focus with multiple topics rather than having all students working in a single subject area.[27] Most sessions were structured as an opportunity for students to report on their progress, provide feedback and suggestions to each other, and ask questions about any difficulties or roadblocks. I found it helpful to learn more about the individual topics than I would have through the single instruction session, as it gave me a sense of whether the library's collections were sufficient for their research, or if we would look at strategies for using resources at partner institutions. Regarding questions from students, my primary role was to offer resource suggestions and research techniques as appropriate. Additionally, the professor was glad to have another (in his words) authority figure in the room to reinforce his suggestions, much as what happens in traditional instruction sessions when the librarian and professor can trade off to emphasize certain points or to offer alternate techniques.

The benefits of embedding extended outside of the classroom. Not only were students more likely to stop by the reference desk when I was on duty, but I saw an increase in the number of questions via my personal phone, e-mail, and chat, plus an increase in outside research consultations. As the weeks went by, I was able to recognize the students by both face and name, which meant that all parties were more likely to greet each other on campus and strike up a conversation about research projects, whether it was passing in the halls on my way to meetings or getting questioned in the middle of my workout at the campus fitness center.

After the semester ended, my relationship with the students continued. All of the students prepared a work plan (presented at the final class session) to get started on their thesis research over the summer, and about one-third of the students contacted me during that time for research assistance and advice. For the handful of honors students who were studying abroad during the spring semester, I was included on all communications with them upon their return. Despite recommendations from the professor, most of the study-abroad students did not contact me for assistance, which in my mind confirms the value of my presence in the classroom and the personal relationships that grow from regular contact. In the fall, the students met on a monthly basis to discuss their progress, and I was there to give advice and answer questions for the group. Outside of the group meetings, I met with half of them for individual research consultations as their theses began to take shape, and even served as an ad hoc reader for one thesis when the official advisers were too busy to meet with the student before the winter break. In 2011, I embedded in a spring semester class of junior-year honors students and, in consultation with the professor, took a more active role during class sessions. We modified the syllabus to include my contact information, give a clearer explanation of my purpose in the classroom, and to direct students to copy me on all submitted assignments. Getting access to their journal entries and all other written assignments allowed me to offer better assistance and ask deeper questions when working with the students. Going forward, the plan is for me to be embedded each spring with the juniors (when my regular library instruction load is lighter) and each fall with the seniors (when the minimal time commitment doesn't impact my intensive work with first-year writing classes), so this model should be sustainable in the long run.

Having heard of the honors embedding experiment, a professor in the communication department asked me to be embedded in an experimental course on acting and interpretation of texts. Her thinking was that my presence in the classroom would allow me to get know the students and help them find texts with greater personal meaning, thus enhancing their performances. She was also aware of my undergraduate training in vocal performance and thought that I could provide input on more than just resources. As opposed to the honors thesis class, this class was scheduled to meet twice weekly and would be a significant commitment of time. I agreed to participate and was ultimately able to attend about 75% of the class sessions, as I had an occasional conflict with a standing meeting. Though the course was offered in the fall semester, it was in a time slot that didn't conflict with instruction for the first-year writing classes (as they have a few dedicated slots), so I was able to juggle my schedule and workload accordingly. Like the honors class, my constant presence in the classroom led to strong relationships with the students, making it easier for them to work with me when they had to find texts for performance. I also led three of the class sessions when the professor was ill or out of town. This would not have been possible had I not been involved from the very start. After the halfway point, the professor started asking for my input to grade the performances, though she still took sole responsibility for grading the associated portfolios and assigning a final grade for the course. The course culminated with a performance of monologues by top students in the library's exhibit area, further underscoring the connection with the library. At the end of the course, students gave favorable evaluations of my participation and said it made their experience more meaningful, as they appreciated my guidance in selecting texts and they felt that their performances were enhanced by having feedback from more than one person. The professor and I met to assess the embedding experiment and ultimately decided to propose the course as a regular offering, albeit with two changes: we would offer the course in the spring (as it would be better for both of our schedules), and we would officially name me as a co-instructor. Our proposal is awaiting final approval from the curriculum committee at this time, but we are excited about the possibility of team teaching and what it could mean for future joint projects by the college and library faculties.

And Now, a Grand Sweeping Conclusion: What Have We Learned?

While the experience of embedded librarianship at Regis may seem like it is happening at two different institutions, we can identify a number of common themes from our separate experiences. In both cases, we took a proactive approach and contacted faculty with whom we knew we could work and, based on past experience with library instruction, we hoped would be open to a new approach. Whether online or in the classroom, the time commitment for embedding librarianship is significant and must be factored into existing workloads. This is directly connected to scalability, which is also a factor for both models of embedding. Whether physically visiting a classroom or spending time in a CMS, there are only so many hours in the day, so embedding projects must be kept at a scale that is sustainable in the long run.

As for differences, there are some that are worth examining and may inform each other's practice in the future. In CPS, the active time for embedding is limited to one week of the eight-week course, while the RC model has the librarian present for the whole semester. We know that sometimes life gets in the way of education, so a student in an online class may miss the one week of active librarian interaction. How this affects the effectiveness of the embedding efforts needs to be studied. Likewise, there were some RC class sessions in which the librarian was an untapped resource. Though there is always some value in hearing the class discussion, the return on investment for time spent in the classroom must be compared to the projects and duties that are competing for our attention. One major difference between online and physical embedding is the ability to develop templates and a knowledge base for online environments. Though there is an investment of time for preparing materials for the initial embedding in an online class, some materials for standard questions and concepts can be re-used each time the class is offered. This also has some impact on the scalability of online embedding, as less time is required for each class after the initial experience, thus allowing more classes to be added over time. In the physical classroom model where the librarian is serving more as a resource than as another instructor, the interactions tend to be more ad hoc and the librarian is less able to use prepared materials. Another difference is the type of student being served: undergraduates of a traditional age versus adult students. However, we don't believe that the difference in student populations is sig-

nificant in our experience. Working with an online class for traditional undergraduates would have the same potential for developing templates and a knowledge base, while embedding in a physical classroom of adult learners would still require the same ad hoc approach for resource questions. Ultimately, we believe the mode of instruction has the greatest impact on our differing experiences.

A hallmark of the Jesuit approach to education is the concept of *cura personalis*, or care for the person, and is defined as "having concern and care for the personal development of the whole person. This implies a dedication to promoting human dignity and care for the mind, body and spirit of the person."[28] This helps explain the development of Regis University into the institution it is today. While still recognizing the value of and demand for a classroom-based experience for our traditional RC undergraduates, our CPS programs for adult learners are geared to meet them where they are, whether it's in evening classes after work or online classes after the kids have gone to bed. Offering multiple educational models for our students demonstrates our respect and care for where they are in their lives. As a single library serving these multiple educational models, we have plenty of experience in customizing our services for our diverse student populations. Extending that same flexibility to our approach to embedded librarianship is just another opportunity to practice *cura personalis*.

Notes

1. College of Professional Studies, "Academic Programs," Regis University, http://cps.regis.edu/academic-programs.php.

2. Regis University, "Regis University Quick Facts," http://www.regis.edu/regis.asp?sctn=news&p1=media&p2=factsheet.

3. P. R. Lowenthal and J. W. White, "Enterprise Model," in *Encyclopedia of Distance and Online Learning (2nd ed.)*, ed. P. Rogers, G. Berg, J. Boettcher, C. Howard, L. Justice, and K. Schenk (Hershey, PA: Information Science Reference, forthcoming), 3. http://www.patricklowenthal.com/publications/enterprisemodelEDOLpre-print.pdf.

4. Ibid., 3.

5. David Kennedy and Tim Duffy, "Collaboration—a Key Principle in Distance Education," *Open Learning* 19, no. 2 (2004): 203-211, http://web.ebscohost.com/ (accessed May 6, 2010).

6. Kay Johnson and Elaine Magusin, *Exploring the Digital Library* (San Francisco: Josey Bass, 2005), 94–95.

7. P. R. Lowenthal and J. W. White, "Enterprise model", 4.

8. Susan Gibbons, "Strategies for the Library: CMS Integration Barriers," *Library Technology Reports* 41, no. 3 (May 2005): 24–32, http://web.ebscohost.com/ (accessed May 6, 2010).

9. Ibid., 26.

10. Nancy Dewald, "Transporting Good Library Instruction Practices into the Web Environment: An Analysis of Online Tutorials," *The Journal of Academic Librarianship* 25, no.1 (1999): 26.

11. Hye-Jung Lee and Ilju Rha, "Influence of Structure and Interaction on Student Achievement and Satisfaction in Web-Based Distance Learning," Educational Technology & Society 12, no. 4 (January 1, 2009): 372–382.

12. Janette R. Hill, Liyan Song, and Richard E. West, "Social Learning Theory and Web-Based Learning Environments: A Review of Research and Discussion of Implications," American Journal of Distance Education 23, no. 2 (January 1, 2009): 89.

13. For more information about this workshop, see Erin McCaffrey, Tina Parscal, And Tom Riedel, "The Faculty-Library Connection: An Online Workshop," *Journal of Library Administration* 45, no. 1–2 (2006): 279–300.

14. See John M. Ivancevich, Jacqueline A. Gilbert, and Robert Konopaske, "Studying and Facilitating Dialogue in Select Online Management Courses," *Journal of Management Education* 33, (April 2009): 196–218 and Ava S. Miller, "Collaborating in Electronic Learning Communities," *Online Submission* (July 1, 2009).

15. Vanessa Paz Dennen and Kristina Wieland, "From Interaction to Intersubjectivity: Facilitating Online Group Discourse Processes," *Distance Education* 28, no. 3 (November 2007): 281.

16. John Battalio, "Success in Distance Education: Do Learning Styles and Multiple Formats Matter?," American Journal of Distance Education 23, no. 2 (January 1, 2009): 71–87.

17. Celeste M. Walls, "Some Strategies for Balancing Economies of Scale and Interaction in Online/Distance Education Courses," E-Journal of Instructional Science and Technology 8, no. 1 (January 1, 2005), http:// web.ebscohost.com/ (accessed May 14, 2010).

18. Mahnaz Moallem, "Accommodating Individual Differences in the Design of Online Learning Environments: A Comparative Study," Journal of Research on Technology in Education 40, no. 2 (January 1, 2008): 217–245. http:// web.ebscohost. com/ (accessed May 14, 2010).

19. Erica Bennet and Jennie Simning, "Embedded Librarianship and Reference Traffic: A quantitative analysis," in *Proceedings of the 14th Off-Campus Library Services Conference*, edited by Timothy Peters and Jennifer Rundels (Mount Pleasant, MI: Central Michigan University, 2010), 25–37.

20. Ibid, 33.

21. Regis College, "Regis College Undergraduate," Regis University, http://www.regis.edu/regis.asp?sctn=rcrcu.

22. Regis College, "Foundational Core," Regis University, http://www.regis.edu/regis.asp?sctn=rcrcu&p1=ap&p2=ccs &p3=fc.

23. Michael R. Hearn, "Embedding a Librarian in the Classroom: An Intensive Information Literacy Model," *Reference Services Review* 33, no. 2 (2005): 219–227.

24. Sarah J. Beutter Manus, "Librarian in the Classroom: An Embedded Approach to Music Information Literacy for First-Year Undergraduates," *Notes* 66, no. 2 (2009): 249–261

25. Russell A. Hall, "The 'Embedded' Librarian in a Freshman Speech Class," *College & Research Libraries News* 69, no. 1 (2008): 28–30.

26. Ibid., 30.

27. Ibid., 30.

28. Regis University, "About Regis: What It Means to be Jesuit," http://www.regis.edu/regis.asp?sctn=abt&p1=mjv.

PART FIVE
Embedding in Graduate and Professional Programs

 ELEVEN

Kresge Library's Embedded Librarian Program: A Student-Centered Approach

Laura Berdish and Corey Seeman

Introduction

The Embedded Librarian Program at the Kresge Library at the University of Michigan is an innovative entry among embedded services in academic libraries. While many academic embedded librarian programs focus on supporting the faculty by providing student instruction and assisting with the creation of information-centric assignments, the program at Kresge Library connects the librarian directly with student teams charged with solving real-world and somewhat ambiguous problems through the school's MAP (Multidisciplinary Action Program). MAP is Michigan's signature action-based learning program and has been in place for 15 years for full-time MBAs. In this program, students work with corporate sponsors/partners on complex business issues in both unfamiliar and narrow markets. In these situations, the valuable assistance that librarians provide them is very well received.

Librarians work very closely with students at the Kresge Library when they are required to research industries and areas that are not well known to them. MAP arrives at the end of the first year of study, when most students have not had full exposure to the resources available to them at the Kresge Library. While the rest of the MBA curriculum at the Ross School of Business at the University of

Michigan has its traditional elements, the MAP keystone program involves working in teams and exploring subjects in a deeper way than students have done in their previous coursework. MAP is often the first instance in an MBA's time at Michigan where they need a guide to help them conduct more detailed research then they have done before. To facilitate this process, the Kresge Library developed a program that connects librarians with these student groups throughout the course of the project.

The result has been a creative embedded librarian program, established almost ten years ago, and continuing to evolve as the number of teams and students participating in MAP grows. The librarian's work varies greatly from team to team, but almost always involves supporting research with resources available from the Kresge Library and beyond. The Library's clear and stated goal from the library is to ensure that each team can find the information that they need. What might be most unique in the academic context of embedded librarianship is that the librarians work directly with the students. The faculty serves critical roles of advising the students on their projects, approaches and deliverables. And while faculty might have little or no interaction with the librarians, that connection is not necessary for the successful completion of a

MAP project. The connection that is critical is that between the students and the librarian.

About the Kresge Business Administration Library

The Kresge Business Administration Library is an independent library at the University of Michigan, reporting to and receiving funding from the Ross School of Business. This relationship mirrors the reporting structure of most law libraries. A leading business school, Ross appears near the top of some of the most prestigious rankings, including number 5 in Business Week, number 7 in the Wall Street Journal, number 12 in both the Economist and U.S. News and World Report.[1] In addition, the school has done very well with specialized rankings, including number 2 (number 1 in the United States) in the Beyond Grey Pinstripes' ranking that explores "innovative full-time MBA programs leading the way in the integration of issues concerning social and environmental stewardship in to the curriculum."[2]

Despite being at one of the largest universities in the United States, the population of students, faculty and staff at the Ross School of Business is relatively small. As of Fall 2010 there are approximately 3100 students at the Ross School (BBAs, MBAs, Evening MBAs, Global MBAs, Executive MBAs, PhDs, and Masters of Accounting Students) and an additional 500 faculty and staff. This population of 3600 is far less than the comparable population of the University's main campus (approximately 39,000 plus faculty and staff) or the system-wide count (approximately 49,000 plus faculty and staff). By virtue of having a relatively small number of students at the Ross School, we are able to provide more individualized support from our eight librarians.

To support the business curriculum at the Ross School, the Kresge Library has acquired and licensed an extensive collection of print and electronic resources. Since Kresge is an independent library and the school maintains a separate Information Technology Department, we are able to

purchase specialized resources just for the students, faculty and staff at the Ross School of Business. This allows us to create a body of resources that few schools can offer. But in most ways, it is during MAP season when we rely most heavily on the resources made available through the University Library at the University of Michigan—in particular when students research developing countries the implications and practicality about a new form of renewable energy, or the science and medical applications behind the drug discovery. During the MAP projects, students will find needs in every corner of the information universe at Michigan, and that will most certainly be uncharted territory.

Action Based Learning and its Impact on Library Interaction

The Ross School of Business has adopted the Action Based Learning (ABL) approach for its curriculum. This is sometimes referred to as "experience-based" or "work-based" learning. It is one of the few alternatives to the case approach that is used at many business schools (including Harvard, where the case-based teaching method was developed at the Law School in the 1870s)[3] The case method allows the professor to present the students with teaching tools that document an issue or a process, and provides the students with a good deal of information to participate in the discussion of the case. Students rigorously study the case prior to class and are responsible for knowing all the contained information for discussion. Columbia has adopted a method that is a modification of the case approach—where the students are presented with much of the information needed to "solve" the business problem featured in the case, but not all.[4] While Ross has adopted Action Based Learning as its signature philosophy, many courses at Ross still use case studies as part of the curriculum.

The reliance on cases for business education might be partially responsible for a perceived under-utilization of the library services by MBA students. While anecdotal in nature, conversations with many members of the Academic Business Library Directors (ABLD) revealed that MBA students are not a primary customer of library services at leading libraries across the United States and Canada. It is plausible that if students are continually presented with case studies that contain all the information that they would need to assess a problem, they might not be required to become strong users of the library. New studies report similar downward trends in reference transactions across the academic campus; a recent study from the Ames Library at Illinois Wesleyan University ranks the "importance" of librarians in solving a specific question below "the Internet", "databases" or even "help from other students."[5] At the Ross School, many of the courses follow an action based learning approach, leaving the discovery and use of information up to the student. They are encouraged to use all the resources at their disposal, including the librarians. To this end, an increase of only 70 MBA students in the FY2010 was one of the factors that contributed to an increase in reference transactions of almost 40% over the previous year.[6] It is our hope that one of the differentiating aspects of the Action Based Learning student is that he/she might be better able to find and uti-

lize a wide variety of information sources than the case-based counterpart. Indeed, the same study at the Ames Library found that "experiential" learning projects, with input from Ames librarians' throughout, increased the students' knowledge of library resources, and provided the "teachable moments" that were the stated goal of the Ames reference staff.[7]

The Action Based Learning approach taken by the Ross School of Business provides a different educational experience for business students. "Action Learning is based on the premise that there is no learning without action and no sober and deliberate action without learning."[8] This instructional method has its origins and greatest adoption among European business schools.[9] Action Based Learning has been adopted by some schools, within certain programs, but few have placed it on the mantle as Ross has. The program is being expanded to include undergraduate business majors (BBAs), evening- and executive-MBAs, as well as being incorporated into Michigan's new weekend MBA program. Since 1992, Ross students have undertaken over 1500 MAP projects, in almost every imaginable industry.

Figure 11-1 showcases how the school conceptualizes Action Based Learning.

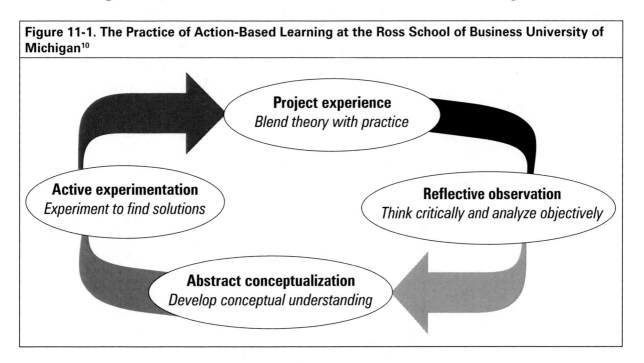

Figure 11-1. The Practice of Action-Based Learning at the Ross School of Business University of Michigan[10]

Project experience
Blend theory with practice

Active experimentation
Experiment to find solutions

Reflective observation
Think critically and analyze objectively

Abstract conceptualization
Develop conceptual understanding

One of the most interesting and important aspects of MAP is that each project offers some level of ambiguity in the mission and objective that students set out to solve. When students bid on projects, there is a general sense and understanding from the sponsor of what the project will entail. That being the case, sponsors can often change projects at a moments' notice. This might happen before the project starts or during the initial meeting with the student teams. This is where flexibility (especially on the part of the students and the librarian) is critical. This also is where we see one of the true distinguishing characteristics of MAP and action-based learning. Unlike a traditional course, where the professor lays out a path that the class will need to complete, MAP teams have few certainties, save a final report and presentation that all teams must do. And because these changes can take place at any time, a librarian that can be counted on to assist (and work quickly) with the new demands for information has been seen as a critical part of the program.

Traditional Embedded Librarian Programs in Academic Libraries

Before understanding the parameters of the Kresge Library embedded librarian program, it would be useful to see how similar programs are implemented in academic libraries. Most of the articles on embedded librarianship focus on providing instruction and guidance for students during a particular course.[11] Many instances also document the librarian's unique position in the course as someone who creates and grades assignments that test the student's knowledge of information resources in a particular area. Ferrer-Vinent and Carello outline their work in this manner with a first year biology laboratory course where the embedded librarians are not only there to help, but also prepare assignments.[12] Manus also outlines this approach as it relates to being embedded to assist with assessing the information literacy skills of students during introductory music classes at Vanderbilt.[13]

The focus might also be on providing a visible library support mechanism for an online class that is conducted far from the library, as was the case at Athens State University.[14]

The Kresge Library approach is more focused on supporting reference and research by students. This is similar to programs that have been effectively used in special libraries to bring librarians and librarian services to the employees who require it. This individualized support is especially critical in corporate settings where teams and groups will often span the globe or work in far corners of vast complexes. The special library model for embedded librarianship is well documented from the model used by Fairfax Media (Australia).[15] Another similar account showcased a program at the Arizona Health Sciences Library, which has placed embedded librarians in academic departments to work closely with faculty on research projects.[16] Because the special library mission is focused on service rather than instruction, librarians operate within a team environment that is very different from the academic setting. As we explain the program implemented at Kresge Library, many of the steps we have taken align with the embedded librarian services found at special libraries.

The Kresge Library's Embedded Librarian Program

The Kresge Library embedded librarian program started initially as an instruction endeavor to train MBA students on how to find resources that would help with their projects. The primary issue was that the students, who have been working with fairly consistently packaged class material (textbooks, course packs, cases, etc.) had difficulty finding resources that sufficiently document very specific markets that were commonplace with MAP projects. As this became a bigger issue for the students, it became clear that creating a formal relationship between MAP teams and Kresge librarians was the best way to proceed. This instruction focus for the early days of our embedded librarian program matches what many programs are currently doing across the academy.

The original and sole participant was the Library's instruction coordinator, who provided library database instruction to these students as they began their MAP projects. While the program now had a dedicated librarian, the sheer size of the student body (over 400 MBA students participating at the time) represented a large burden for a single librarian. By expanding the program to include other librarians, one could create specialized training to help the students find the research materials that would support their individual projects. As the program continued to expand, it also became clear that this was more than an instruction and reference opportunity; students were continually returning to the librarian who provided MAP training for additional research.

The structure of the program changed around 2002, because the library's reference desk was becoming swamped by all of the additional work required by the MAP teams. The library director then decided that each team would work with a specific librarian to assist with their information needs during the projects. This connection would allow the library to provide instruction, but, more importantly, it would allow a single person to have a far better understanding of each team's research needs. Not only would that person be able to understand the project, but would supply the students with resources and suggestions on an ongoing basis, without requiring the students to repeatedly explain what they were doing. In this regard, the librarian became the information specialist on the team, allowing for more efficient interaction with the library. Originally, participation as a MAP librarian was limited to the four references and instruction librarians. By 2006, it was expanded to include all of the librarians at Kresge (including the library director), cementing this role as an important core activity. This was critical in 2010 as the size of the MBA class increased, pushing the number of MAP teams from 80 to 96.

Critical to the success of the embedded librarian program is the ability to ensure that the increased reference load does not overwhelm the librarian's schedule. Workload balance has been identified as a common pitfall for many embedded librarian programs.[17] And while MBA MAP is the primary responsibility during the months of March and April, we need to ensure that regular work of the library is covered during this period. As any other library, we have important administrative work that cannot be ignored for seven weeks while we are working with the student teams. Although most of the teams are covered by reference staff, all librarians participate including the library director, the digital services librarian, the head of technical services and the collection development librarian. All of these positions have day-to-day responsibilities that need to be continued during the MAP season.

By knowing when MAP 'season' is, we have been able to preemptively curtail some reference, administrative and project activity during the time periods when we are busiest with MAP. While we cannot completely cut off our daily work, we can ensure that we take on no major projects during the time when our reference demand is the greatest. Occasionally, there are factors beyond our control and we need to adjust accordingly by giving librarians fewer teams or reassigning teams as needed. Additionally, during MAP season, we alleviate some of the job responsibilities that would normally fall onto the librarians by not scheduling library instruction sessions and by using part-time staff, including graduate students and reference interns from the Michigan School of Information. These schedule adjustments allow most of the librarians to primarily focus on meeting the needs of the MAP teams.

The MAP Research Process—The Librarian Perspective

As with many academic research libraries, the Kresge Library reference staff works primarily with students during the school year on an ad hoc basis—relying on students coming into the library, emailing the librarians, connecting via IM, or using the general reference email from the website. The students' perception of need for research assistance is often based on an immediate assignment or paper requirement; students will often visit us in a panic—"I checked the databases and I 'Googled' for two hours but I still couldn't find anything! Can you help?"

As is also the case with some other research libraries, Kresge is constantly striving to approach the reference process in a more proactive manner—through more hours at the physical reference desk, extended IM reference coverage, wiki pages focused on courses and coursework, podcasts and more. This often requires a lot of preliminary legwork and marketing, forming relationships with individual instructors and professors, trying to work some research instruction directly into the course curriculum; an often slow, and sometimes frustrating process, and an indirect path to the ultimate patron—the student. The MAP program offers a unique opportunity to further our goal of proactive research assistance—as a member of a team working on a project literally from the start. It also offers a different way of working with our student patrons, which has carried into our relationships with these students throughout their remaining time in Ross programs, and in some cases into their alumni years.

The "MAP season" kickoff begins with a half day orientation to the program, and its rules and schedule. This is an exciting and chaotic time, with student teams working through meetings with faculty members and communication coaches, trying to better understand the scope of their project. At this stage of the process, a MAP librarian assigned to the team will make initial contact, usually via an email introduction. Although most teams will not meet their librarians on the first day, nearly all will make some kind of contact during the first week. As with similar projects within the spon-

sor organizations, research needs at this point are very focused on broader overview and background information and data. Team members will often request background information about their sponsor organization or company, and relevant industry market reports if applicable. Kresge librarians can much more quickly identify the best resources for this process, and more easily evaluate how well (or not) these may meet the teams' current and future information needs.

Once a preliminary understanding of the sponsor organization and its business has been gained, the student teams are much more confident meeting with their sponsors for the first time. For many business reference librarians this initial packet of information with important background and overview material is relatively easy to acquire and can be done far more efficiently than the student could acquire the same content. With all that the students need to concentrate on in these early days of the projects, this background information takes a daunting task off their plate and allows them to start off with the sponsors in a better light. Alleviating the stress with students in this way from the beginning can be key to the team's success—and is a key connection between the librarian and the student team.

Most MAP groups will request an initial meeting with the team librarian, to get some help researching their company, industry, competitive landscape and market environment. This is a great opportunity for the librarian as well, to meet the team, get some clarification on the project goals and generally open the lines of communication for the duration of the project. This meeting tends to be more fruitful if the groups have already had the first meeting with the company sponsors; some librarians actually request that the teams do that meeting before sitting down with the team librarian, though this is not always possible, especially with international site visits which can take up 5 of the 7 weeks for the program. Additionally, the research that the student team believes they need may have little to do with the industry they are exploring. A computer software firm might be looking at new opportunities in a different industry altogether; an airline might be looking at more efficient workflow; an automotive company might be looking at means to engage the workforce; or a nonprofit organizations might want to investigate franchising as a means to extend their reach to broader communities. Looking at the project from a company or organization profile, it is not always clear what resources would be useful to support the team.

As the project continues through the seven week session, students will require assistance with more and more narrow research needs. As markets are investigated, products are understood, and teams get more immersed in their sponsors' organizations and culture, the students' questions become more sophisticated—and the need for details becomes more crucial. Smaller and smaller market segments, and the corresponding financial and other data related to them are defined; specific programs and industries are explored; specific recommendations to sponsor organizations are fine-tuned—with data backup and other information for validation required for each step.

As with the initial research, the Kresge librarians are in a unique position to help teams not only find the data required, but also to help the teams' understanding of their own work. Their knowledge of a wide range of industries and the information sources dedicated to specific industry information is extremely helpful, both in terms of saved time, and efficient knowledge acquisition by the team members. And the expertise gained through experience working in business, with other MAP and student teams, and with Ross professors and researchers comes with the librarians serving on the teams.

Kresge librarians field a wide variety of reference and research questions to assist with this learning process. Most groups require a substantial amount of general information on their market and the in-

dustry; as the teams work through their projects, requests become more specific (and challenging!):

- *"We need to know ad spending in local markets for a variety of industries"*
- *"I need a list of every small to medium-sized business in Europe…Why does my list from ORBIS not include every company?"*
- *"We are looking to learn anything recent on what companies are doing to engage customers when they register for baby showers"*
- *"We've heard that there are regulations in India that require only trained, certified clinicians can administer eye drops, but we haven't been able to verify this"*
- *"I need to find the uses and size of the gourmet pickle market in the United States."*

Invariably, the questions that we receive during MAP season are some of the most complicated and interesting ones we receive all year. While we are able to get answers to a great many of these requests, there are some that are truly too difficult or narrow to answer. Many of these instances are related to the way transactions are tracked and the way that students would like to see the information (which are not always in sync). Furthermore, some of the questions that the teams pose have no real answer, and the way that we communicate this to the team can sometimes lead to dissatisfaction. In this case, the focus for the librarian is to work with the team on finding a solution. In some instances, that involves identifying a series of databases to explore in hopes of finding the answer. But in more cases, it involves the librarian working with some of these resources in order to find where the data might lie or if there is proxy information that might help illustrate what the student is looking for. Since the students are being judged on how they use information, not how they found it, this approach makes perfect sense from everyone's perspective.

As the projects wind down to the final weeks, the teams' research demands become even more defined—and the requests even more detailed.

Here the librarian may need to work harder to find the requested information—for example students might be seeking the potential market for drugs targeted at autoimmune diseases in Ireland and this is not covered in the report they already viewed. Students appreciate the ability to work with a partner who knows what resources they have, so they do not have to explain what they have viewed and what they are looking for. At this point, the librarians will call on a different expertise—the "knowing where to look" vs. "knowing". The students can get quite stressed during this phase of the MAP projects, and their demands can get desperate; the librarian's ability to provide assistance at this point is critical for success, and for sanity. Additionally, this is when having eight librarians supporting MAP pays dividends. Kresge Librarians are very good at asking one another when a particular research question has them stumped. The goal, from the director's point of view, is to ensure that these requests are answered and that we look to our colleagues to help with that.

As the team reaches the final presentations to their faculty team members and sponsor organizations, the librarians' knowledge of how to report and present the data, use and cite various resources used, and the proper use of copyrighted material will be called upon. While most of us probably take this knowledge for granted, and can recite those rules in our sleep, to the student teams working on this phase of the project we can seem like angels of mercy, swooping in and saving them yet another frustrating search for information. The student teams not only learn about and discover business information resources and processes, they also gain a new understanding of the role of the librarian—the information expert assigned to the team.

As participants in MAP and other action-based learning programs at the Ross School, Kresge librarians are also involved in a constant knowledge-acquisition process—moving from industry to industry, from marketing programs to product development, from technology to yet another new technology. We gain not just a broad understanding of more industries, or a deeper understanding of practical application of marketing techniques or of customer relationship management packages, but a broader and deeper understanding of the student experience at Ross, creating tighter bonds with our Ross colleagues involved in MAP. There can also be a "trickle up" effect with regards to our relationships with Ross faculty and other staff as a result of our work with student MAP teams; as key participants in the most important program at the School, the library and its staff continually build ties with the broader Ross community, resulting in more (and better) faculty research projects, and more work with other organizations within the school. We are also able to use our new relationships to get in on the ground floor with instruction, wiki pages and other more proactive reference services for more and more of our Ross teaching faculty.

The librarian's role as guide also needs to include some advice as to what the group will likely be able to find, as well as what they most likely will not be able to get from the Kresge resources. This might take the form of a discussion of the difficulty in obtaining information about private companies or start-ups; a guide to other University of Michigan libraries or departments (i.e. how to work with the medical library and librarians, databases available from the University Library); or a conversation about the process and guidelines for requesting research reports or other materials that Kresge does not currently own.

The physical location of the MAP teams will often dictate communication with the team librarian. Some teams may be at a remote location for the duration of the seven weeks, in areas where database access is not always reliable, or where time zones increase the difficulty of actual conversations. Others may be working with sponsors that are located in or near Ann Arbor, and may want to meet with their MAP librarian several times throughout the project. Most teams are away for at least some part of the first weeks of the project, and reappear at the end with research needs related to completing the final recommendations or plans to present to their sponsors. Some librarians like to attempt to put some parameters around the nature of communication with their team—and request that inquiries be passed to them via email if at all possible, for example, or that the team designate a library liaison to communicate research requests to avoid the problems of multiple, identical requests from the team members—with the knowledge that they need to remain flexible when dealing with the groups at the different points of their projects.

The MAP Process—Student Perspective

For most MAP teams, the inclusion of a research librarian seems like a great idea, even before they are actually using our reference services. As more and more faculty become familiar with the process and the individual librarians working in the program, the likelihood that a team will begin communication with their librarian from the beginning has grown. From a student perspective, this contact can be quite beneficial—a few well-researched overview reports and a company profile can provide a lot of peace of mind for the student meeting with a sponsor for the first time. The start of the MAP projects, when the students are busy trying to get up to speed about an unfamiliar industry and learn about the business of doing business at the same time, can be intimidating; having a research specialist on the team at this critical time is a significant help. Quick access to these resources is also important—the additional expertise brought to the process by the librarians' knowledge of what is available and where to get it can greatly reduce the stress level at all stages of the seven-week projects.

Although there is no longer a formal instruction element to the MAP program, there is a potentially more effective introduction to the business research process that can be gained from the inclusion of the librarian on the MAP team. As the librarian passes along selected research reports,

articles or datasets, she/he makes the research process more visible—pointing out where the research came from, why it's an important resource to consider for the project, how it fits into the other background and overview information already passed along, how to use the database used to generate it for the next set of data—and the student becomes more comfortable with the process, unconsciously developing an individual research process to bring to the next phase of the MAP project, as well as to their next Strategy course, or their first marketing plan at a new company following graduation.

The very nature of the MAP projects and action-based learning, has helped to make the librarian's role increasingly important to student team members; the librarian assignment has become a critical part of the MAP process. Project goals and targets can change quickly, and quite dramatically, in some cases; a team working with a computer vendor may also need to suggest new opportunities in the education or banking industry—all of which leads to another round of business research. The wealth of resources available at Kresge, and at the University of Michigan, creates an excellent environment for this demanding work; having a research professional who can guide the team through all of these resources can mean the difference between being completely overwhelmed and running out of time and being prepared, with the right information, at the right time.

Among the many benefits of this approach from the student perspective are two in particular. First, the student teams work with dedicated librarians who are familiar with their project. This is a critical and essential aspect of the embedded librarian process in every way, shape and form. And while we have addressed the strong possibility and likelihood of project scope shifting and getting more narrowly focused, the general theme typically remains the same. So to this end, the librarian who is working with the team will not require the student members to start at the beginning when they interact with the library. Since the librarian has been working with the team, she/he knows what they have found and what ground they have covered already. Second, the librarian is very aware of the class calendar and where they are with the project. This allows the librarian to be able to measure the team's ability to appreciate and respond to a teachable moment. Early during a project, the team might be able to spend more time doing independent or mediated research on a subject. But as the group moves towards the end of the term, the librarians are typically more empathetic and will help the students more directly, especially in light of last minute changes and tweaks. While some might argue that this approach amounts to librarians doing the work for the team, we would argue that the students are not in a position to learn information skills with the mounting pressures of finishing this project.

One of the most significant aspects of embedding librarians with each and every MAP team is the focus on student, rather than faculty, research needs. This, more than any other individual research request, or the nature of the projects or sponsors, is what truly makes the embedded librarian program for Ross MAP teams a student-centered approach. As academic and research librarians, we are used to prioritizing the needs of the faculty and the research scientists. While most of the embedded librarian programs within the academy focus on the connection between the library and the faculty, the Kresge program is almost exclusively designed to enhance the connection between the library and the students. We see this manifested in several different ways, from increased reference use outside of the MAP program, individual librarians hearing from repeat customers as a result of working with the student on a team, to the lovely gifts some of have received as a thank you from our student teams.

Assessing Kresge's Embedded Librarian Program

Working with MAP teams not only involves the Kresge librarians in a highly visible, challenging and interesting process with the Ross School of Business; it also provides guidance on a wide variety of Kresge Library functions. From suggestions for how to catalog previous MAP project reports as examples for future MAP teams, to how to staff the reference desk during the MAP season, to assigning an additional budget for MAP-specific market research reports, MAP influences every department and most every employee at the Kresge Library.

Reference services are also positively affected by the work we do with the MAP teams. As the teams move on to the second year of their MBA program, they are much more aware of the role that the library and the library staff can play in their studies; most of us have experienced the instances of repeat customers and can name a new group of "library ambassadors"—not only returning when they need research assistance for coursework, internships and project work, but also advising their fellow students and even some faculty that they need to come to Kresge to take advantage of the library resources and staff.

The embedded librarian program we have at Kresge serves many functions.

First, it puts us with the group, be it literally or intellectually. We are seeing the project unfold in all its glory and responding accordingly. By being embedded with these teams, we are able to better understand what their needs are at different times during the term. This is very critical to any embedded librarian program—the need to match library services with the desires and needs of patrons.

Second, the embedded librarian program provides students with someone who knows where they are, where they have been and where they are going. This is critical, especially for a reference-based program. Were students working on a MAP project or any detailed research project strictly to go to the reference desk every time for assistance, they would have to explain what they are looking for, what they have already used and what they are missing. In an embedded librarian program, especially one focused on reference, the first two steps can be avoided. One of the best benefits to the student (as previously mentioned) is that they do not have to explain their research project or what they have used, because the librarian has been there, helping find material and advising on future research. This ability to dispense with the background information on the request seems to make students more likely to seek out help and focus in on what he or she wants and needs. Additionally, by working closely with the team over the course of the term, we can gauge if their request provides an appropriate teachable moment. While early in the term, we might suggest more exploration on their own, late in the project we might simply work with them to quickly get an answer.

Third, we can easily identify gaps in the collection, enabling Kresge Librarians to preemptively seek out and evaluate other available resources. Fulfilling this information need is critical to the success of the embedded librarian program since many MAP projects involve new markets and applications. Rarely, do we find pre-packaged reports and articles that will serve as a Rosetta Stone for all MAP teams.

Fourth, it helps us with projects that are very demanding in terms of information needs. MAP projects involve seven weeks' worth of work for the students and it is expected (by both the faculty member who assigns a grade and the sponsors) to be well researched and documented. Students are expected to make a business case with hard data that will support other decisions that the company might make. To that end, students working on MAP projects are looking at dozens, if not hundreds of reports, articles and datasets. This makes the entire project larger in scope than any individual project or paper that a student might be required to complete.

In evaluating this program, we continue to build upon the foundation of work that we have done, but also seek to address the needs of students as they embark on these yearly projects. As Action-Based Learning becomes a more central means of teaching at the Ross School of Business, we have moved with the school to ensure that we offer other students and other projects the same service. In 2008, we surveyed MBA students directly about MAP library services and presented the data in a presentation at the Special Libraries Association Conference.[18] Since then, we have worked with the MAP office to be included in the end of program survey for MAP students. We have not conducted any other assessment. With an increase in demand, we have not undertaken any new assessment programs for MAP, but are hoping to utilize information from the official MAP survey.

Overall, we feel that we have done a great job of connecting with the students and showcasing our individual skills and abilities as researchers. We are bridging the gap between academic and corporate library models of embedded librarianship. In many instances, we follow the academic library model in providing students with instruction on how to use the resources. In many more instances, we follow the corporate library model in providing students with the actual information and reports through our own introductory and advanced searching. The happy medium, as we are discovering, is almost always somewhere between these two library models. What is most important, from our library's perspective, is that we provide the means to connect the students with the information that they require.

Notes

1. For more information on the school, please visit: http://www.bus.umich.edu/NewsRoom/FastFacts.htm (accessed June 1, 2010)

2. http://www.beyondgreypinstripes.org/about/index.cfm (accessed June 1, 2010)

3. Katherine K. Merseth, "The Early History of Case-Based Instruction: Insights for Teacher Education Today." *Journal of Teacher Education* 42, no. 4 (1991): 243–249.

4. Geoff Gloeckler. "The Case Against Case Studies." *BusinessWeek* no. 4069 (02/04, 2008): 66–67

5. Lynda M. Duke, Jean B. MacDonald and Carrie S. Trimble. "Collaboration between Marketing Students and the Library: An Experiential Learning Project to Promote Reference Services." *College & Research Libraries* 70, no. 2 (2009): 109.

6. Based on Library's submitted budget document. Final statistics will be on the Kresge Library's Annual Report which is available here: http://webservices.itcs.umich.edu/mediawiki/KresgeLibrary/index.php/Kresge_Library

7. Duke et al, 109.

8. Stephen M. Ross School of Business website, http://www.bus.umich.edu/MAP/ABL.htm (accessed June 1, 2010).

9. Don Antunes and Howard Thomas, "The Competitive (Dis)Advantages of European Business Schools." *Long Range Planning* 40, no. 3 (06, 2007): 382–404.

10. http://www.bus.umich.edu/MAP/Dev/ABL.htm (accessed April 20, 2010)

11. Martin A. Kesselman and Sarah Barbara Watstein. "Creating Opportunities: Embedded Librarians." *Journal of Library Administration* 49, no. 4 (06, 2009): 383–400.

12. Ignacio J. Ferrer-Vinent and Christy A. Carello. "Embedded Library Instruction in a First-Year Biology Laboratory Course." *Science & Technology Libraries* 28, no. 4 (2008, 2008): 325–351.

13. Sara J. Beutter Manus, "Librarian in the Classroom: An Embedded Approach to Music Information Literacy for First-Year Undergraduates." *Notes* 66, no. 2 (12, 2009): 249–261.

14. Susan D. Herring, Robert R. Burkhardt, and Jennifer L. Wolfe, "Reaching Remote Students." *College & Research Libraries News* 70, no. 11 (12, 2009): 630–633.

15. Deborah Brown and Dean Leith, "Integration of the research library service into the editorial process. "Embedding" the librarian into the media." *New Information Perspectives* 2007;59(6):539–549.

16. Gary Freiburger and Sandra Kramer, "Embedded Librarians: One Library's Model for Decentralized Service." *Journal of the Medical Library Association* 97, no. 2 (04, 2009): 139–142.

17. David Shumaker, "Who Let the Librarians Out?" *Reference & User Services Quarterly* 48, no. 3 (Spring 2009): 239–242.

18. Laura Berdish and Corey Seeman, "Spanning the Straits of Business Information: Kresge Library's Embedded Librarian Program for MAP (Multidisciplinary Action Program)—A Contributed Paper for the Special Libraries Association Meeting in Seattle, June 2008." (2008).

References

Antunes, Don and Howard Thomas. "The Competitive (Dis)Advantages of European Business Schools." *Long Range Planning* 40, no. 3 (06, 2007): 382–404.

Berdish, Laura and Corey Seeman. "Spanning the Straits of Business Information: Kresge Library's Embedded Librarian Program for MAP (Multidisciplinary Action Program)—A Contributed Paper for the Special Libraries Association Meeting in Seattle, June 2008." (2008).

Brown, Deborah and Dean Leith. "Integration of the Research Library Service into the Editorial Process."2007.

Duke, Lynda M., Jean B. MacDonald, and Carrie S. Trimble. "Collaboration between Marketing Students and the Library: An Experiential Learning Project to Promote Reference Services." *College & Research Libraries* 70, no. 2 (2009): 109.

Ferrer-Vinent, Ignacio J. and Christy A. Carello. "Embedded Library Instruction in a First-Year Biology Laboratory Course." *Science & Technology Libraries* 28, no. 4 (2008, 2008): 325–351.

Freiburger, Gary and Sandra Kramer. "Embedded Librarians: One Library's Model for Decentralized Service." *Journal of the Medical Library Association* 97, no. 2 (04, 2009): 139–142.

Gloeckler, Geoff. "The Case Against Case Studies." *BusinessWeek* no. 4069 (02/04, 2008): 66–67.

Herring, Susan D., Robert R. Burkhardt, and Jennifer L. Wolfe. "Reaching Remote Students." *College & Research Libraries News* 70, no. 11 (12, 2009): 630–633.

Kesselman, Martin A. and Sarah Barbara Watstein. "Creating Opportunities: Embedded Librarians." *Journal of Library Administration* 49, no. 4 (06, 2009): 383–400.

Manus, Sara J. Beutter. "Librarian in the Classroom: An Embedded Approach to Music Information Literacy for First-Year Undergraduates." *Notes* 66, no. 2 (12, 2009): 249–261.

Merseth, Katherine K. "The Early History of Case-Based Instruction: Insights for Teacher Education Today." *Journal of Teacher Education* 42, no. 4 (1991): 243–249.

Shumaker, David. "Who Let the Librarians Out?" *Reference & User Services Quarterly* 48, no. 3 (Spring 2009): 239–242.

# TWELVE

More Than a One-Shot: Innovative Faculty-Librarian Collaboration

Lisa Coats and Bojana Beric

Introduction

This chapter outlines the process of developing a collaborative approach to teaching and learning in higher education, and provides an analysis and discussion of a faculty-librarian collaboration experience and students' responses to an assessment conducted over the course of three semesters. Our case study represents collaboration as an innovative teaching strategy in health education developed for the senior-level college perspectives course *AIDS and the Global Society* (PR 422) at Monmouth University (MU) in New Jersey. Our experiences may be the grounds for possible replication in health education courses, as well as any courses requiring extensive library research to support projects.

The inspiration for this faculty-librarian project came from a campus-wide workshop promoting collaborative teaching. As a teaching institution of higher education, MU has been increasingly focused on identifying ways to enhance the level of information literacy skills of students across campus. In the fall of 2008, after we both, Bojana Beric, health faculty, and Lisa Coats, librarian, attended a workshop on linked learning communities and information literacy which emphasized faculty collaboration and co-teaching, we decided to expand on our previous, one-shot library instruction in a senior-level perspectives course. We were both

aware of the information literacy need within our own disciplines as well. In addition to the university's outlined direction, we received strong departmental support for our proposed project since a collaborative faculty-librarian teaching relationship should foster improved information literacy. However, as Given and Julien attest, "forging and maintaining strong working relationships between faculty and librarians is no easy task." Kotter further asserts, "the improvement of relations between librarians and classroom faculty is a key to the continuing viability of academic libraries and librarianship." In pursuing this collaborative project, we sought to bridge this divide and encourage more collaborative efforts between librarians and teaching faculty members at MU and more generally in the field of Health Studies.

Theoretical and Practical Background

In designing a course, teachers must consider several variables. How do we develop teaching strategies in our courses to facilitate skills, knowledge, and a solid understanding of the basic concepts in the discipline? The term "facilitator" has been in use rather than "teacher" for those who create strategies to stimulate or facilitate learning of knowledge and skill in health education. The term is embedded in the widely used definition of health education. According to Green, Kreuter, Deeds, and Partridge, health education is "any combination of learning experiences designed to facilitate voluntary adaptations of behavior conducive to health." Often, the construction of knowledge in health education classes is a result of a group process, or a dialogue in social interactions. Very rarely does learning happen in isolation; especially in schools and colleges, teaching and learning tend to be inseparable, interactive processes.

Social constructivism is an approach to learning in a group context or through interaction with other people who may be teachers, librarians, other students, mentors, or facilitators, where the focus is on a learning-centered classroom. Vygotsky defines a Zone of Proximal Development ("zpd") as a maximum potential that every student or learner can reach with scaffolding, or purposeful guidance, of a teacher, mentor, or facilitator. Therefore, when teachers design strategies, they ought to try to construct them in such a way that each student will reach that maximum potential in learning, to achieve a step up in the development, a level that without outside support the student would not reach. On the other hand, Freire introduces "conscientizacao" or active, engaged learning where students become active learners as opposed to being passive receptacles in the "banking system" of schooling. How do we as teachers, mentors, or facilitators help students reach their maximum potential and transform a passive learner into an active, engaged mind or active learner?

A lecture-style approach to teaching should be perceived as an oppressive, imposing, and intimidating process that contributes to the passivity of young minds. How do we break this process that seems to be comfortable for some teachers, but not effective for all students? How do we move away from traditional lecturing to stimulate learning? How do we develop a strategy for health education classes that will transform the traditional roles of a teacher and a student, and even more, how do we transform our classrooms from being teaching-

centered to learning-centered? The *Community of Philosophical Inquiry* that Lipman proposes as a prototype of a transformed and engaged classroom may be an answer to these questions, and serve as an environment conducive to active learning. In a community of inquiry, students and teachers exchange roles where the students become teachers and the teachers become students. Anyone participating in the community of inquiry becomes a teacher, or a facilitator, and therefore an active learner. To be able to teach, or explain some content or idea, one needs to understand and know the concepts.

Librarians have been working closely with teaching faculty for many years. However, the term *embedded librarian* is a relatively new Millennium invention. Dugan writes that the term "'embedded,' though appropriated early on, has not been uniformly applied to identical academic activities and the label appears in several different models" after its infusion into instructional librarianship. We sought out literature and questioned librarians via listservs to discern if others had conducted embedded collaborations in health education. While some librarians on the listservs reported that they were participating as a co-facilitator in class management systems or other online formats in health-related courses, only a few were embedded in the classroom. Furthermore, while the literature indicates that many librarians are embedding in-person in a variety of disciplines from engineering to music to sociology, we did not locate any reports on primarily in-person embedded librarians in health education. At MU, the one-shot model is the primary format by which students receive library instruction, and all freshmen receive at least one library instruction session during their first year. While the MU librarians are assigned liaison departments, no collaborative, embedded projects have been implemented in recent years between the faculty and the librarians. Since the Health Studies major was only established in 2007, and the librarian in this collaboration serves as the Library Liaison to the School of Nursing & Health Studies, she has been steadily working on library resources for the major and developing a relationship with the Health Studies faculty. Because of her in-depth involvement, we decided to develop our own collaborative model and focused our study in the field of Health Studies.

Collaboration

We proposed a semester long, faculty-librarian course collaboration on multiple levels, including a library instruction session, in-class sessions, and online communication with the students. It was also important, particularly from the librarian's perspective, to encourage a new dimension in the students' relationship with the library, not only for this class assignment, but in general. Therefore, our objective was to develop a collaboration between the librarian and the teaching faculty member that allowed students to learn and increase their knowledge on the subject, develop and refine library skills, and deepen their comfort level in using quality, reliable published resources while working on the specific class assignment for the perspectives course.

Our planning and collaboration began in December of 2008, after establishing strong support from our respective Departments for the project. We met several times to discuss the structure of the course as defined in the syllabus, including a time-line, specific dates, the requirements for the assignment, and an outline of the library assistance that would be provided to support the research required to complete the assignment. In addition, we considered including two other health education courses requiring extensive research for the assigned projects and taught by the same health faculty (Table 12-1).

The two health education courses continued to have a single library session as control groups to measure student satisfaction with the faculty-librarian collaboration. To be able to survey the students and gather their perceptions about the faculty-librarian collaboration, research permission was obtained from the MU Institutional Review Board (IRB).

The Case Study

Our collaboration focused on *AIDS and the Global Society*, an undergraduate senior-level health promotion class, listed as a general education perspectives course at the University. One of the projects required in this course is a study of vulnerable populations with HIV/AIDS globally and a presentation of the research findings. Students worked in small groups to complete the assignment by selecting a vulnerable population (e.g., adolescents, bisexual men and women, children, commercial sex workers, elderly, gay men, homeless people, incarcerated persons, lesbians, people with hemophilia, substance abusers) infected with HIV and having AIDS. They needed to identify literature and resources to support their presentations. To present

Table 12-1. Courses Surveyed with Number of Students Enrolled and Responses		
Semester	Course	Number of Students (N=197)/Responses (161)
Spring 2009	PR 422 AIDS & Global Society	27/24
	HE 420 Principles of Health Ed	18/15
Fall 2009	PR 422 AIDS & Global Society	26/21
	HE 420 Principles of Health Ed	24/21
	HE 335 Community Health	23/20
Spring 2010	PR 422 AIDS & Global Society	29/26
	HE 420 Principles of Health Ed	24/18
	HE 335 Community Health	26/16

the research on the topic, students developed a self-standing poster, which included the following information: 1) A global perspective on HIV/AIDS; 2) A description of the population, including demographics, risk factors and common health issues prevalent in this population in addition to HIV/AIDS; 3) Information about the access and barriers to health care and treatment options for this population globally; 4) A discussion of prevention programs with possible suggestions for improvement of the existing programs. Students were required to use at least five references in their study to support the poster presentation, and references had to be listed or displayed on the poster.

To demonstrate the learning on the topic, students in each group had a fifteen minute presentation per poster in class. Each student received an individual grade for the oral presentation and the ability to answer questions during the presentation. The entire group received one common grade for two components of the poster: a) content and b) appearance. Students enrolled in the perspectives course offered during the spring semester also held a poster session at the university-wide Global Understanding Convention (GUC) during the first week of April.

The library research component of the collaboration consisted of: 1) one 75-minute library session, early in the semester; 2) one 75-minute library research consultation session in the classroom about one to two weeks after the initial session; 3) individual student-initiated communications with the librarian; 4) the librarian's attendance at some of the poster presentations in the classroom and the GUC poster session during the spring semesters. A description of the collaboration with the librarian was included in the syllabus so that the students knew the plan and schedule at the beginning of the semester regarding this particular assignment.

During the first two semesters in the library instruction sessions for the classes presented in Table 12-1, we provided the students with a general re-

search guide for the Health Studies major at MU in the form of a handout. (Appendix A). This guide, also available as a PDF on the library's Web site, was developed by the librarian based on suggestions by the MU Health Studies faculty. It included search tips for finding books, both circulating and reference, a section on database research for finding scholarly, peer-reviewed articles with suggestions on subject-appropriate databases, links to professional associations and government resources, as well as some basic information on how to get more assistance from the library. For the third semester of the study in the case study course and both control classes, we introduced course-specific research guides online that were developed by the librarian with the Springshare product LibGuides. Because LibGuides are interactive, online, user-friendly guides, with hyperlinks that can be tailored for general or specific disciplines, topics, classes and assignments, we anticipated that the students might utilize the resources from these guides more readily than from a print guide. The online guides provided a feedback box for users' comments and suggestions, from which statistics on usage can easily be drawn, as well as contact information with a photo of the librarian. These guides were prepared in consultation with the health faculty to assist students with research for specific assignments in each course. A few days before the library instruction sessions in all three courses, the librarian e-mailed students directly, introducing herself and the online research guide that had been created for their class, specifically for the assignment on which they were currently working. In addition, at the library session, each student received a one-page handout including the contact information for the librarian, the link to the online subject research guide tailored to their assignment, as well as the link to a general LibGuide for Health Studies.

The in-classroom session was scheduled one-to-two weeks following the initial session at the library, just for the case study course, during all three semesters of study. During her visit, the librarian spent time with each group of students studying the vulnerable populations. Both the health faculty and the librarian were guiding groups, answering questions, and providing directions to students who were now well immersed in their projects. The students were more focused and questions and inquiries were better defined at this second session. Individual contact (e.g., via e-mail, phone, drop-in at Reference Desk, one-on-one appointment) was encouraged in both the library session and the in-class meeting with students. During the spring semesters, the librarian attended the GUC poster presentations. In all three semesters, both of us evaluated the in-class presentations, and we consulted each other about grading, while the final grade was assigned to students by the health faculty.

To gather feedback on the students' perceptions regarding the effectiveness of the faculty-librarian collaboration, we developed a survey: "Faculty Librarian Collaboration: A Student Questionnaire." (Appendix B). The first section of the survey asked about students' use of the library as a general resource and as a resource for this assignment, as well as their perceptions about the faculty-librarian collaboration. The second section was about demographic information of respondents. The initial version of the survey was minimally revised with the IRB approval for the use at the conclusion of second and third semesters of study. The surveys were administered by graduate assistants in all classes towards the conclusion of the semester. A total of 197 surveys were administered in eight classes and 161 were returned and completed, with an 82% response rate.

Analysis and Findings

The participants in the case study course were all undergraduate students enrolled in a senior-level perspectives course during three academic semesters at a medium-sized private university. They represented a variety of majors with about 10-25% of the students enrolled in Health Studies, depending on the semester, and 75-90% enrolled in other majors offered at the University. Participants

ranged in age between 21 and 44 years, with the majority (80%) being 21 to 22 years of age. The participants were predominantly female (70-75%), having a White or Caucasian racial/ethnic background (98%). The participants in the two control classes were similar in demographic characteristics, with the only difference being their academic majors; all were enrolled as Health Studies majors.

Some of the students' perceptions and responses to the survey are depicted in Tables 12-2, 12-3, and 12-5. Based on survey results, the participants appreciated our collaboration when it helped them with the specific class assignment. (Table 12-2) The students benefited from the librarian's assistance and guidance with their search for references. They also liked the fact that class sessions were devoted to library search or work on the posters and assignments. In the case study course, they embraced the librarian's involvement and continuous connection with her, as well as the helpful resources that were prepared and developed by both faculty members.

The students found some aspects of our collaboration less useful, mostly because of the type of information offered initially, which was perceived as basic, general library skills and repetitive in nature, as represented in Table 12-3. After assessing the students' survey responses and verbal feedback in the first semester, it became evident that most of the students felt they did not need any general introduction to library resources, because they were upper classmen. They reported that they knew all the general library research information presented by the librarian, stating that they learned how to use the library earlier in their studies, as most of the students at MU are exposed to a one-shot library instruction session in a general Information Technology (IT 100) course required by all freshmen. Another common complaint was the location of the library. The Monmouth University Library is in a beautifully converted mansion surrounded by pines and landscaped lawns. It has over 100 computers, five study rooms, and many picturesque areas for reading and studying. However, it

Table 12-2. What Students Liked Most About the Collaboration		
Semester	Case Study PR 422	Control Health Courses
Spring 2009	• Learning about tools like Noodletools • Librarian was very helpful • Time allotted during class to use the library • Understand database search more easily • Librarian was there to help • Librarian was very willing to help • Information session with librarian was very helpful • Helpful with research and finding new ways to search for info • The primary informational session • Showed the citation links • How friendly they are • Finding out that the journals are already put in APA formatted citations online • Librarian was friendly, helpful and interested in our project • Asking question • Librarian's tutorial was very informative • Real knowledge about online resources • They informed how to do things, not just did it • Always available for help	• Organized and well informed • Librarian provided the new ways to search for articles & she was very helpful • I did not like any aspect • A walk through the best possibility • Their willingness to be of assistance • Helped us research our health topics through different databases effectively • The general helpfulness of the staff • They taught us how to narrow the search • They knew a lot about online library • They get journal articles for you • Helped use databases • Helped me cite • Helpfulness/learning what words to search
Fall 2009	• The info session • Links suggested • Librarian checked back with us after • Seminar in the library, very informative • Ability to ask for help when needed • They worked well together to help students • Guest speaker • Good advice what sites to use • They were willing to help • Her help in finding resources • Nothing	• Assistance with relevant websites • Research ideas • Information • PowerPoint on research • Helpful • Friendly • Nothing
Spring 2010	• The interaction • The website librarian made • Librarian coming to presentations • The ease of use • Q&A • She was very friendly, helpful and interested in our projects • Librarian • Knowing librarian was there if needed • That it had all resources grouped together • Willing to help • Having her be the health studies rep. • That librarian consolidated all the pertinent information • In-class time for meeting • In-class information session • Librarian had a great personality • Having to attend library research session • Easily accessible • Everything was very accessible • Research databases • Help with research • LibGuide	• Its helpfulness • The resources made available • Online resources • Was made aware of better search engines • Librarian was friendly an very helpful • Nice people • Nice • Made it a little easier • The website • Session • Nothing • Easy to research • In person • The resources made available • Availability • Felt as though help was readily available • The preparation the librarian had

is on the edge of the campus, about a 10-minute walk from the center of campus where most of the academic buildings are located. While there are designated parking spots for library users, parking can be problematic during regular class times. A few other students reported that more one-on-one assistance from the librarian would have improved their research experience, as shown in Table 12-3.

Table 12-3. What Students Liked Least About the Collaboration		
Semester	**Case Study Course PR 422**	**Control Health Courses**
Spring 2009	• Having to walk to the library • Walking around campus in the cold • Repetitive in some areas • I already knew how to use the databases • I did not learn anything that I did not already know • I did not think it was very necessary • I already knew how to find articles, so it was repetitive • There is only one of them • I did not find it helpful • Repetitive because I've been to the session already in the past and it's a far walk • I know how to research. I do not need help. • Being seniors it was a waste of time. • Walking to the library in the cold • I already knew how to use library service • It was hard to cite. • Knew a lot of it already • None!	• It was repetitive, did not learn anything new • Felt I knew a lot. Should be question based. • Took too long to explain. • Repetitive, nothing new • They taught the basics that everyone knew • None • Didn't seem clear for searching topics • I have seen it before
Fall 2009	• Going to the library for orientation, because most are seniors and have gone before • There were too many students in there, not enough time for one-on-one time • So many students, not enough one-on-one time • Learned info from fresh year • Going to the library unnecessary, because it can be done on any computer • Confusion • The class held in library because I've done so many times • Nothing	• Having to go there • The whole aspect. Taught nothing. • Sometimes it was too much work • Research methods • Felt elementary • Information I did not need • The availability of them • Learning new info
Spring 2010	• Nothing • Nothing • Nothing • Not enough info on my topic • Going over the resources at (?) • The in-class-session. I already knew what was talked about. • That we had to be taught how to use it • Having to go to the library • Faculty obviously explained exactly what kind of info was needed • Not needed—in school for four years, I know how to use the library • No parking • Having a class about how to research • Not much access of info	• None • Specific population info was somewhat hard to find • Boring • Boring • Search • None • Nothing • Too long • Library session; as seniors we know it

As a result of students' comments and suggestions, general library research information was cut back in the second semester with more emphasis placed on searching for resources for the specific assignment. From the beginning of our collaboration, we allotted time during the initial library session for hands-on research, assisted by both of us. However, the time devoted to hands-on research and one-on-one assistance has increased as a result of a feedback from the students. Although some students found the library research sessions to be "repetitive" and not particularly helpful (Table 12-3), several of them made positive references to the hands-on, focused research assistance when answering what they liked the most about the collaboration. (Table 12-2) Therefore, we decided to increase the librarian's in-class presence during the third semester in the case study course by adding more class time with the librarian and having her attend poster presentations in class. The case study participants' responses in the third semester reflect this adjustment, as they reported liking the in-class sessions. (Table 12-2) Similarly, while the librarian was particularly interested in the quality of the references and the content as an outcome from the embedded collaboration, we expected that her attendance during class presentations and the GUC poster session in the spring semester would also show the students the investment the librarian had in their projects and presentations. The comments made by students via e-mail and from the feedback form on the subject research guide corroborated this notion, confirming the meaning and value of the librarian's increased participation. Dugan concludes, "our value and success were directly aligned with our presence; so in the future, we must raise our profile in the class." We also believe that the increased involvement of the librarian in our health education classroom setting contributed to students' more active participation in library research. We attribute the improved quality of selected resources to this active engagement of students with the embedded librarian collaboration.

Both the analysis of the surveys formally administered and the informal dialogue and discussion with the students showed that they did utilize the library resources, including the librarian's expertise, more as the librarian's presence increased both online and face-to-face, as presented in Table 12-4. The questions in Tables 12-4 & 12-5 were added to the survey in the fall of 2009 to better assess student satisfaction and gain insight on their opinion of the collaboration from another angle.

It is significant that most of the participants 88% (23 out of 26) from the case study class in the third semester would recommend the faculty-librarian collaboration for other classes. This was an increase from 67% (16 out of 24) in the first semester, and 70% (14 out of 20) in the second semester. We attribute this shift in perception of the need for library guidance to the increase in direct contact from the librarian for the case study course over the semesters. During the first semester, the librarian did not contact students before her session in the library, nor did the students directly contact her for assistance after the initial session. However, during the third semester while only the case study course had more scheduled face-to-face time with the librarian planned in advance and outlined in the syllabus, the control classes were contacted by e-mail at least once directly by the librarian, and the reported increased satisfaction is depicted in Table 12-4. The introduction of the LibGuide before the initial library session in the third semester gave the students contact information for the librarian, making it easy to contact her even before the face-to-face session. That initial e-mail prepared them for the library session and their work with the librarian much more than before. Because of this added e-mail contact and connection, the librarian was more associated with the research for the assignment, making it easier for students in all three classes. (Table 12-4) Similarly, in the third semester students began contacting the librarian directly for research help, particularly in the case study course, after the library session.

One group came to the library while the librarian was working at the reference desk and she assisted them with their poster assignment there. Others e-mailed with questions regarding statistics about the vulnerable population or country on which they were focusing. Since the students could see a photograph on the LibGuide and met the librarian in person several times, they appeared to feel more comfortable contacting her directly. Some students even did so for other course assignments as well,

Table 12-4. The Reasons why Work on the Poster/Assignment Was Easier

Semester	Case Study PR 422	Control Health Classes
Fall 2009	• CDC website & WHO website • Library searches • That we were working in groups to split the work • The information was easy to find from different websites • Working in groups • My group members • Having the resources right there to help us • The websites such as CDC that were given • Library research lab on site • The information was laid out nicely • Creativity could be used • All facts easy to find • Being with a partner • Partners • The Library website • Knowing what resources to use • Groups • Nothing	• By myself • You were able to get your point across using pictures • More opinion on assignment • Websites suggested by the librarian • Having articles available online • Accessibility of articles • Learning what to look for when searching for material • Having a librarian help us • Resources from the library • Online resources • It was a creative process • Nothing
Spring 2010	• The tutorial from the librarian • There are a lot of websites • Having the common websites on a page for our class • The research database the librarian put together for us • Having a group • We had some time in class to work on it • Class time • The info available • Knowing where I can find the information • Access to research databases • Having a credible sources so easy to access • Having all the info in one place • The topic • The library guide created for us • Help from the librarian in class • Session with librarian in library • Librarian help & suggestions • The assistance of librarian and her helpful site • They provided websites to use for research • Having many useful sites available in the website librarian set up for our class • Group work • The fact that we were working in groups • Research help • Librarian guiding the information & compiling info that was accurate	• The resources available from the library's page • Using the online resources • The links that librarian provided • The help from the librarian • The online periodicals • The site dedicated to this class • The sources • Having the library guides • Access to research databases • Online databases • Library session helped • Help from librarian • It wasn't easier • The resources for our class • In person session • The resources provided by the librarian • Using the journal articles under health • Knowing where to go • It was online form-not paper • The internet • Knowing how to work the website/journals • The time we were given to complete it • Nothing really • Nothing

such as for a paper for an English class, a Women's Health class, and for a Strategic Management class in Business.

In analyzing the responses to the question, what made work on the poster/assignment difficult, we found that participants did not attribute any difficulties to our collaboration. (Table 12-5)

Mainly, the critiques included the physical location of the library, the type of resources they were able to find online, and working in groups. These responses are in concert with the students' preference for online work, as well as individual differences allowing them the freedom to choose the time and place for work.

Table 12-5. The Reasons why Work on the Poster/Assignment was Difficult		
Semester	**Case Study Course PR 422**	**Control Health Classes**
Fall 2009	• Not being able to find information on some countries • It was a bit hard to find some information even with the aid of the librarian • There were many websites to find some information • Finding good sources to pertain to the project • The format of the paper. It was difficult to find all the information requested • Too much information to include it all • Not having specific directions • I am not creative • Prevalence of info • Working in a group • Doing it with a group • Guidance during the library session • Needed to look for a lot of information • Lack of info	• Lib's location • Nothing • Hard time management • Some of us are not good artists or creative • Trying to decide on one topic to focus on • Having many articles not available online • Getting to the library to print • Trying to think of ways to effectively teach a specific age group • Finding information • Hard to get ideas at times
Spring 2010	• Not a lot of info on hemophilia/AIDS • Lack of information on other countries • Having a group • It was a lot of different info • Working in the group, finding the time to meet • The lack of information on other countries • Originally I couldn't find anything on my topic (wrong terminology) • Finding exact info • Not enough information available on subject • Lack of statistics online about adolescents and HIV • The terms we were given: ex: elderly when research states "older adults" • Looking facts up about other countries; not enough • Information on the assigned population is very hard to find • Finding information • Our topic • Finding global information • Looking at the population on a global scale • Finding time to complete it • It was easy • Nothing	• It was boring • The length & finding the appropriate articles • Finding information I could use • Finding journal articles specific to class • Finding info from home • A lot of research • Finding information I could use • Finding journal articles specific to class • Finding info from home • A lot of research • Hard to find research • Finding articles • Getting to Library • What the teacher exactly wanted • Some journals were not available • The lack of direction • Nothing

Even though a specific question was not asked on the survey regarding the LibGuides, the comments from students were very positive, many mentioning the guides specifically in all three classes. Students reported that the work on the poster or assignment was made easier with the LibGuide. (Table 12-4) Similarly, results from the LibGuides feedback forms that thirteen out of twenty-nine case study students submitted, show that all checked "yes" in response to the question about helpfulness of the site. Finally, in an informal discussion with the students at the GUC poster session spring 2010, many of the students other than the Health Studies majors expressed how useful they found the extra help they received on Health Studies resources from the librarian and the subject research guide. The science and health majors also reported using the subject research guide for other classes besides the case study course, which was apparent in the usage statistics for the case study course after the posters were already completed, presented and graded (Figure 12-1). Some students admitted to going directly to government Web sites (e.g., CDC), and United Nations Web sites (e.g., UNAIDS) that were suggested in the class, on the syllabus, or in the library instruction sessions. Others said they found the government and organization Web sites on the guide useful and did access them from the "Government & Organization Resources" section (e.g., AVERT, WHO) of the LibGuide. One student confessed to being "not a very good student" and only using Google Scholar, but we were happy to see it was "Scholar."

In evaluating some of the reference lists the students in the case study used for their posters, we found that while the vast majority relied primarily on Internet resources, all of those resources appeared to be reliable government, educational and organizational Web sites. In addition, all of the students fulfilled the minimum requirement of five references, many going well beyond, with a few scholarly journal articles and books listed among the resources as well. The quality of the resources and the number of credible resources used in the assignments has increased since the librarian's involvement with the students and through our collaboration over the semesters. The quality of the work on poster presentations, in terms of content and the relevance of resources, has also been improving. It could be attributed to our collaboration

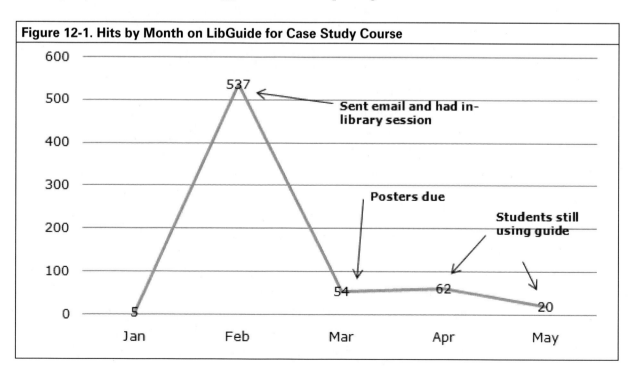

Figure 12-1. Hits by Month on LibGuide for Case Study Course

and the librarian's involvement and careful guidance through the resources available and required. Students are guided by both of us on how to identify scholarly papers and publications, as well as credible on-line resources.

Mentoring and scaffolding in a social context should allow all students to reach their maximum potential in learning and development, so the grades should also reflect that. Students worked with each other, with the librarian, and with the health faculty to study HIV and AIDS in vulnerable populations globally and to manifest their learning and understanding on the topic by sharing with others and answering questions. As a result of this collaborative work, students are better prepared, more confident, and ready for their presentations. Some of the students still used cards as a reminder, although most were comfortable talking about their topics just referring to the information they selected for the poster. Similarly, like professionals when they go to meetings to present posters, students engaged in discussing the content they chose to display on the poster. Vygotsky's "zpd" and mentoring have been supported through many recent reports in the literature discussing the social constructivism approach in teaching and learning and in classroom community of inquiry in a variety of forms. Mentoring and careful guidance increase students' capacity on many levels, such as academic and social, and stimulate conscious learning, allowing for the transformation that Freire suggests in his writings. Through this assignment, guided carefully by two skilled and knowledgeable facilitators through our collaboration, students learned the task while performing and actively working through it, and not just in isolated drills.

Conclusion

Based on our study results and analysis, on students' responses and comments, and our own observations and insight, it may be concluded that collaborative teaching or co-teaching, is an effective strategy in teaching health topics that require extensive literature research. Interdisciplinary collaboration incorporating the expertise of two professionals stimulates meaningful and purposeful learning. In addition, the embedded librarian is a valuable member of the learning community of inquiry in the perspectives course *AIDS and the Global Society*, as well as in other health classes. It is important for effective teaching that instructors *meet the students where they are* in terms of the library and research skills and provide them with an opportunity for expanding in areas of need, because as the students' ability to evaluate sources and the selection for inclusion in posters improves, information literacy increases. In these types of experiential courses, the students learn by doing when they search for the content, and their communication skills are enhanced through presentations in class or at the GUC.

A valuable lesson learned from our collaboration was that at the senior-level college course there is no need for basic, general instruction on library research, but rather focused instruction on specific resources and guidance in task-oriented support. Online research tools seem to be effective for continuous student learning after instruction and provide good connections to library support as an easy access to resources through links.

Therefore, we recommend that the embedded faculty-librarian collaboration in health education classes be instituted as a valuable and meaningful teaching strategy in courses that require extensive research for completion of assignments. Based on our experience, we suggest that the embedded librarian could be instituted even earlier in the students' academic career for courses requiring a research component, ideally in the freshman or sophomore year. Finally, we recommend replication of the collaboration with other MU faculty and librarians to bring more personal insight and critique into the evaluation of research projects, and replication in other university and college settings to add to the validity of the process.

Appendix A. General Research Guide for the Health Studies Major at MU

Health Studies

Subject Research Guide

Contained within this document are selected resources at the Monmouth University Library useful for locating information in the field of Health Studies. For additional resources, search the Library catalog or call the reference desk at 732.571.3438.

Finding Books

Visit http://millenium.monmouth.edu/search.html to find books in the Monmouth University Online Library Catalog. For help using the Catalog, go to the Library Help Pages http://library.monmouth.edu/help/tutorial/tutorial3.htm

Search Tips

Health Studies topics should be searched as "**Keyword**" to maximize the number of references to a topic. When a subject heading is known, search the "**Subject Heading**" index. To find subject headings in the medical field, try the *Medical Subject Heading (MeSH)* online: http://www.nlm.nih.gov/mesh/MBrowser.html

Reference Books

Dictionaries & Encyclopedias

REF QH332 E52 2004	*Encyclopedia of Bioethics* (5 vols.)
REF QH427 E53 2004	*Encyclopedia of Genetics* (2 vols.)
REF QP356.45 H433 2002	*Hormones, Brain and Behavior* (5 vols.)
REF QP771 E53 2004	*Encyclopedia of Vitamins, Minerals and Supplements*
REF R121 M89 2002	*Mosby's Medical, Nursing, and Allied Health Dictionary*
REF RA790.6 M46 2001	*Mental Health: Culture, Race, and Ethnicity*

Handbooks & Guides

REF R733 A475 1999	*Alternative Medicine Sourcebook*

REF RA790 W69 2005	*Mental Health Atlas 2005*
REF RM666 H33 N38 2005	*Natural Standard Herb and Supplement Handbook*
REF RT98 S783 2001	*Handbook of Public and Community Health Nursing Practice*
REF TX551 P385 2005	*Bowes & Church's Food Values of Portions Commonly Used*

Finding Journal Articles

Visit http://library.monmouth.edu/researchdb/researchdb.php to locate databases and journal articles available at Monmouth University.   Databases specific to "Nursing & Health" are found on the Research Database page under the subject listing:

- **Abstracts in Anthropology** – thousands of fully indexed abstracts in anthropology and archaeology
- **ALT-HealthWatch** – complementary, holistic and integrated approaches to health care and wellness
- **Biomedical Reference Collection** – over 200 full-text medical, clinical and research journals
- **CINAHL** – electronic version of the *Cumulative Index to Nursing and Allied Health Literature*
- **Cochrane Library** – collection of several evidenced-based healthcare databases
- **Health Source: Nursing/Academic Edition** – over 500 scholarly full-text journals and the Lexi-PAL Drug Guide
- **Highwire Press** – high impact journals in the areas of science, technology and medicine
- **Science Direct** – full text scientific, technical and medical articles from Elsevier Publishing
- **Wiley InterScience** – offers full-text access to certain journals available via Wiley InterScience that are commonly held by libraries involved in the New Jersey Knowledge Initiative

Career Resources

Print Resources in Reference Career Collection

REF Career Coll. R690 P45 2000   *Peterson's Job Opportunities: Health & Sciences*

REF Career Coll. HD8051 A62 2008-2009   *Occupational Outlook Handbook*

Professional Associations

American Association for Health Education	http://www.aahperd.org/AAHE/
American College Health Association	http://www.acha.org
American Public Health Association	http://www.apha.org
American School Health Association	http://www.ashaweb.org
Gerontology Society of America	http://www.geron.org
International Society of Behavioral Nutrition	http://www.isbnpa.org
International Union for Health Promotion and Education	http://www.iuhpe.org
National Wellness Association	http://nationalwellnessassociation.com/
Society for Public Health Education	http://www.sophe.org
Society of Behavioral Medicine	http://www.sbm.org
New Jersey Public Health Association	http://www.njpha.org
New Jersey Society for Public Health Education	http://www.njsophe.org
World Health Organization	http://www.who.int/en/

Online Government Resources

Centers for Disease Control (CDC) is a clearinghouse for credible health information, easy for everyone to navigate with very current disease and health information. http://www.cdc.gov/

Fedstats is *the* place to go for statistics gathered in the last decade from more than 100 federal agencies, ranging from agricultural to social services. Click on "Health" via the dropdown menu for links to many government health-related websites. http://www.fedstats.gov

MedlinePlus has authoritative information from National Library of Medicine (NLM), the National Institutes of Health (NIH), and other government agencies and health-related organizations.   http://www.nlm.nih.gov/medlineplus/

Morbidity and Mortality Weekly Report (MMWR) is a free online version of the classic publication published since 1976. Article topics include the effects of prison violence on juveniles, tobacco use, and disease and health conditions for meatpackers. http://www.cdc.gov/mmwr

National Center for Health Statistics contains up-to-date state and federal statistics relating to many health issues. This resource provides the quantitative evidence to support research theses. http://www.cdc.gov/nchs/howto/w2w/w2welcom.htm

National Institutes of Health (NIH) is one of the nation's top medical research agencies. The NIH website publishes the latest studies in all medical fields with online reports used by many medical professionals in scholarly journals. http://www.nih.gov

Occupational Safety and Health Administration (OSHA) aims to ensure employee safety and health in the United States by working with employers and employees to create better working environments.   http://www.osha.gov

PubMed Central is a free digital archive of biomedical and life sciences journal literature at NIH developed and managed by NIH's National Center for Biotechnology Information in the NLM.   http://www.pubmedcentral.nih.gov/

Substance Abuse and Mental Health Administration (SAMHSA) was created by an act of Congress in 1992. SAMHSA is a public health agency that confirms the accountability and effectiveness of programs that deal with mental health and substance abuse. Scholarly researchers contribute to and cite the information gathered by SAMHSA.   http://www.samhsa.gov

Need more help?

- Access the Monmouth University Library Page at http://library.monmouth.edu/
- Access the Research Help Page at http://library.monmouth.edu/help/help.php
- Use our Ask-a-Librarian service at http://library.monmouth.edu/help/ask.php
- See the Library's hours at http://library.monmouth.edu/about/about.php#hours
- Call the reference desk at **732.571.3438**.

Appendix B. Faculty Librarian Collaboration: A Student Questionnaire

Please read all instructions carefully. Do not put any marks on this questionnaire that could identify you. The survey is anonymous. Please mark your answers clearly.

Section I: This section asks about your use of library as a resource and your perceptions about the **Faculty/Librarian collaboration** over the past semester in the health course. Please place an **X** on the line next to appropriate answers, circle the response, or fill in an answer.

1.   **In the past, how many times did you typically go to the library during the semester?**
   a._____   Never
   b._____   1-2 times a week
   c._____   3-4 times a week
   d._____   5 or more times a week

2.   **During this semester, how many times did you typically go to the library?**
   a._____   Never
   b._____   1-2 times a week
   c._____   3-4 times a week
   d._____   5 or more times a week

3.   **How many times did you use the Library services (in person or online) for this class' library assignment?**
   a._____   Never
   b._____   1-2 times a week
   c._____   3-4 times a week
   d._____   5 or more times a week

4.   **How many times did you contact a Librarian for this class' library assignment?**
   a._____   Never
   b._____   1-2 times a week
   c._____   3-4 times a week
   d._____   5 or more times a week

5.   **Did your research process for this class differ from your research processes for other classes?**
   YES   NO

   If you answered yes, please explain how:

   _____

   _____

6. **What made working on this poster easier?**

    _____

7. **What made working on this poster difficult?**

    _____

8. **What aspect of the Faculty/Librarian collaboration did you like best?**

    _____

9. **What aspect of the Faculty/Librarian collaboration did you like least?**

    _____

10. **Would you recommend Faculty/Librarian collaboration for other classes?**
    YES   NO

    Please explain further your answer above:

    _____

11. **What is the name of the Librarian who worked with the class on the library assignment?**

    _____

Section II: This section asks more about you. Please place an **X** on the line next to appropriate answers or fill in an answer.

12. **What is your year in college?**
    ____   Freshman
    ____   Sophomore
    ____   Junior
    ____   Senior

13. **What is your academic major in college?**

    Please specify _____

    Undeclared _____

14.   What is your racial/ethnic background?

_____ *Black, non-Hispanic*: a person having origins in any of the black racial groups of Africa (except those of Hispanic origin).

_____ *American Indian or Alaskan Native:* a person having origins in any of the original peoples of North America who maintains cultural identification through tribal affiliation or community recognition.

_____ *Asian or Pacific Islander*: A person having origins in any of the original peoples of the Far East, Southeast Asia, the Indian Subcontinent, or Pacific Islands. This includes people from China, Japan, Korea, the Philippine Islands, American Samoa, India, and Vietnam.

_____ *Hispanic*: A person of Mexican, Puerto Rican, Cuban, Central or South American, or other Spanish culture or origin, regardless of race.

_____ *White, non-Hispanic*: A person having origins in any of the original peoples of Europe, North Africa, or the Middle East (except those of Hispanic origin).

_____ *Race/Ethnicity Unknown or Unavailable*: A person whose race or ethnic identity is either unknown or information about that person is unavailable.

15.   What is your age?   _____

16.   What is your gender?

_____   Female

_____   Male

Thank you for your cooperation.

Bibliography

American Library Association. "Information Literacy Competency Standards for Higher Education." http://www.ala.org/ala/mgrps/divs/acrl/standards/informationliteracycompetency.cfm (May 21, 2010).

Beric, Bojana. *Empowerment in College Health Classes: Perceptions and Determinants.* Saarbrucken, Germany: VDM Verlag Dr. Muller, 2009.

Beric, Bojana. "The Relationship between Students' Participation in Class Discussion and Perceived Control in Personal Health Issues Classes." *The International Journal of Interdisciplinary Social Sciences* 3 (2008): 61-74.

Callison, Rachel, Dan Budny and Kate Thomes. "Library Research Project for First-year Engineering Students: Results from Collaboration by Teaching and Library Faculty." *The Reference Librarian* 43 (2005): 93–106.

Dugan, Mary. "Embedded Librarians in an Ag Econ Class: Transcending the Traditional." *Journal of Agricultural & Food Information* 9 (2008): 301–309.

Freire, Paulo. *Pedagogy of the Oppressed.* New York, NY: Continuum Publishing Company, 1999.

Given, Lisa M. and Heidi Julien. "Finding Common Ground: An Analysis of Librarians' Expressed Attitudes Towards Faculty." *The Reference Librarian* 43 (2005): 25–38.

Green, Lawrence W., Marshall W. Kreuter, Sigrid G. Deeds and Kay B. Partridge. *Health Education Planning: A Diagnostic Approach.* Palo Alto, CA: Mayfield Publishing Company, 1980.

Gunawardena, Charlotte N., Penne L. Wilson and Ana C. Nolla. "Culture and Online Education." In *Handbook of Distance Education,* edited by Michael G. Moore & William G. Anderson, 753–775. Mahwah, New Jersey: Lawrence Erlbaum Associates, 2003.

Kotter, Wade R. "Bridging the Great Divide: Improving Relations between Librarians and Classroom Faculty." *Journal of Academic Librarianship* 25 (1999): 294–303.

Lipman, Matthew. *Thinking in Education.* Cambridge, UK: Cambridge University Press, 2003.

Lipman, Matthew. *Philosophy Goes to School.* Philadelphia, PA: Temple University Press, 1988.

Manus, Sara J. Beutter. "Librarian in the Classroom: An Embedded Approach to Music Information Literacy for First-Year Undergraduates." *Notes* 66 (2009): 249–261.

Rootman, Irving and Diane Leven-Zamir. "Health Literacy: Concept, Measurement and Practice." Symposia, International Union for Health Promotion and Education Global Conference, Vancouver, British Columbia, Canada, June 11, 13, 14, 2007.

Smith, Susan Sharpless and Lynn Sutton. "Embedded Librarians: On the Road in the Deep South." *College & Research Libraries News* 69 (2008): 71–4, 85.

Stage, Frances K., Patricia A. Muller, Jillian Kinzie and Ada Simmons. "Creating Learning Centered Classrooms: What Does Learning Theory Have to Say?" *ASHE-ERIC Higher Education Report* 26 (1998).

Vygotsky, Lev S., Michael Cole, Vera John-Steiner, Sylvia Scribner, et al. *Mind in Society: The Development of Higher Psychological Processes.* Cambridge, MA: Harvard University Press, 1978.

THIRTEEN

Starring the Literature Review: An Integrative Approach

Deborah S. Garson and Eileen McGowan

Research Question and Research Strategy

The concepts of asking good questions and effectively locating relevant information go hand in hand. If you work with doctoral students, you undoubtedly know many who, despite approaching the literature with good questions, have frittered away precious time using archaic methods searching for the most current literature on their topics. These students, who could Facebook and Twitter in their sleep, are likely oblivious to the power of citation indexes. Why does this gap in skill levels exist in this technologically savvy demographic? Unfortunately, the root cause is that less than effective academic pedagogical practices for researching the literature persist in academe. Isolated research skills workshops are offered, often online. Literature review courses are devoid of the essential embedded librarian. Why?

We suggest there is no conspiracy to deprive students of the requisite skills or to isolate librarians. Rather, we believe the importance of a collaborative pedagogical paradigm for integrating topic development with search strategy has not yet been widely recognized within the academy. There are few examples of effective collaboration to emulate between faculty instructors and research librarians. In this chapter, the head research librarian and a faculty research methodologist at the Har-

vard Graduate School of Education describe and analyze the development and implementation of a course aimed at bridging this obstructive and unnecessary divide.

The Literature Review as Research

Documented and anecdotal evidence reveals that doctoral students in all research areas struggle with creating a scholarly and comprehensive review of the literature relevant to their fields.[1] A 2006 article states that disciplinary fields have been negatively affected by poorly researched and written literature reviews.[2]

Thomas Boote and Penny Beile argue that the literature reviews of most educational doctoral students are insufficient and deficient.[3] Their 2004 findings concluded that most doctoral candidates were not "on the cutting edge of current research in their field," and that most candidates have not "learned to critically analyze and synthesize research in their fields."[4] The education dissertation literature reviews simply summarized large amounts of information rather than analyzing and synthesizing the information. The quality of dissertation literature reviews has had an impact on the educational research community. If education dissertations are offering less than high quality research to the education community, there is cause for concern on the part of academe. The process of analysis and synthesis is required of any researcher in order to add new and informative insight to bodies of knowledge. A 2007 study concluded: "educational researchers need to place greater emphasis on the literature review."[5] Sadly, "the dirty secret is known by those who sit on dissertation committees that most literature reviews are poorly conceptualized and written."[6]

The quality of doctoral literature reviews and literature reviews in general is widely discussed and critiqued by the research and academic communities. The question of why literature reviews are often lacking has not been subjected to sufficient research as to offer the community reasonable and documented causes. We can only surmise what is lacking within the doctoral process that causes students to produce less than stellar literature reviews, and subsequently dissertations that do not strengthen social sciences research. Boote and Beile's study focused explicitly on education doctoral dissertations, but the findings can certainly be used as a possible indicator for other social sciences dissertation work.

Research Challenges and the Literature Review

To consider and identify factors relevant to the quality of literature reviews, we can begin with the new landscape of academic research. The ever-evolving and fast-paced role of technology in producing and providing information is both an opportunity and a challenge to today's student, scholar, and researcher in academe. The doctoral process is recognized as a complex and challenging venture in all disciplines. Most graduate students face several challenges in their doctoral career, including finding their intellectual home as defined by their research question. Given the recognized hurdles doctoral students face when constructing a research question and conducting research, the shifting landscape of technology adds another hurdle. The undertaking of doctoral research today

presents a challenge to even the most information literate student. Technological advances continue to alter and have an impact on the information landscape almost daily.

Despite the increasing complexity doctoral students face in navigating the literature review process, the academic community has continued to rely on student initiative or supplementary resources. Current instructional approaches to the literature review process range from "how to" documents, dissertation boot camps, online tutorials, in-class explanation/discussion, literature review rubrics, information literacy workshops which address the literature review in a generic format, and recommended articles and/or books. These silo approaches can be instructionally viable and valuable, but taken independently they do not constitute a holistic approach where both research content and strategies are integrated into the process of conducting and writing a literature review. The doctoral student must understand the place of the literature review in research: what good research is; what is involved in researching fields of literature; and the necessary skills of an effective researcher.

Joseph Maxwell states, according to Golde, that "research skills are often neglected" or less than adequate in doctoral students' work.[7] Kwan goes further and writes, "finding the 'right' direction of reviewing is a particularly grueling experience, a practical concern seldom addressed in thesis manuals."[8] Doctoral students, as part of their induction into the community of scholars, must learn to communicate their ideas using the discourse genre and conventions of academe, and an important convention is the literature review. Beyond the immediate need for the doctoral student to have sufficient and efficient research skills is the question of what is required of academe to produce qualified researchers in all disciplines. Across academic disciplines, the current literature highlights the ongoing challenge of training and educating researchers who subsequently produce quality research in their fields. The challenge has become more complex with information technology's impact in every sphere of research from the hard sciences to the social sciences.

Research Challenges and Information Literacy

The complexity of the research landscape requires skills identified and defined by the field of information literacy. A researcher's skill level with searching, finding, and evaluating can have a direct impact on the resulting research.[9] The challenges of researching for a literature review require a mastery of information literacy skills. An extensive body of literature on information literacy principles and best practices in academe is widely disseminated to support this argument. The focus of the documented research and practice, however, is information literacy instruction for undergraduates. There is minimal research on, and subsequently, a lack of best practices regarding graduate students' information literacy skills. A notable exception is Barbara Blummer's article offering an overview of library instruction for graduate students from the 1950s to 2000.[10]

As with the literature review, academe has addressed the issue of information literacy and the graduate student through the lens of long-held assumptions. One assumption is that the graduate student, having been an undergraduate, knows how to do research. The academy's understanding is that a student seeking an advanced degree has been indoctrinated into the research process via undergraduate information literacy experiences, such as library workshops and course or curriculum-based research requirements. Underlying assumptions and existing current approaches do not adequately address graduate students' unique instructional needs for acquiring advanced research skills. Indeed, these commonly held assumptions and approaches by academe have proven to be less than effective in ensuring strong graduate research. This is evident in the academy's focus on and discussion of literature review quality and the subsequent conclusion of an overall lack of quality. Undergraduate coursework does not necessarily ensure that a graduate student has information literacy skills such as building a search strategy, using Boolean logic to construct the search question, employing keyword vs. subject searching, or understanding the benefits and limitations of cross-database searching. Library workshops give students an opportunity to gain information literacy skills. Many library instructional opportunities, however, are optional and/or not at the students' point-of-need. Although students do acquire "informal knowledge" about doing research, this "informal knowledge" merely allows students to achieve a semblance of research skill but not an authentic understanding of the process.[11] As a librarian and a faculty member, we argue that to achieve the necessary critical thinking skills required by a researcher there must be an integrated approach to teaching information research. In 1958 an information literacy survey conducted at twenty-four university libraries produced the following opinion; "...the optimal method of training [graduate students] centered on collaborative efforts with the faculty" by librarians.[12] A 1972 repeat of the survey concluded that little progress with information literacy programs for doctoral students had been made over the years, and at best these "efforts remained poorly organized" and lacked innovation and "imagination."[13]

Researching is not just a skill but also an intellectual approach to information. Instruction on how to research requires a pedagogy focused on teaching for understanding. Today's researcher must be able to use the requisite information literacy skills and to have a basic understanding of information seeking behavior, collaborative technologies, human-computer interaction, knowledge construction, and resource evaluation. As instructors in a graduate education program, we hypothesize that the current academic response to learning how to research does not go far enough or deep enough to support the development of "intellectual inquiry that manifests itself in creative scholarship and research."[14]

Faculty/Librarian Collaboration in a Research Institution

Our institution's teaching and learning environment fosters a high level of expectation and support for both master's and doctoral students to develop advanced information literacy skills. The institution is mission and goal oriented to building and sustaining a community of learners and researchers. A tenet of the School states *'the nexus of practice, policy, and research is the most powerful way to advance education.'* The Library is an integral unit within the School's academic life. Research and Instruction Librarians are colleagues of the teaching faculty, researchers, and administrators of the School. The School's faculty and teaching staff have a history of a strong working relationship with library staff. The librarians have key roles in the School's educational and instructional mission and goals. Librarians are embedded in the doctoral orientation, the School-wide orientation, classroom library sessions, research consultations, and contribute to School initiatives, faculty committees, and administrative projects

During the fall doctoral orientation, the librarians establish relationships with incoming doctoral students, a cohort of about twenty, and maintain a relationship with individual doctoral students throughout the student's academic tenure at the School, and often beyond. In other words, doctoral students can and are encouraged to work with an individual librarian during their academic career at the School. Shumaker and Talley's final report on *Models of Embedded Librarianship* lists the librarian's strong relationship with a community or customer base as an important characteristic of embeddedness.[15] Our institution has fostered and supported a highly collaborative and respectful relationship between the librarians and the School that presents numerous embedded opportunities for the librarians. The School's highly collaborative

framework of librarians and faculty and doctoral students provided us with a unique opportunity to address the challenges of the doctoral literature review process.

An Innovative Course: Librarian/Faculty Proposal

The impetus for our course began with a student's request for a research methods class that included library research skills. In appealing to Eileen, the faculty instructor teaching the research methods class, the doctoral student also proposed the idea of officially including the research librarian in the course structure. The student emphasized the instructional disconnect between the research methods course and the acquisition of information literacy skills. Based on this conversation, Eileen approached the head of research and instruction services at the library, Deborah, and together we developed the idea of a co-taught seminar specific to the literature review. We informally surveyed a number of doctoral students and found that they echoed a frustration of trying to integrate research questions with effective search strategy. The students expressed the reality that a single library session did not address the diversity of challenges they encounter conducting research for their literature reviews. Additionally, the library sessions were often not held at the doctoral student's specific point-of-need, which varied considerably depending upon the student's academic progress and topic. Realizing that a new paradigm was necessary to overcome this dichotomous approach that isolated the research question from the research search, we worked collaboratively to bridge this divide.

Based upon these identified student concerns, we developed and wrote a course proposal and received official approval from the School of Education. We designed the year-long seminar to prepare doctoral students to research and write a critical literature review, whether constructed as a qualifying paper or as background for a qualifying paper proposal or a dissertation proposal. The holistic model we have developed for our course, *Researching and Writing a Critical Literature Review,* addresses the defined issues above through an innovative approach by combining the critical expertise of two disciplines, library science and research methods in education. Structured to guide students throughout the research process, the seminar is focused on identifying and developing individual research interests, searching for relevant information resources, refining research questions and strategies, and the writing of a research proposal or literature review.

Our seminar scaffolds the development of information literacy strategies with the exploration and refinement of the research topic. We designed our course meetings to investigate the construction and purpose of a literature review, exploring questions such as

- why is a literature review integral to producing quality research?
- what are the debates in the field regarding the structure/function of a literature review?
- how are students' interests coalescing and evolving into meaningful research topics; what bodies of knowledge are relevant to their interests?
- how can specific research questions be formalized to guide their inquiry?

We focused course meetings on developing principles and practices associated with information research and applying those processes directly to each individual student's evolving research agenda. We believe this approach informed and supported the critical thinking skills necessary to develop a relevant and distinguished literature study and, subsequently, the dissertation.

Designing a Course with an Embedded Librarian

The course, *Researching and Writing a Critical Literature Review,* engages both instructors and stu-

dents every other week in a limited enrollment three-hour seminar with the overarching goals of individual student progress and the development of a community of learners. With our knowledge of the challenges specific to the literature review, we are committed to assisting doctoral students in the analysis and synthesis of the literature in their selected fields, and to support and reinforce good research. The students' interests are diverse and often multi-disciplinary. The topics range from public policy to issues of human psychology and development, to teaching and learning in urban contexts and more, all of which require the students to develop and utilize inter-disciplinary research knowledge and skills. The seminar content is primarily the students' own research agendas that are developed through the class sessions and the syllabus framework. We introduce students to research as integral to academe, but challenge their thinking about research as requiring "a leap of faith" into the new landscape of research and scholarship. Our pedagogical approach is to guide students to examine and consult classic research literature in their fields, "standing on the shoulders of giants," and simultaneously, we engage and explore the new research landscape and its impact on scholarship, such as open access publishing and a wide range of electronic resources. Although there is emphasis on the individual student's topic, we incorporate best practices to develop a community of learners and researchers within and beyond our classroom. As a community, we explore, debate, and define what research is and how an individual assumes the mindset, role, and confidence of a researcher.

We frame the seminar's work through the doctoral students' approach towards knowledge construction. Our students enter with passions, ideals, and commitments to a broad range of educational issues, and then conduct preliminary research to provide a foundation for their own research agendas. In many ways, they are looking for their intellectual home. As a community, we support the individual student's construction of this intellectual home. The tools required are those of both research methods and research skills. It is important to lead students past the standard articles and fields of literature to the gray or emerging literature that can take them to the cutting edge of research, and widen and further their own thinking. Exploring the research value of established literature with our students as well as the developing literature is a key to moving the students into researching beyond Google. The introduction of citation indexes is often an "aha" moment. This past fall, we used the analogy of car headlights and rear lights to illustrate how previous and current research help guide the researcher on their individual journey. To further this analogy, we demonstrated and explored citation mapping of authors and topics that created a lot of in-class discussion and excitement. Introducing research skills or resources at the critical point-of-need is a 'best practice' for ensuring student understanding of information literacy's relevance to their individual research process. Within this course we have that opportunity and we strive to ensure that our students' learning constitutes a deep understanding of the presented concepts and ideas.

The seminar is designed to build a lifelong orientation towards researching that is highly interactive. Researchers must understand how to find and use information in a continually shifting landscape of new formats for information packaging and delivery. To address these goals and learning objectives, we specifically teach graduate students how to develop and refine their topics through concept mapping; the importance of record-keeping using Refworks or other bibliographic management tools; and how to stay current with new developments relevant to academic research.

Co-Teaching—Welcome to Our Classroom

The challenge of co-teaching has been highlighted in the educational literature from K–12 to higher education to lifelong learning. Recently the *Chron-*

icle of Higher Education published an article titled "Co-teaching is more work not less."[16] A 2003 *Academic Exchange Quarterly* article discussed the shared teaching experience of two instructors.[17] Both the *Chronicle* and the *Academic Exchange Quarterly* articles address the challenges faced by instructors engaged in co-teaching.

Deborah's instructional experience and expertise was largely with one-time workshops, classroom sessions, or one-on-one consultations. Eileen's experience, on the other hand, was with traditional classrooms. Our collaborative effort began with very little shared instructional experience. An article on faculty-librarian collaboration highlights the greater challenges this teaching method presents and the effort required in order to be instituted and effective. In the article, Hollander, Herbert, and DePalma address specific 'obstacles' often encountered in a faculty and librarian partnership for teaching purposes. Obstacles identified by the authors include faculty members undervaluing librarians as instructors, viewing librarians as support staff rather than teaching staff, and assuming that graduate students are research literate.[18] Eileen, in fact, did not subscribe to any of these points of view or obstacles. Generally speaking, from the librarian's perspective of co-teaching with faculty, librarians may tend to view themselves as important but supporting colleagues, and thus not necessarily a full participant in the classroom teaching experience. From practice-based teaching experience, librarians' instructional expertise is often to teach independently, whether a workshop or classroom session or an individual consultation. As co-instructors we did not have to overcome all of the Hollander obstacles above, but we did face other challenges in developing the course.

As cited earlier, the *Chronicle of Higher Education* article captured the challenges and rewards we have experienced in our collaborative venture between a librarian and a faculty member.[19] The article author, Jackson, argues that co-teaching is harder than individual instruction "because to really do it right, to do it well, means many more hours of preparation beforehand: debating the very structure of the course, comparing notes/takes on the material, and doing justice to two distinct perspectives on the subject matter."[20] For us, co-teaching is an iterative process, but each class's experience affirmed our instructional goals to explain and highlight the critical importance of both interplay and integration with 'doing research' and 'producing research.' After three years of sharing a classroom, both physically and intellectually, we are a very complementary team in our instructional approach. While we have developed shared instructional goals and objectives, our distinct professional experiences continue to enrich and expand our course content and teaching. Although we are the course instructors, we are just as often learners within our classroom—learning from each other and from our students.

What were the hesitations we each brought to the table? What were the questions we had for each other? What did we initially share? What did we have to educate the other about? How did we establish common goals? These are a few of the many questions we addressed in our initial collaborative work. An important foundation piece was to articulate individual educational beliefs for the course learning objectives, and then work to integrate these into a shared learning base. From initial pedagogical discussions, we established a shared overarching goal that good educational research requires good educational research skills and we implemented best practices to ensure this learning outcome. We continued to find 'common ground' as we worked to integrate our distinct individual expertise and styles of teaching and our commonly shared and defined learning outcomes for the course. Our goal to achieve a holistic approach to the literature review process and to the learning outcome of students gaining lifelong research skills gave us the foundation to find the commonality in our individual experiences and backgrounds.

The Ever Evolving Course: A Balancing Act

Our own conceptualizations of an effective integration of research question development and information literacy are continually evolving and being refined as the course continues to be offered and taught. In the initial development of the seminar format we considered several approaches to the information literacy component. We were in agreement about the importance of the information literacy content being equal to the research methods content, and thus requiring equal instructional time. The students need to recognize the value and legitimacy of research skills to the educational research process. An initial draft of the syllabus divided the three-hour class into distinct hours of instruction with the 'education' hour followed by a 'library' hour. While this model would still have been an embedded instructional opportunity, it did not provide a true co-teaching experience between a faculty member and a librarian.

Additionally, we immediately recognized that the separateness of the subjects might replicate the very divide we were striving to bridge. As we engaged in long conversations, often late into the evening, the syllabus began to reflect truly integrated content and collaboration. The syllabus emphasized research skills and the information literacy knowledge critical to understanding and advancing the process of a literature review through both readings and class activities. The syllabus reflected and confirmed the commitment to an embedded librarian within the course.

We continue to refine and adapt the seminar during the academic year. In an intense review during the summers, we look to our past year's teaching experience and investigate new research regarding the doctoral process and information literacy. In our commitment to co-teaching we have established a practice of shared reflection and conversation throughout the week. We value our after-class hour as time to share individual instructor perceptions of class activities, offer comments on specific student issues, and examine the day's class dynamics. Often, we discover new instructional insights based on the other instructor's view of a classroom activity or discussion. We revise content and/or classroom activities to ensure the course is supporting student work and the course goals throughout the academic year. Each year's community of students brings new challenges to our instructional practices and course content.

Using course evaluations and other qualitative feedback from our students we continue to investigate and document our learning goals framed by the following questions:

- Can an integrated course that promotes conceptually based understanding and an integration of research skills and methodology facilitate the researching and writing of the literature review?

- Does the course fill a need for formalized instruction on researching and writing a literature review?

- Do the course-enrolled respondents believe the course improves their understanding and development of the literature review?

- Do the course-enrolled respondents believe they have the skills and knowledge necessary to do good educational research?

Evaluation of a Co-Taught Course

Currently, we are investigating student learning outcomes based on teaching the course for three years. From the course evaluation data we have developed a theoretical perspective on the course's learning outcomes, and implicitly the embeddedness factor. The initial data and feedback support that the course content, format and pedagogical approach result in students producing an effective literature review. Our data is drawn from three sources: student course applications, in-class feedback memos, and end-of-year course evaluations.

Over the first three years of the course, 33 doctoral students have enrolled in *Researching*

and Writing a Critical Literature Review taught at the Harvard Graduate School of Education. The students range from second year to fourth year in their doctoral program; their fields of study range from higher education to mind, brain and education to teacher education to educational leadership. Students apply to and are accepted into the course based on an instructor-designed questionnaire. The course has been oversubscribed, and not all interested students were accepted.

Our primary data is from the student evaluations. The student evaluations contain fourteen questions including narrative-response boxes and Likert scales. The institution's student evaluation is aimed to assess students' perceptions of teaching, program, and course quality. The course evaluations have four primary purposes: 1) to help instructors improve the design of their courses and strengthen their teaching, 2) provide information about courses to students, 3) encourage student reflection upon their own learning and, 4) as part of the professional review process for faculty members. All responses are entirely confidential, and no identifying information is ever reported or shared.

As stated earlier, four research questions have guided our preliminary descriptive study's data analysis. Given the relatively small sample, analysis of the quantitative data is best accomplished through descriptive study rather than inferential statistics. Additional analysis of the qualitative data allowed us to understand better the impact and perceived benefit of the course in descriptive study.[21] Preliminary findings suggest that students find the course to be both necessary and effective, that they have learned a valuable skill, and that they are well poised to be proficient researchers. Although the initial sampling collected and examined for this book chapter as well as the anecdotal feedback is quite favorable, it is primarily an assessment of students' perceptions of their learning and understanding. It is not an assessment of the student's ability to critically analyze and synthesize research. This assessment is for future research.

It is obvious that our students have reaped the benefits of this faculty/librarian collaboration. The course evaluations have documented the students' academic progress and their appreciation for our innovative approach. From course evaluations we have gathered student-based feedback, which continues to guide course content refinement and development. Over the past three years the course has garnered student comments such as "I've learned several best practices, not just for conducting literature reviews, but also for approaching academic research, in general." This one comment is indicative of the course's highly positive student feedback. Our students are engaged, active, and together we build a community of learners throughout the academic year and beyond.

Summary Discussion

The course was developed and continues as part of our on-going shared goal to educate and support doctoral graduate students in their understanding and development of a literature review. Based on the descriptive study results the instructors' argue that in addition to the literature review the course contributes to broader doctoral challenges in the following ways:

- Modeling and supporting interdisciplinary research
- Integrating research strategies and the use of technology as a tool at point-of-use
- Embedding research skills into dissertation development
- Advancing understanding of the doctoral process and responsibilities as future faculty within academe or professionals of practice
- Addressing identified issues such as the lack of scholarly substance in literature reviews
- Teaching critical thinking skills necessary to develop a substantial and relevant literature review
- Providing a model for teaching about the role and development of an effective literature review within the doctoral process and beyond
- Building a community of learners, and thus lessening the isolation often reported by doctoral students
- Promoting a model of librarian embeddedness within academe

As instructors we believe we have a responsibility to address the information literacy challenges of researching for and developing the literature review by integrating research skills with research questions. Each class presents content, interactive activities, and discussion with the goal to integrate research skills and research questions. This approach guides the research trajectory of doctoral students precisely at the most critical point-of-use moment—the research and development of the literature review. Ultimately, our students must understand the place of the literature review in research and the place of their research questions within the broad spectrum of the education field, and the importance of information literacy in accomplishing these goals. Lovitts states that by "focusing on the skills and abilities relevant for success as a researcher, graduate programs may produce more creative and innovative work in graduate schools and beyond."[22] We suggest a beginning is an integrated literature review process as exemplified in our course, *Researching and Writing a Critical Literature Review.*

Proactive initiatives such as this are critical to university culture and provide students with the knowledge necessary for academic success. We all acknowledge, as Golde states, that "...competently working with or knowing the literature of a field is important for scholarship in all disciplines"[23] Our shared vision and implementation of a course to address the literature review process can be a model for other initiatives. The preliminary descriptive study supports our course's effective learning outcomes and highlights the importance of collaboratively incorporating effective instructional practices early in the doctoral process as well as the value of embeddedness at point-of-need. This model is scalable to other types of academic communities whether on-site or online. We believe this innovative model will contribute to the importance of embedding librarians into academic programs.

Notes

1. Kjell Erik Rudestam and Rae R. Newton, *Surviving your dissertation: A comprehensive guide to content and process* (2nd ed.). (Newbury Park, CA: Sage, 2001)

2. Yair Levy and Timothy J. Ellis, "A systems approach to conduct an effective literature review in support of information systems research". *Informing Science Journa*l, 9 (2006): 181–212.

3. David N. Boote and Penny Beile, "Scholars Before Researchers: On the Centrality of the Dissertation Literature Review in Research Preparation". *Educational Researcher*, 34(6) (2005): 3–15. Retrieved July 11, 2009, from ERIC database.

4. David N. Boote and Penny Beile, "The quality of dissertation literature reviews: A missing link in research preparation". (paper presented at the annual meeting of the American Educational Research Association, San Diego, CA, 2004): p.5.

5. M. Harris Fitt, Andrew E. Walker and Heather M. Leary, "Assessing the Quality of Doctoral Dissertation Literature Reviews in Instructional Technology". (paper presented at the Annual Meeting of the American Educational Research Association, San Diego, CA, April 2009). p.10. This paper is posted at DigitalCommons@USU.

6. Fitt, 4.

7. Christopher Golde and Timothy M. Dore, "At Cross Purposes: What the Experiences of Today's Doctoral Students Reveal about Doctoral Education". (www.phd-survey.org) Philadelphia, PA: A report prepared for The Pew Charitable Trusts.

8. Becky Kwan, "The nexus of reading, writing and researching in the doctoral undertaking of humanities and social sciences: Implications for literature reviewing. *English for Specific Purposes*, 27(1) (2008): 42–56. doi:10.1016/j.esp.2007.05.002.

9. Richard A. Dreifuss, "Library instruction and graduate students: More work for George". *RQ* 21(2) (1981): p.121–123.

10. Barbara Blumer, "Providing Library Instruction to Graduate Students: A Review of the Literature". *Public Services Quarterly* 5 (1) (2009): p.15–39.

11. Barbara E. Lovitts. "The Transition to Independent Research: Who Makes It, Who Doesn't, and Why." *The Journal of Higher Education* 79, no. 3 (2008): 296–325. http://muse.jhu.edu/ (accessed July 21, 2010).

12. Barbara Blumer, "Providing Library Instruction to Graduate Students: A Review of the Literature". *Public Services Quarterly* 5 (1) (2009):15–39.

13. Blumer, 16–17.

14. Barbara E. Lovitts, "Who makes it through?" *Academe*, 93(1), (2007): 80–82. Retrieved July 11, 2009, from Academic Search Premier database.

15. David Shumaker, and Mary Talley, *Models of embedded librarianship: Final report*. Chicago: Special Libraries Association. (2009) Retrieved from http://www.sla.org/pdfs/EmbeddedLibrarianshipFinalRptRev.pdf.

16. John L. Jackson, Jr., "Co-teaching is more work, not less". *Chronicle of Higher Education*, 4 February 2010, p.1.

17. Greg Conderman and Bonnie McCarty, "Shared insights from university co teaching". *Academic Exchange Quarterly.* 7 (4) (2003): 2461-3z.

18. S. A. Hollander, B.R. Herbert and K. S. DePalma, "Faculty-librarian Collaboration". *APS Observer*, 17 (3)(2004):

19. Jackson, Ibid.1.

20. Jackson, Ibid. 1.

21. William E. Hanson and John W. Creswell, "Mixed methods research designs in counseling psychology". *Journal of Counseling Psychology, 52* (2005): 224–235.

22. Barbara E. Lovitts, "The Transition to Independent Research: Who Makes It, Who Doesn't, and Why." *Journal of Higher Education* (Columbus, Ohio), 79(3) (2008): 296–325. Retrieved July 11, 2009, from Education Abstracts database.

23. Chris M. Golde, "Signature Pedagogies in Doctoral Education: Are They Adaptable for the Preparation of Education Researchers?" *Educational Researcher*, 36(6) (2007): 344-351._ doi: 10.3102/0013189X07308301.

Bibliography

Beile, Penny M., and David N. Boote. 2002. Library instruction and graduate professional development: Exploring the effect of learning environments on self-efficacy and learning outcomes. *Alberta Journal of Educational Research* 48 (4) (12/01): 364–67.

Beile, Penny M., David N. Boote, and Elizabeth K. Killingsworth. 2004. A microscope or a mirror?: A question of study validity regarding the use of dissertation citation analysis for evaluating research collections. *Journal of Academic Librarianship* 30 (5) (09): 347–53.

———. 2003. *Characteristics of education doctoral dissertation references: An inter-institutional analysis of review of literature citations.*

———. 2003. *Characteristics of education doctoral dissertation references: An inter-institutional analysis of review of literature citations.* ERIC, .

Blummer, Barbara. 2009. Providing library instruction to graduate students: A review of the literature. *Public Services Quarterly* 5 (1) (01/01): 15–39.

Bodemer, Brett, Karen Brown, and Jennifer Crowther. 2009. Eyes wide open. *Public Services Quarterly* 5 (2) (01/01): 148–54.

Boote, David N., and Penny Beile. 2006. On "literature reviews of, and for, educational research": A response to the critique by Joseph Maxwell. *Educational Researcher* 35 (9) (12): 32–5.

———. 2005. Scholars before researchers: On the centrality of the dissertation literature review in research preparation. *Educational Researcher* 34 (6) (August): 3–15.

Bruce, Christine Susan. 1994. Research students' early experiences of the dissertation literature review. *Studies in Higher Education* 19 (2) (06): 217.

Bruce, Christine, Ian Stoodley, and Binh Pham. 2009. Doctoral students' experience of information technology research. *Studies in Higher Education* 34 (2) (03): 203–21.

Cole, Karen. 1992. Doctoral students in education and factors related to the literature review process.

Dillon, Patrick. 2008. A pedagogy of connection and boundary crossings: Methodological and epistemological transactions in working across and between disciplines. *Innovations in Education & Teaching International* 45 (3) (08): 255–62.

Dreifuss, Richard A. 1981. Library instruction and graduate students: More work for George. *RQ* 21 (2) (12/01): 121–23.

Earp, Vanessa J. 2008. Information source preferences of education graduate students. *Behavioral & Social Sciences Librarian* 27 (2) (08): 73–91.

Fleming-May, Rachel, and Lisa Yuro. 2009. From student to scholar: The academic library and social sciences PhD students' transformation. *Portal: Libraries and the Academy* 9 (2) (04/01): 199–221.

Golde, Chris M. 2007. Signature pedagogies in doctoral education: Are they adaptable for the preparation of education researchers. *Educational Researcher* 36 (6) (August): 344–51.

Green, Rosemary. 2006. Fostering a community of doctoral learners. *Journal of Library Administration* 45 (1) (11): 169–83.

Green, Rosemary, and Mary Bowser. 2006. Observations from the field: Sharing a literature review rubric. *Journal of Library Administration* 45 (1) (11): 185–202.

Hanson, William E., John W. Creswell, and Vicki L. Plano Clark. 2005. Mixed methods research designs in counseling psychology. *Journal of Counseling Psychology* 52 (2) (04): 224–35.

Harrington, Marni R. 2009. Information literacy and research-intensive graduate students: Enhancing the role of research librarians. *Behavioral & Social Sciences Librarian* 28 (4) (Oct): 179–201.

Kesselman, Martin A., and Sarah Barbara Watstein. 2009. Creating opportunities: Embedded librarians. *Journal of Library Administration* 49 (4) (06): 383–400.

Kwan, Becky S. C. 2008. The nexus of reading, writing and researching in the doctoral undertaking of humanities and social sciences: Implications for literature reviewing. *English for Specific Purposes* 27 (1) (01): 42–56.

Leshem, Shosh, and Vernon Trafford. 2007. Overlooking the conceptual framework. *Innovations in Education & Teaching International* 44 (1) (02): 93–105.

Lovitts, Barbara E. 2008. The transition to independent research: Who makes it, who doesn't, and why. *Journal of Higher Education* 79 (3) (May): 296–325.

———. 2007. Who makes it through? *Academe* 93 (1) (Jan): 80–2.

———. 2005. How to grade a dissertation. *Academe* 91 (6) (Nov): 18–23.

Macauley, Peter, and Rosemary Green. 2009. Can our relationships be reconceptualized? librarians, information literacy, and doctoral learners. *Journal of Education for Library and Information Science* 50 (2) (Spring): 68–78.

Maxwell, Joseph A. 2006. Literature reviews of, and for, educational research: A commentary on Boote and Beile's "scholars before researchers". *Educational Researcher* 35 (9) (12): 28–31.

———. 2004. Causal explanation, qualitative research, and scientific inquiry in education. *Educational Researcher* 33 (2) (03): 3–11.

Pierce, Deborah L. 2009. Influencing the now and future faculty: Retooling information literacy. *Notes* 66 (2) (12): 233–48.

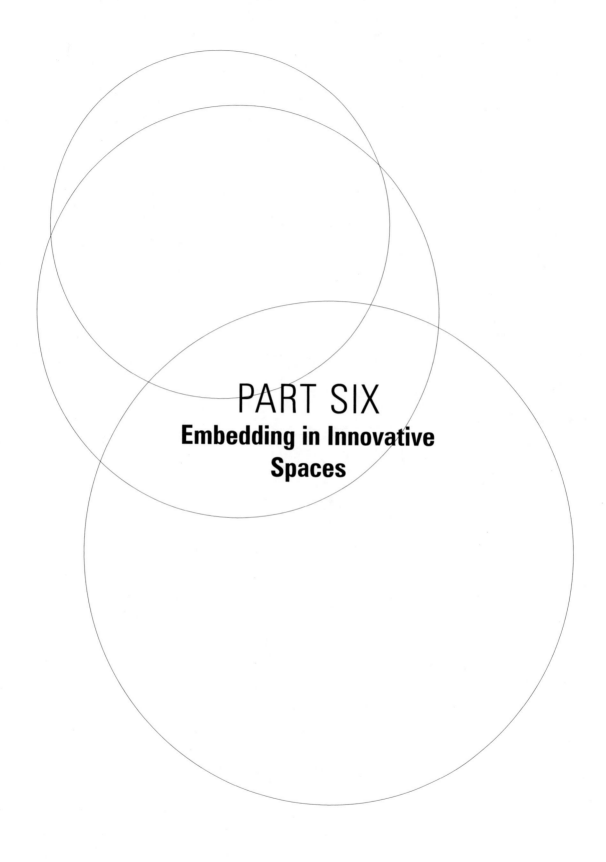

PART SIX
**Embedding in Innovative
Spaces**

 FOURTEEN

Embedded Right Where the Students Live: A Librarian in the University Residence Halls

Dallas Long

Introduction

"Good morning!," I exclaim cheerfully to the family who has just finished unloading boxes, a computer, and a micro-fridge onto to the sidewalk. The parents and daughter look anxious and uncertain about what to do next. I pull a small wagon over to their car and ask, "Do you want help moving your belongings into your dorm room?" It's Move-In Day, and more than 7,000 new students and their families are descending on the University of Illinois, preparing to move into the undergraduate residence halls and start a brand new year. "Are you our daughter's residence hall director?" the mother inquires. "No," I respond, "I'm your daughter's librarian!"

Most of the university's faculty and staff avoid the carefully controlled chaos of Move-In Day, and often the only staff to be found are the Student Affairs professionals and resident advisors greeting families and checking students into the rooms that will be their home for the next ten months. I love participating in Move-In Day because my participation means that I'm often the first librarian the students meet during their college years. It is a wonderful opportunity to show the students that I care about their experiences on campus, but also provide tours of the libraries to interested parents. What a great way to make an impression on the students by being a friendly face during their first

day on campus. Later, students tell me often that when they call home to their parents and express frustrations with their classes, their parents suggest that they visit the librarian that helped them move into their room.

I am the Residential Life Librarian at the University of Illinois. I serve approximately 7,000 first-year and 3,000 upper-division students who live in seventeen undergraduate residence halls and apartments on the campus. We do not have a first-year experience program at the University of Illinois. Instead, we have a strong academic component embedded at University Housing and Residential Life, two of our Student Affairs divisions. Resources for academic support are rich within University Housing. Many of the students participate in one of the nine living-learning communities, where floors or entire residence halls serve as classroom environments. The students who reside there share an interest in an academic theme, such as learning about the allied health professions or exploring globalization and the cultures of the world. The general education curriculum is often taught in classrooms within the residence halls, and students participate in a variety of programs that explore concepts connected to the themes of their living-learning communities. Academic advisors, career counselors, health educators, tutors for math, science, and writing—and yes, a librarian—are all available for the students who live there.

As the Residential Life Librarian, I am fully embedded in the residence halls. I manage eight small libraries in the residence halls, each with a collection that is carefully tailored to support the general education curriculum and especially the living-learning communities that operate in the halls. The collections include textbooks and supplemental reading material placed on reserve by instructors, popular reading material, guides that help students explore academic majors, and career and internship resources. I manage two full-time library assistants who support the libraries' acquisitions, cataloging, and processing of new materials. Teams of more than fifty student assistants staff the circulation desks. The libraries are principally open in the late afternoons until 2 o'clock in the morning—the hours when the undergraduate residence halls are typically busiest. The libraries are prime destinations for students seeking quiet places in which to study or work on group projects. The residence hall libraries' strength is their availability for students—located in the areas where they live, and operating at hours when other libraries on campus are closed. Another great strength is the residence hall libraries' collections related to diversity. The collection encompasses works of nonfiction and fiction written by or about historically oppressed groups or groups under-represented in literature, ranging from Pakistani poetry to collections of narratives by lesbian, gay, bisexual, and transgender writers to scholarly works on the Korean immigrant experience in America. The emphasis on diversity is a fundamental aspect of the libraries' mission: to ensure that the libraries reflect the identities of the many peoples who reside in the residence halls and to ensure the visibility of students who do not belong to the majority culture.

My office is a converted dorm room, and I eat all my afternoon meals alongside the students in the dining halls. I am a full member of the Student Affairs professional staff, and I participate in Student Affairs activities such as hiring and training resident advisors, chaperoning student events, and mediating roommate conflicts. I am extremely visible in the students' lives—I attend hall programs at night, advise a student organization, and generally "hang out" in the residence halls getting to know many of the students by their name and major. I receive the same professional development and training as other members of the student affairs staff, and I attend student affairs conferences as well as library conferences.

Unlike other librarians at the University of Illinois, I am not connected to an academic discipline and do not support the research of faculty. Instead, the student affairs professionals often jokingly call me "their" librarian because I often help them with literature searches and supply them with current news and articles relevant to their work. I maintain a strong relationship with the University Library and serve on many committees, but my position is otherwise exclusively devoted to working with students. My mission is to help the students develop strong academic skills as they transition to off-campus living and successfully navigate our complex research-intensive university. I am often engaged in the administration of my eight libraries, especially in collection development, but principally I see my role as an instruction and outreach librarian. I introduce first-year students to information literacy and research skills in a fundamentally different way than the instruction they receive as part of their general education curriculum.

Emerging Trend or Rediscovered Resource?

Despite the emerging trend of embedded librarianship, a librarian in the residence halls is a very old idea. The first residence hall libraries were founded in 1928 at Harvard University, where a library was developed within each of seven residences for male students.[1] The house libraries, as the residence hall libraries were called then, were considered the "the integration of tutors and students, under the guidance of resident librarians, to make these houses genuine living and learning centers and to breathe new life into the instructional methods of Harvard College."[2]

By the 1950s, libraries and librarians in undergraduate residence halls had appeared at dozens of colleges and universities throughout the United States.[3] Stanford supported librarians in residence halls as serving a strong academic purpose. He states,

There is increasing interest in experimental new types of campus housing that will contribute directly to the intellectual, cultural, and social development of students. New awareness of the educational potential of residence hall libraries is indicative of growing interest in creating student living quarters and facilities where enriched learning, as well as rooms for sleeping and eating, are provided.[4]

Subsequently residence hall libraries became the center of academic programs based in the halls.[5] At the University of Illinois, there was a strong emphasis on the residence hall libraries' role in community building and these libraries were marketed to new students as 'neighborhood' libraries in which they could find their local newspapers and other familiar items. The residents of the respective halls shaped the library collections, with most requests for new purchases coming from residents and fulfilled by librarians from the University Library. Consequently, each library evolved to illustrate the culture of the hall in which it was based.

Scant literature regarding residence hall libraries exists after the mid-1980s. This can arguably be attributed to the closure of residence hall libraries at many institutions. The reasons for the closures of most residence hall libraries vary, from lack of student interest and support, cuts in institutional budgets, and the need to convert facilities into living quarters to accommodate the growing number of first-year students.[6,7] Indiana University, the University of Michigan, and the University of Illinois

at Urbana-Champaign are the only institutions of higher education where residence hall libraries are known to still be operating as late as the 1990s.[8]

The residence hall libraries at the University of Illinois were founded in the 1960s, and a full-time librarian was hired a few short years afterwards. University Housing maintained the libraries' facilities and contributed wages for the student assistants and funds for collections, while the University Library paid the librarian's salary.[9] The Residential Life Librarian's reporting line and salary were transferred to University Housing in the early 1990s, making the librarian and the libraries fully integrated into the Student Affairs Division.[10] As one of the few remaining Residential Life Librarians, I take my role seriously and make myself highly visible to the student community. What better way to make a librarian accessible to the students than to place one right where the students live?

Teaching Information Literacy

I begin introducing library skills to the students by training the resident advisors to encourage good study habits among the students living on their floors. Resident advisors are often my best allies in reaching out to the students who live in the residence halls. They know the students on their floors intimately, and they are well trained in the advising, counseling, and other student services that exist for our students' emotional and physical well-being. Academic affairs, however, is often a mysterious dimension of the university for the resident advisors. This is where I step in to provide the resident advisors with a comprehensive training program; I train the resident advisors to be experts in the variety of academic resources that exist on campus. This means teaching the resident advisors to understand when and why they would visit a librarian and what resources exist in the libraries to support their own academic endeavors. During the several weeks of training that the resident advisors receive prior to Move-In Day, I hold a workshop in which the resident advisors brainstorm about good study strategies. I coach the resident advisors on how to talk to students about their classes, how to identify students who may be struggling academically, and how to recommend the students visit a librarian, tutor, professor, or academic advisor for assistance.

In turn, the resident advisors invite me to floor meetings in the first two or three weeks of the fall semester. At the floor meetings, I am able to meet with many of the new freshmen at once. We talk about effective study skills and time management, and I describe how librarians can help them develop thesis statements and locate information for their papers. I offer one-on-one research consultations right where they live—no need to come even as far as the libraries in the residence halls. I have a laptop that I bring with me to the common lounges, and we can have a research consultation wherever it is most convenient for the student.

The residence halls include living quarters for upper-division students, too. I take a different approach with the older students since they are not as likely to attend floor meetings or require their resident advisor's assistance as often as the freshmen. Free food always brings students out of their rooms. I put up flyers in the halls advertising dinner with the librarian, and I bring free pizzas to the student lounges. I do not generally have a large turnout of students, but there are always new and curious students who are happy to meet with me. We enjoy our pizza dinner, and I talk about what the library can do for them, hand out brochures and study tips, and answer questions about the library's hours, policies, and ways of contacting the librarians.

Getting to know the students personally and building a sense of trust are vital steps to being successful as their embedded librarian. I must be highly visible in those first few weeks of the semester—especially as I build a rapport with the freshmen. The key is showing up and simply getting to know the students. I attend hall programs, eat in the cafeterias, go to musical performances and guest speaker lectures, attend social events, and spend time—along with the rest of the Student Affairs staff—learning who my students are, where they come from, and what they hope to get out of college.

The first few weeks of the semester tend to be my slowest times of the year in terms of the number of students who actively seek me out for research consultations, but they are often my busiest time of the year creating visibility. By the time students are preparing their first papers of the semester, they begin to remember that I'm not just a friendly face; I'm a librarian too. My calendar fills up quickly with one-on-one research consultations, and I help the students develop better thesis statements, select the best sources, and develop searching skills for the library's online databases.

Personal research consultations are not my only way of providing instruction to the students. One of my most effective strategies for helping students develop information literacy skills is holding workshops in the residence halls' computer labs—but I disguise such workshops as fun activities. My most popular workshop is "Become an Editor on Wikipedia—Anyone Can Be an Expert!" The students select a subject—whether it's their favorite pop star or a baseball team—and they build a page for it on the social networking encyclopedia, Wikipedia. Of course it's difficult to find a subject that isn't already extensively covered on Wikipedia, but creating an unique entry isn't the point; I instruct them how to register as an editor on the site, identify the social conventions involved with writing an entry, and how to follow the discussion threads in which editors debate the finer points of an entry's validity.

Interwoven through the lesson, we discuss the features that make a "good" Wikipedia entry: fact checking, citations from credible sources, unbiased language, neutral points of view, and integrating opposing viewpoints.[11] They do not want their entries to be deleted or edited by someone else because their entry lacks credibility, so I teach them how to search other sites for information to include in their entries, how to evaluate those sources for credibility and authority, and how to appropriately cite those sources on their own entry. The students love it, and they learn research skills at the same time. Of course I caution the students against relying on Wikipedia entries as sources for their academic coursework; we discuss how Wikipedia's very nature as a social networking tool that can be altered by anyone at any time can undermine its credibility.

I emphasize the importance of information literacy in an everyday context for my students. I meet regularly with the instruction librarians at the Undergraduate Library at the University of Illinois to discuss core competencies for information literacy, essential library resources, and changes to the library's catalog and electronic journals. Such meetings, however, do not always provide appropriate context for mapping core competencies to life skills outside the classroom. Serving as an embedded librarian, however, provides me with the unique opportunity to connect information literacy with a real world context for the students. The Wikipedia workshop is arguably a good example of how the concept of information literacy extends beyond teaching students how to use library resources but also encompasses information as a facet of perceiving knowledge. Library literature on information literacy, too, emphasizes the need to provide a real world grounding for teaching information literacy to students. Funes asserts:

Information literacy is more than library instruction; it includes an understanding of the landscape of information in today's world and knowledge of how to gather, evaluate and use information… Information literacy is the ability to understand the concepts and values of information in the context of…knowledge. Further, it is the ability to understand where information comes from, where it goes, and what the relationship is between the learner and the information world. It means being able to gather, analyze, and use information in an effective and meaningful manner.[12]

As an embedded librarian working in the residence halls, I take such statements to heart. I attempt to make as many of my lessons as possible relate to the students' living experiences and their daily lives as college students rather than making instruction sessions always connect to their classroom environments. Learning does not happen exclusively in the classroom—it is the whole of the student experience on the campus.

I teach traditional instruction sessions as well. Many of the living-learning communities have classes that meet regularly in the classroom spaces of the residence halls, and the students take classes there that support the academic programs of the living-learning communities. I invite the instructors to bring their students to the residence hall libraries, where I provide orientations to the students on the libraries' resources and collections. We also use the computer labs in the residence halls for traditional instruction sessions, where I introduce the students to the University Library's website and catalog, and I teach them how to locate resources that are specific to the curriculum of their class.

To ensure that my teaching is consistent with the instruction sessions taught by the librarians at the University Library and to ensure that my knowledge of the University Library's catalog and resources are current, I meet regularly with the instruction librarians and participate in their professional development opportunities and discussions. There is sometimes confusion on the part of the librarians regarding my role in the students' educational process. I explain the nature of my work frequently, and the burden is generally on me to seek out collaborations with librarians and to obtain information about professional development opportunities that are facilitated by the University Library. It's easy to forget an embedded librarian when the librarian does not work in an office within the University Library itself—it is up to me to remain connected.

Another strategy I use to introduce students to the concepts, if not the skills, of information literacy is through a scavenger hunt conducted in the eight libraries that are located in the residence halls. Programming is an essential component of a resident advisor's responsibilities at many departments of Residential Life and Housing.[13] At University Housing at the University of Illinois, the resident advisors are required to produce two hall programs each semester—one program can be purely recreational, while the other must have an educational basis. The resident advisors are occasionally stumped for programming ideas that are simultaneously educational and engaging for the students. At least once per year, I suggest to the resident advisors that they organize a scavenger hunt with the residence hall libraries in mind.

The educational purpose of the scavenger hunt is to acquaint students with the elements of information literacy, such as learning how to find a copyright date on a published work or three subject headings in the catalog in which students can locate books on social justice. I design the scavenger hunt with the resident advisor, and together we design clues that will send students on a journey through the libraries' resources. The scavenger hunt is a surprisingly popular activity, but my only regret is that I haven't yet devised a way to integrate an opportunity for reflection into the hunt. I would like the students to think about the strategies they used to discover the items on their lists and why those strategies are important for their learning. A structured educational moment *does* occur at the conclusion of the scavenger hunt, where we examine the items left on the list that the students did not discover or had trouble locating and I demonstrate to the students where in the libraries they would find the missing items.

Information literacy is not the only area in which I provide instruction to the students. I also regularly hold workshops on media literacy. Once per semester, I teach workshops on video-sharing sites. Students learn how to search for and use video clips from YouTube and other sites and how to integrate those clips into class presentations. We discuss parameters such as copyright and fair use, and I teach the students how to recognize political and cultural bias in the perspectives that are represented in the video clips. Additionally, I teach them that YouTube is not the only video-sharing site available, and point them to other sites that are equally useful and provide video sharing and international news clips.

I have also collaborated with the professional staff member who manages the closed-circuit television broadcasts for the residence halls. University Housing maintains a closed-circuit television channel whose broadcasts reach the approximately 10,000 students who live in the residence halls and apartments as a way to convey important information, such as room contracts for summer break housing, meal plan options, and upcoming hall programs and recreational activities. University Housing purchases feature films from distribution companies for broadcast over the closed-circuit channel, with students selecting the films through special requests. I help the resident advisors select films to complement their programs, particularly if they want to use a film to frame a critical discussion on social issues. University Housing tries to avoid broadcasting a film more than once in a three-year period, and some films prove popular choices among resident advisors (such as the movie "Crash" for facilitating a discussion about race and race relations). To minimize repetition in the film selections, I research movies with similar themes that could be acceptable substitutes for facilitating such programs.

As a librarian embedded in the residence halls, I've had the unique opportunity to engage the students socially and educationally. There are substantial opportunities for teaching information literacy to students in environments that are not wholly connected to the classroom experience but are instead relevant to the context of their daily living experiences. However, creating such opportunities requires creativity, flexibility, and a significant investment of personal time to be present in the students' lives and recreational activities. It is also important for me to remain connected with the librarians affiliated with the University Library. Such a connection helps ensure that lessons for information literacy remain a consistent experience for the students as they receive instruction sessions with the Library's liaisons to the students' academic departments as well as in the residence halls.

Outreach to Under-represented Students

Teaching information literacy to the students in the residence halls is only one dimension of my role as the Residential Life Librarian. The University of Illinois is a diverse campus, and the first-year students who traditionally make up the majority of the students living in University Housing represent a greater breadth of diversity than the upper-division students. Approximately 22% of the first-year students self-identify as Asian or Asian American, 8% as Latino/a, 7% as African American, and 12% as international students.[14] African American and Latino/a undergraduate students have a significantly higher rate of attrition than their White and Asian peers at white-majority institutions, with as many as 50–70% leaving white-majority colleges and universities before they reach their fourth year of study.[15] Many African American and Latino/a students report pressure from families to study at an institution close to home, greater issues with college affordability, and negative experiences with institutional racism.[16] While the reasons for their departures from the University of Illinois are shared only anecdotally amongst university faculty and staff, the proportion of African American and Latino/a students who leave the university by their fourth year of study appear to mirror national trends.[17]

Concerned about the high rate of attrition of under-represented groups of undergraduate students nationally and at the University of Illinois, I emphasize outreach to under-represented students as part of my mission as an embedded librarian. I have asked myself the questions, "What can

librarians do to help create a sense of belonging for under-represented students? Are libraries contributing to institutional racism? If librarians and other professionals who provide academic support demonstrate that we care about the students' success, will the rate of attrition decline?" I concluded that as an embedded librarian who enjoyed greater access to the students' lives outside the classroom, I was well positioned to understand better the college experience of our under-represented students and help remove the barriers that impede their academic success.

While it is important to be visible in the lives of the students in the residence halls, I must be even more highly visible to the students who belong to under-represented groups. Building a sense of trust with the students is paramount. I attend student organization meetings, social functions, and guest speaker lectures. If a student wins an award for an accomplishment or receives recognition from the university, I make sure that I attend the event to cheer the student on. One of my strongest relationships with the under-represented students on campus has developed with La Casa, a cultural center dedicated to serving our Latino/a students. Once per semester, the cultural center invites a librarian from the University Library and me to a pizza lunch sponsored by the center. (The center staff call this a "Lunch and Learn.") The other librarian and I provide a fifteen-minute talk on the University Library and the residence hall libraries' resources and services, and we answer any questions the students might have about the libraries. The other librarian and I always bring new concerns back to the University Library and to the Student Affairs Division for their consideration. One year, the University Library canceled its subscriptions to Spanish language popular magazines and newspapers. The students who attended our "Lunch and Learn" at La Casa explained to us that the subscriptions' cancellation deprived a minority of students of the ability to read recreational materials in their native language and thus sent an unintended message to the Latino/a student community that their presence was not particularly valued by the University Library. Armed with this information, the library quickly purchased Spanish language popular magazines again and prominently showcased them in visible areas of the library.

The students at La Casa also reported that many of them attended primary and secondary schools without libraries or grew up in immigrant families where the parents had received little formal education themselves. As a consequence, libraries were not part of their educational experience. Whereas other students might have been encouraged to visit the library by their parents when they called home to express their frustration with school assignments, the parents of students at La Casa did not. "We simply do not think about going to the library. We're not sure what the Library is supposed to do for us," I'm often told by the students during my visits to La Casa.

Students and staff at La Casa appreciated the dedicated outreach they received, and we realized that we needed to devote more attention to building awareness of the libraries amongst our Latino/a students who may not participate in La Casa's programs. As a result, I staffed a booth along with a Spanish-speaking colleague from the University Library at Latino Family Day, an informational session held in Chicago and designed to educate Latino high school students and their parents on the breadth of services available at the University of Illinois. We answered questions from parents and students about how the libraries support academic pursuits and resources for tutoring, but most importantly we made contact with prospective students and their families at a very early stage of their educational journey—hopefully laying the foundation for a strong relationship with the University Library before they were even registered for classes.

Sometimes the nature of my outreach efforts is shaped directly by the students themselves. An officer of a student organization for Lesbian, Gay, Bisexual, and Transgender (LGBT) students that meets regularly in the residence halls approached me and said that the LGBT students had noted the visible minority groups on campus enjoyed attention from academic support services such as the library, but LGBT students—who surely face their own unique and complex set of challenges on college campuses—had no such rapport. I was subsequently asked to consider forging a relationship with the Lesbian, Gay, Bisexual, and Transgender Resource Center to provide regular outreach hours for the students who congregate there as their cultural space on campus. As a consequence, I hold office hours there. I bring a laptop and am available for several hours each Wednesday afternoon for research consultations.

At first, the students who frequent the LGBT Resource Center made only small talk with me, but asked me why a librarian is spending time in their space. I explained what librarians can do for the students, and that I am there because I want to help the students who associate with the LGBT Resource Center have a librarian dedicated to their academic support. I have found that instead of being focused on academic research, much of the assistance I lend to the students at the LGBT Resource Center facilitates the exploration of their identity—helping them locate health and legal information within the local community and teaching them to search the library's catalog more effectively for LGBT literature and history.

Providing outreach to under-represented students on the campus was never a formal expectation for me as an embedded librarian. In a way, outreach was a natural growth from my work serving the students who live in the residence halls as I noted the educational inequity that appears to exist between groups of students on the campus. Crafting outreach opportunities was less difficult with the LGBT students, who invited my presence and whose identities as LGBT students were not necessarily visible to others. Therefore my status as an "outsider" to the group was less of a concern. The other under-represented student groups, however, noted immediately that I did not share their cultural identity. Building a sense of trust with the students required a significantly greater period of time before they saw me as a genuine ally and someone who demonstrated an earnest commitment to their success as students at the University of Illinois.

Not all Fun and Games

Providing instruction that is not connected to a class or academic discipline is not easy. I am challenged to invent sessions that are interesting and will appeal to a wide audience of students. If the instruction session is not immediately useful or is simply uninteresting, students will not attend. I have learned not to advertise my workshops as "developing your research skills" or anything that sounds remotely academic—students will not come. They will come, however, if what they are learning is fun and different. I have to figure out how to disguise information literacy as something that happens not just in the classroom, but also in their everyday lives. I am also challenged to re-invent my workshops frequently. My workshop "Become an Editor on Wikipedia!" was hugely popular four years ago, but interest from the students has steadily declined. Students are increasingly savvy about using social networking sites, and Wikipedia's exponential growth has left many students feeling as if "everything is already written—so why should I contribute to it?," as one student told me. I have to truly stay on top of my game and understand youth culture to find innovative ways for introducing information literacy into their lives.

Remaining unaffiliated with a class or academic discipline is a significant disadvantage for assessment. I am not receiving formal feedback from the students; there is no evaluation form to distribute at the end of the workshop—doing so dispels the idea that the workshop is fun, not learning. With the exception of the instructors who invite me to teach traditional instruction sessions with the classes associated with the living-learning communities, I am unable to follow up with instructors to determine if the skills I teach are translating to increased performance in the classroom. It is possible that students have difficulty making the connections between applying the same skills to academic pursuits as they do to personal endeavors. Nonetheless, the lessons I have learned for teaching information literacy successfully outside of an academic class or discipline are, "Make it fun, make it interactive, and make it relevant."

Successful performance as a librarian embedded in the residence halls is difficult to measure. I justify my position's existence with the number of information literacy sessions I teach, headcounts of the sessions and other activities I facilitate, and the gate count and circulation statistics of the residence hall libraries I manage. Anecdotal evidence is, however, the most compelling evidence accepted by University Housing. I include notes and e-mails from students who thank me for my assistance in helping them develop thesis statement, finding sources for them, or simply stopping by their room in the residence hall to answer questions as they work on a paper late at night. Such appreciation demonstrates that embedded librarianship is providing academic support and instruction in a way that is fundamentally non-traditional for librarians.

The challenges associated with outreach to special populations as an embedded librarian are similar to the challenges associated with teaching information literacy. Assessment is difficult to quantify. Which is more important: the number of students who seek my assistance through the outreach venues, the quality and depth of the assistance I provide, or the value that the students attach to my presence and availability? It just might be possible that I helped demonstrate to an underrepresented student that the university cares about that student's success.

Embedding a librarian in the residence halls is not going to be an overnight success. Building a rapport with the students is paramount for a successful experience. The venture will not work unless the students know that I am there, understand my reason for being there, or value my presence. I spend a significant amount of time thinking about creative ways to market my services and embed myself into students' daily lives in a meaningful way. Unlike traditional librarianship, where the librarian may wait at a reference desk for a student to come them, I go to the students. My success is dependent on being available to the students at the times when they are most likely to be in the residence halls—and that means many evenings and weekends spent in the halls. Too many evening and weekend commitments can make it difficult to balance the committee meetings and other professional obligations that are inevitably scheduled during traditional work hours. Finding a work/life balance and maintaining a high energy level can be challenging.

Conclusion

The practice of an embedded librarian in university residence halls is not a new concept. Residence hall libraries and librarians have existed in various forms since the 1920s but declined in number through the decades. As embedded librarianship emerges (or re-emerges) at many colleges and universities, perhaps the idea of librarians working principally in the residence halls will be revisited and reinvigorated.

My position is sometimes professionally isolating, as I have one foot in the University Library and one foot in the Student Affairs Division. As a full member of neither, I must be an active participant in my own professional development and stay abreast of changes to the University Library's catalog, resources, and curricula for information literacy. However it is a very rewarding experience to participate in the daily lives of the students and demonstrate that information literacy skills can play a strong part in their everyday living environment. Developing programs to engage the students requires building knowledge of the students' culture and emerging technologies and a willingness to continually update and experiment with my techniques. If there is a lesson that I can impart to other colleges and universities considering developing an embedded librarian program in the university residence halls, it is "Make it fun, make it interactive, and make it relevant!"

Notes

1. Kenneth Morgan, "The Harvard House Libraries." *Library Journal* 56, no. 6 (1931): 536–539.
2. Ibid., 538.
3. Edmund Griffith Williamson, "Students' Residences: Shelter or Education?" *Personnel and Guidance Journal* 36, no. 2 (1957): 386–397.
4. Edward B Stanford, "Residence Hall Libraries and Their Educational Potential." *College and Research Libraries* 30, no. 3 (1969): 197–203.
5. Williamson, "Students' Residences," 397.
6. Gail Oltmanns, "Purposes and uses of residence hall libraries." *College & Research Libraries* 46, no. 2 (1985): 172–77.
7. David Alan Flynn, "There's No Place Like Home: A History of Residence Hall Libraries at Indiana University." *Indiana Libraries* 12, no.1 (1993): 2–10.
8. Flynn, "There's No Place Like Home," 7.
9. University of Illinois, *Residence Hall Libraries Annual Report*, 1978.
10. University of Illinois, *Residence Hall Libraries Annual Report*, 1993.
11. Eric Jennings, "Using Wikipedia to Teach Information Literacy." *College & Undergraduate Libraries* 15, no. 4 (2008): 432–437.
12. Carolyn H. Funes, "Palomar College Develops an Information Literacy Course." *Community & Junior College Libraries* 12, no. 3 (2005): 61–65.
13. Susan R. Komives, "The Relationship of Hall Directors' Transformational and Transactional Leadership Factors to Resi-

dent Assistant's Perceived Outcomes." Journal of College Student Development 32, no. 6 (2001): 509–515.

14. University of Illinois, New Freshman Demographics Fall 2009. Available at: http://www.dmi.illinois.edu/stuenr/index. asp#new. (Accessed March 22, 2010).

15. Sue R. Rankin and Robert D. Reason, "Differing Perceptions: How Students of Color and White Students Perceive Campus Climate for Underrepresented Groups." *Journal of College Student Development* 46, no. 1 (2005): 43–61.

16. Ibid.

17. University of Illinois, New Freshman Demographics Fall 2009

References

Flynn, David Alan. "There's No Place Like Home: A History of Residence Hall Libraries at Indiana University." *Indiana Libraries* 12, no.1 (1993): 2–10.

Funes, Carolyn H. "Palomar College Develops an Information Literacy Course." *Community & Junior College Libraries* 12, no. 3 (2005): 61–65.

Jennings, Eric. "Using Wikipedia to Teach Information Literacy." *College & Undergraduate Libraries* 15, no. 4 (2008): 432–437.

Komives, Susan R. The Relationship of Hall Directors' Transformational and Transactional Leadership Factors to Resident Assistant's Perceived Outcomes. Journal of College Student Development 32, no. 6 (2001): 509–515.

Morgan, Kenneth. *"The Harvard House Libraries." Library Journal* 56, no. 6 (1931): 536–539.

Oltmanns, Gail. "Purposes and uses of residence hall libraries." *College & Research Libraries* 46, no. 2 (1985): 172–77.

Rankin, Sue R., and Robert D. Reason. "Differing Perceptions: How Students of Color and White Students Perceive Campus Climate for Underrepresented Groups." *Journal of College Student Development* 46, no. 1 (2005): 43–61.

Stanford, Edward B. "Residence Hall Libraries and Their Educational Potential." *College and Research Libraries* 30, no. 3 (1969): 197–203.

University of Illinois, *Residence Hall Libraries Annual Report*, 1978.

University of Illinois, *Residence Hall Libraries Annual Report*, 1993.

University of Illinois, New Freshman Demographics Fall 2009. Available at: http://www.dmi.illinois.edu/stuenr/index.asp#new. (Accessed March 22, 2010).

Williamson, Edmund Griffith. "Students' Residences: Shelter or Education?" *Personnel and Guidance Journal* 36, no. 2 (1957): 386–397.

 FIFTEEN

Extending Our Reach: Embedding Library Resources and Services within Extension

Kristen Mastel

Introduction

Extension staff has a unique set of needs ranging from document delivery to off campus locations, instruction on citation tracking, file management, and technology trends. Through the hire of a dedicated librarian to serve Extension, the University of Minnesota Libraries were able to capitalize on a perfect storm brewing within Extension.

This chapter will discuss how the University of Minnesota is seeking to reach out to previously underserved Extension staff through virtual and personal services. A variety of techniques have been used, such as trend spotting, lurking and active engagement, to identify the strengths and weakness in our library programming and services for Extension staff; with this information we are able to develop strategies for outreach opportunities. A discussion of several digital projects underway will highlight how we are working towards integration within Extension's place, policies and preservation.

History of Extension

The University of Minnesota started as a preparatory school in the Territory of Minnesota in 1851. The school was designated as the land-grant institution for the state under the 1862 Morrill Act. All universities have the mission of research and teaching, but land-grant institutions have a third

mission, outreach. The Smith-Lever Act of 1914 established the Cooperative Extension Service and provided federal funds for extension activities. In 1909, the state legislature created the Extension division within the University of Minnesota, providing funds thereafter. The mission of Extension furthers the University's outreach efforts by "providing Minnesotans with access to practical, research-based information to help improve their lives. Extension faculty and staff live and work across the state, in regional and county offices as well as University campuses and research and outreach centers."[1] Currently, Extension has five units designated as Extension Centers. These Extension Centers include: Family Development; Youth Development; Community Vitality; and Food, Agricultural and Natural Resource Sciences. Each Center includes numerous program areas. Some examples include, students using science, math, engineering and technology to design and build robots in 4H and nutrition educators training to improve the nutritional content of school lunches and food handling techniques.

Library Liaison Role

Previously, Extension staff had to funnel their reference questions, instruction requests, and copyright inquiries to the appropriate subject liaison within the University of Minnesota Libraries based on academic disciplines, rather than program areas. Often questions were passed around to different experts in the areas of copyright and instruction. There was no designated Extension contact providing continuity of service in the Libraries.

Before the Outreach and Instruction Librarian position was advertised in 2008, the Agricultural, Biological and Environmental Sciences department within the Libraries analyzed their needs and determined that they desired a dedicated liaison to two colleges that were previously underserved. My position, as it stands today, is one that combines outreach to the Saint Paul campus community and the surrounding area, along with coordinating instruction. In addition, my position is the liaison to the College of Continuing Education (CCE) and Extension, both of which cover numerous discipline areas, making the position uniquely interdisciplinary.

Challenges and Opportunities

Hiring the first dedicated librarian for Extension brought many opportunities for the Libraries. At the time of my hire, Extension was restructuring and implementing a new promotion process for their staff. Additionally, Extension staff members were excited about having a personal librarian to assist them.

In 2003, due a severe budget cut of 7 million dollars or 13% of their budget, Extension considered new structures and models of organization.[2] Prior to 2004, Extension educators were located in all 87 counties in Minnesota. After 2004, Extension became a regional/county model. Extension realigned its program teams to topic-based groups mapped to an overarching area. For example, the program team Agricultural Drainage is aligned to the topic of agriculture, and this falls within the Extension Center for Food, Agricultural and Natural Resource Sciences (EFANS). Though most of the staff was retained, everyone had to adjust to the new business plans of the program teams and smaller budgets.

Extension staff has embraced technology as an affordable means to get their message out to the community and amongst themselves. The staff members already use tools to create webinars to reach community members who are spread out over numerous counties. Though they still do in-person training, they have been able to reach more residents with the addition of online technologies. Numerous program teams also make use of course management systems, such as Moodle, for ongoing education regarding new developments in their areas, such as federal legislation, standards and other factors that can influence their outreach and educational programming. Technology has been integrated into Extension's workflow, which provides the Libraries an opportunity to partner with the Extension community and staff, while keeping the Libraries budget reductions for site visits and on-site training during the recession in account.

Because few extension staff members are located on a University of Minnesota campus, accessing the Libraries' resources can be challenging. A proxy server allows off-campus staff to authenticate to the University of Minnesota and access the Libraries' web-based resources.[3] Staff also may request items to be delivered from Document Delivery via e-mail. This does not address the disparity of broadband access that exists within regional offices and within the general community in parts of the state. According to a broadband study, 94% of Minnesotans have access to broadband.[4] However, examining rural Minnesota reveals drastically different numbers. Only 73% of households in outstate own a computer, and 68% maintain an internet connection.[5] All Extension staff members have access to a computer and e-mail is the most common communication medium, however the Internet report illustrates that not all connections are equal. Some Extension offices have relatively slow upload/download times, making developing resources and content for staff more challenging.

Another inequity that off-campus Extension staff experience is the lack of access to physical materials within the Libraries. Currently, offsite extension staff may request materials to be delivered to their offices through the program *Documents to U*. However, this is a fee-based program, with a cost associated for each item requested and for postage. Extension staff use personal or Center professional development funds to request delivery of materials from the Libraries to their offices. As a work around, many extension staff off campus will request University of Minnesota library materials through the public library system. Through the statewide network, *MnLINK*, residents of Minnesota may borrow materials from other Minnesota library systems, including many academic libraries, at no charge. However, most public libraries have a two-week loan period, while staff and faculty at the University may borrow materials for thirteen weeks with unlimited renewals. This inequity needs to be resolved, as numerous other institutions offer direct mailing of materials to off campus Extension personnel.[6–9]

In addition to new programming directions and the consolidation of regional offices in 2004, Extension recently reviewed their promotion process. Extension educators are now evaluated on leadership, scholarship, teaching, management, and service. The scholarship section plays a larger role than it has in the past, giving the Libraries an opportunity to work with Extension staff as they publish and promote their research and evidence-based programming.

One of the major challenges in working with Extension is that being a subject expert in all areas of Extension is perhaps not realistic for a single Libraries liaison. Rather, as Extension liaison, I illustrate how I can assist with the tools and strategies for research in their respected areas and look to them to provide the content expertise.

Working with staff throughout the state makes outreach and communication challenging. There are numerous factors to take into consideration, including those areas the Libraries has little control over, such as network connectivity, and policies that should be reconsidered, such as our loan policy and process for offsite staff.

In the Know

Communication is the key to keeping current and relevant with Extension staff throughout Minnesota. Knowing the programming under development allows the Libraries to be a potential partner in creating content and providing research support. Being present within Extension's communication channels allows the Libraries to provide information regarding our resources and services within their workflow. I use six communication channels to remain informed and disperse content as needed: email lists, Twitter, blogs, video, Extension meetings, and connecting with influential technology and community personnel within Extension.

Email lists are an obvious choice when it comes to being an effective subject librarian. We use them across the University to keep up-to-date on student and faculty research, to monitor department efforts and to communicate what the Libraries have to offer that specific population; Extension is no different. The Extension all-staff list provides updates on the Dean's vision for Extension and procedural changes, but it is the Center lists that I have found to be most useful. Rather than subscribing to almost a hundred program team email lists, which would be unmanageable in my workflow, I subscribe to each Center's general list. Most Centers put together weekly or monthly highlights regarding developments among their program teams. To manage all the messages, I have a strong filtering system in my e-mail, along with a tagging system to mark the e-mails for follow-up for various reasons: new program, policy change, program cancellation, new initiative, and research.

Tagging can also be found on Twitter. Extension is often at the forefront of new technologies as the staff members try new ways to communicate with their community and the profession. Many extension staff use Twitter, a microblogging site that allows for 140 character messages. Using a program called TweetDeck to manage my Twitter account on my desktop and mobile phone, I have created a group for all the Extension staff I follow. I keep track of what they are discussing and advertising to the community and add to the discussions with comments and links to useful resources. In addition to following Extension employees and groups, I follow Extension hashtags for the program teams, such as #trotttweet for the Horse Program Team, and official Extension communications at #UMNExt. Not only does this afford me an easy, nonintrusive way to engage Extension staff, but it also has increased my visibility. Numerous Extension staff now follow my account, @KLMLibrarian, and often repost my tweets to share with their community at large. I have also been able to gain valuable feedback regarding presentations based on the immediacy of a post on Twitter. As soon as I enter a message on Twitter it is posted, unlike the mediated Extension email lists which may take a few days to be approved and sent out.

Blogs are another immediate mode of communication that I use. Like Twitter, I subscribe to blogs from individuals and Extension programs through RSS feeds. Again, the use of folders, filters and tagging allow me to organize the blog posts and focus on those that are relevant to the Libraries. I also use a blog (http://blog.lib.umn.edu/meye0539/kristenmastel/) to communicate with Extension staff. To aid Extension staff in their scholarship, my blog posts highlight useful reports and University sources, as well as quality free resources that could be useful in their programming with the general public. I embed YouTube video screencasts, welcome messages, and productivity tips I want to present visually in less than five minutes within the blog. One of the main reasons I use YouTube instead of other video-sharing sites is the accessibility component. In YouTube, I can offer closed captioning to assist those with hearing impairments and to reinforce the message to

international Extension staff. Since Twitter only allows 140 characters, I can have a longer discussion about a resource or topic on my blog and link to that post via a tweet on Twitter.

Since there was strong buy-in from Extension administration to having a dedicated Libraries liaison, I have been invited to participate as an ex-officio member on many of the Extension teams. For example, I am invited to attend all monthly Extension Center for Food, Agricultural and Natural Resource Sciences Program Leader Team meetings. In each of their meetings one program team is highlighted. This allows me to hear the latest accomplishments and annual goals from the administrative perspective. Again, this reinforces the support that the Libraries play within Extension, and allows me to strengthen our ties with Extension leadership.

Serendipitously I have met many influential and informed personnel within Extension. One of the first support groups I met within extension was EDTech. This group of Extension staff is interested in educational technology, and many of them are early adopters. This group has become a sounding board for outreach possibilities and has introduced me to upcoming initiatives and projects. Through one of the members of EdTech I learned that the Center for Community Vitality was interested in organizing all of the personal libraries Extension staff have across the state about community economics and other areas. After analyzing their situation, we developed a group RefWorks account and came up with custom fields to help organize the data. I helped train the administrative assistant on efficient and effective citation tracking strategies and uploading to RefWorks. She then imported the Center's circulating library, along with the administration's personal files. Instructions were developed and dispersed to Community Vitality staff who were invested in the program. One can never underestimate the power of networking within an institution to lead you down new program and outreach paths.

Some of these methods to embed within Extension's communication workflow are from the top down and others bubble up from the bottom. Twitter and blogging are grassroots methods of connecting directly with the Extension staff and their communities to share information at a point of need. Attending various meetings with administration allows for the Libraries to strategically assist in accomplishing Extension goals, and potentially be incorporated in the future.

Marketing Resources

The Libraries are embedded in two core areas of Extension: the promotion process and the intranet. Marketing and assessment of resources for both areas is possible by embedding within the communication system.

When the promotion guidelines for Extension educators changed, there was a great deal of unease about what scholarship meant and how it would be evaluated. To relieve apprehension about the review process, Extension administration developed numerous tools and strategies to inform and educate staff. Many Centers offered webinars, handouts and worksheets that discussed assessing evidence-based programming, building a dossier, writing a narration, and examples of curriculum vitae.

Building on the key pieces of information needed for promotion, I was invited by the Community Economics Team to develop a webinar on conducting literature searches to support the area of scholarship. A communication channel was in place to archive the presentation. In the hour-long session I introduced familiar indexes and databases, along with strategic searching strategies, such as using controlled vocabulary. Creating a search alert was also demonstrated, as staff members often work on projects over a period of time. Locating grey literature, illustrating bibliographic mining and cited reference searching were also discussed.

The Community Economics program team endorsed the quality of the webinar and posted it on the internal Promotion Initiatives for Educators (PIE) website. The webinar is cited as a tool to consult as staff moves through the promotion process. This successful partnership led to more than ten one-on-one consultations via Skype and conference calls with Community Economics Extension educators. Since the Community Economics presentation, I have developed five other presentations covering similar strategies for other topic areas of Extension.

The PIE website exists within the intranet for Extension, which uses the MyU Portal. In addition to creating content to populate Extension's websites, I have created a custom myLibrary page within their Portal, which is a part of their daily workflow.

MyU is a web portal "created by the University's Office of Information Technology and Office of the Vice Provost for Distributed Education and Instructional Technology. The site is intended as 'the first stop for University of Minnesota information and applications' for students, staff, and faculty."[10] The portal is a one-stop-shop for work and student life here at the University. Undergraduate students can register for courses, access course management systems, check their e-mail, and pay bills through the portal interface. The staff can access their e-mail, view their pay statements, and other core work life related tasks. This is all embedded within Extension's customized MyU Portal, which also serves as their intranet. Both groups are able to have customized content delivered to them.

The Libraries have a dedicated tab within the portal, titled myLibrary. Undergraduate, graduate, staff and faculty all receive different pieces of content produced by the Libraries. To reach Extension staff where they are virtually I created a custom myLibrary template for the portal.

The Extension myLibrary page has components that are standard for all myLibrary pages, such as a widget featuring a library catalog search box at the top, another box that allows you to save your favorite databases, e-journals and citations, along with listing items you have checked out, and in the footer a list of Libraries. I was able to customize all of the other boxes of content throughout the page with assistance of the coding skills of the Libraries developers.

I created a custom "Search Key Resources" widget that recommends databases, indexes and other web resources for Extension. Ideally, I would be able to push economics related information to the Extension Community Economics Program Team within the Center for Community Vitality, or horticulture resources to the Master Gardeners. However, this is not currently possible, as the human resources records do not have unique job codes for each Center or Program Team. Therefore, we had to create one list that would reflect the five Centers of Extension equally. This is a difficult task, as the first ten items alphabetically I mark as core resources on my subject guide are pulled into the myLibrary interface. I strategically identified less than ten core resources: two general interest databases and one subject specific database appropriate broadly for each Center. In the widget there is a link to "More" which links out to the longer Extension subject guide. However, I wanted to do more than simply pushing content out. Extension staff is familiar with a wealth of resources for their specific areas of interest, and I wanted to provide an opportunity to gather their feedback and additions to a subject guide, which the current technology the Libraries uses does not allow.

To allow user feedback and contributions I decided to link to all the relevant library resources via social bookmarking. Social bookmarking allows users to share and organize bookmarks of web content. I decided to use the social bookmarking site Delicious (http://delicious.com/). Since I knew other Extension staff was using that particular program to manage their personal and professional bookmarks, I went where the people were already invested, although other social networking tools would work as well. I bookmarked databases and

free web resources and tagged them with the appropriate Center names to group the items. I also added other items of interest, such as literature searching, writing a literature review, and copyright and intellectual property. I included a link to my Delicious account in the core resources of the Extension subject guide; therefore it appears at the top of the alphabetical list of "Key Resources." In the short time since creating the Delicious account I have received over a dozen recommendations of resources to include. Another way I hope to revise the "Key Resources" area is to incorporate the most popular online resources Extension staff has saved to the e-journals and database favorites section. This illustrates the importance of not only pushing content to our users, but also pulling in their suggestions to make our resources more robust.

Another custom widget in the myLibrary tab is "Library News." I wanted to create a custom feed rather than linking to the Libraries' general RSS feed, which populates all other myLibrary templates. Most Extension staff is located offsite and the general RSS feed lists onsite events, workshops and other information that does not always apply to this population. The developers used my blog's RSS feed to populate "Library News." Now, Extension staff receives highlights of resources, embedded screencasts, and discussions regarding current projects and partnerships between the Libraries and Extension delivered to their myLibrary page.

The last area I was able to customize was "Library Links." There I featured our chat reference service, recorded workshops, copyright information and other sites relevant to distance learners.

The custom myLibrary page within the portal allows Extension staff to have a personalized virtual library to fit their needs and interests. In the future, by examining the items people click on and archive in their "Saved Resources" section, the Libraries hope to build in a recommender system.

Through the myLibrary and Promotion Initiatives for Educators projects, research assistance has been provided to Extension staff located on and off campus. A recent small sample study at a similar sized University found that 71% of off campus Extension personnel access the Libraries website less than once a month.[11] By integrating the Libraries resources into Extension's workflow and interface I hope to increase awareness and ease of access to library information.

Embedding Services

In addition to being embedded within the communication methods of Extension, and within the portal tools, library services have been embedded into numerous Extension programs to provide reference support and document archiving.

Many libraries that serve Extension staff offer reference assistance in-person, on the phone, via chat and e-mail, and the University of Minnesota is no different. Extension staff members are welcome to contact the Libraries though whatever medium is most comfortable for them. However, when I started working with Extension I tried an additional approach. Three months after I started in 2008, the Center for Youth Development was hosting their annual conference online, due to budget considerations. In collaboration with the conference organizer and Associate Dean of the Center for Youth Development I created a welcome video to introduce myself to the Extension staff and a library scavenger hunt to acquaint staff with relevant resources and services on the Libraries website. In addition, I offered an optional drop-in chat session to meet Youth Development staff. Of the eighty Youth Development staff that participated in the conference over fifteen introduced themselves to me during the one-hour chat session and/or asked questions. Since this was a success and only a short period of time was invested, I have offered drop-in virtual chat sessions quarterly or biannually, with similar attendance. As other Extension Centers have started to move their more in-depth professional development opportunities online I have been able to extend this service.

In addition to attending the Center's smaller professional development events I have been involved with Extension's fall conference every year. While attending my first conference I participated in the poster session and presented on the customized myLibrary tab in the portal. There were over fifty research-based posters being presented and there was no archiving precedent for their work. After the conference, I worked with the organizers to issue a call to the poster session presenters to add their work to the University's digital repository, the University Digital Conservancy (UDC). The majority of poster session presenters participated and submitted their materials to the UDC. This project has expanded the UDC's collection to include national presentations and posters by Extension staff as a part of their workflow after they present.

The Libraries need to be present from the beginning of the research process to the end product. The personal connections made during the drop-in chat sessions have led to collaborations on additional projects and the pursuit of adding Extension publications to the University Digital Conservancy.

Conclusion

Two years ago the Libraries connection with Extension was ad hoc. Some librarians had relationships with Extension faculty in their subject liaison areas, but there was no systematic effort for reference, instruction, collection development or outreach. Through buy-in and risk taking within Extension the Libraries has become part of their communication channel. Through this open dialogue, opportunities for partnerships on projects and resources have emerged, as the Libraries continue to understand and fulfill the needs of Extension staff.

The University of Minnesota Libraries is a land-grant library system with a mission to provide information to the people of Minnesota. Similarly, the mission of Extension is to provide useful information to the people of Minnesota anchored in current research done within the University. The alignment of outreach within both the Libraries and Extension provides opportunities for growth and development which stretch beyond embedding Libraries resources and services within Extension to informing the Minnesota community of state-wide resources and services.

Notes

1. University of Minnesota Extension. "Extension History, since 1909." University of Minnesota Extension Service. http://blog.lib.umn.edu/extmedia/centennial/ (accessed May 15, 2010, 2010).

2. O'Brien, P. and G. W. Morse. "Minnesota Extension's Mixed Regional/County Model: Greater Impacts Follows Changes in Structure." *Staff Papers* (2006).

3. Faiks, A. H. "Libraries and Extension: Engaging in Partnerships." *Journal of Agricultural & Food Information* 4, no. 3 (2003): 21–27.

4. Minnesota. Ultra High-Speed Broadband Task Force. *Minnesota Ultra High-Speed Broadband Report.* Minnesota: The Task Force, 2009.

5. See note 4 above.

6. Tancheva, K., M. Cook, and H. Raskin. "Serving the Public: The Academic Library and Cooperative Extension." *Journal of Extension* 43, no. 3 (2005).

7. McKimmie, T. "Reaching Out: Land Grant Library Services to Cooperative Extension Offices, Experiment Stations, and Agriculture Science Centers." *Journal of Agricultural & Food Information* 4, no. 3 (2003): 29–32.

8. Neely, T. Y., N. Lederer, A. Reyes, P. Thistlethwaite, L. Wess, and J. Winkler. "Instruction and Outreach at Colorado State University Libraries." *The Reference Librarian* 32, no. 67 (2001): 273–287.

9. Davis, V. "Challenges of Connecting Off-Campus Agricultural Science Users with Library Services." *Journal of Agricultural & Food Information* 8, no. 2 (2007): 39–47.

10. Hanson, C., S. Nackerud, and K. Jensen. "Affinity Strings: Enterprise Data for Resource Recommendations." *The Code4Lib Journal* 5, (2008).

11. Brazzeal, B. "Library use by Extension Service and Experiment Station Personnel." *Journal of Agricultural & Food Information* 8, no. 3 (2008): 33–41.

# SIXTEEN

Embedded Librarianship at the Claremont Colleges

Jezmynne Dene

Background Information

The Claremont Colleges consists of seven separate institutions, five undergraduate colleges of Harvey Mudd College, Pomona College, Pitzer College, Claremont McKenna College, and Scripps College, and two graduate universities, Keck Graduate Institute and Claremont Graduate University in Claremont, California. The full time enrollment for the Claremont Colleges is approximately 6000 students and full time faculty total 800. The seven institutions share many centralized services based on the Oxford model, including a library system, governed by the Claremont University Consortium.

The shared nature of the library has advantages and disadvantages. The biggest advantage is the shared purchasing and services power the distributed cost provides as each of the individual colleges could not afford such rich collections and services on its own. One major disadvantage is that library staff and facilities are cut off from the communities that they serve. The library building itself is centrally located between the colleges, and is not affiliated with any one school. Furthermore, the library is on a separate computer network, and is further separated as each individual college has its own separate, closed network. Overlap between the networks is very sparse and intermingling is

not encouraged. Because of the separate networks, librarians find it difficult to be included on the campus email lists. Each academic year, as the student, staff, and faculty email lists are created, they are done so by domain and registration information. Since the librarians are not on the same domain, special permission and additional work must be done in order to add a librarian to any email lists. Additionally, this is often a political battle, as the librarians must justify why they feel they need to be on the campus-specific lists. These disadvantages make working with the colleges challenging for the library and its staff as each campus has its own unique culture, email lists, physical spaces, services, and works to cultivate use by its own campus community.

The physical spaces are a challenge, as well. The library sits centrally located to all the colleges, but often students and faculty choose to find a location on their own campus to work, collaborate, and research. Each campus has its own café and dining areas, recreation areas, computing and study areas, and campus living rooms. Geographically close to classrooms and dorms, these spots are often the first choice for users to gather and work. Often these spaces are not open to the general public and are accessible only via swipe card authentication access. This poses an issue for librarians as the swipe cards are created and managed internally by each college and specific only to those college campus members. Librarians again must meet the challenge of why their cards should gain them access to these areas on campuses to meet and work with students and faculty.

The individual campus cultures, networks, and physical spaces necessitate that librarians in Claremont actively engage with users in the user's home environments. Because of the separateness that each college maintains and cultivates, it is imperative that the librarians initiate embedded programs to integrate into those campus cultures within the physical boundaries of the campus communities. In doing so, the librarians gain a deeper understanding of the community of users and the research and information needs unique to each. To rise to this challenge, three embedded initiatives were launched: the Writing Center Initiative, the Sakai Initiative, and the Embedded Campus Initiative.

The Writing Center Initiative

Most academic institutions have a writing center, which provides students with assistance organizing and structuring writing assignments such as research papers, essays, and lab reports. In 2006 the librarians of the Claremont Colleges created formal ties with each writing center at the colleges that had a writing center (Keck Graduate Institute does not have a writing center for its students). In order to establish relationships, the embedded librarian coordinator hosted a lunch for the writing center directors and their assigned librarians. After lunch and conversation, the leaders and librarians discussed topics specific to each of the writing centers, identifying frequent questions, issues, problems, and concerns in the centers. The writing center coordinators talked about the average competencies expected of the students they assist, brought up frequently asked questions, and shared high use times and other relevant data. The librarians asked about the level of bibliographies

the students supplied, and if content was an issue the writing centers experienced. This discussion proved helpful for all involved, as each side addressed competencies that were important to one side but were unknown to the other. For example, the librarians were concerned about the quality of resources used and how those resources were discovered and identified, whereas the coordinators were concerned with levels of grammar and cohesive writing flow. This brainstorming led to a better understanding of the workflow the writing centers manage and assisted in the creation of effective expectations for the initiative. The group then outlined a common approach for the program.

Tutors are typically hired at the beginning of the academic year, so each fall, the embedded librarian assigned to the college in question works with the writing center coordinator to meet with the hired tutors. The librarian builds relationships with the tutors while assessing their level of research competency through conversation, asking each tutor their declared major and minor, year of college, and how long they've been a tutor (it is very common that tutors are retained multiple years). Following the relationship building, the librarian gives the tutors an instruction session tailored towards dealing with typical issues brought to the tutors by students. These issues are predefined by the writing center director and the embedded librarian, based on individual issues encountered by the center and suggested competencies outlined by the librarian. Examples include how to format a bibliography, writing in-text citations, issues of plagiarism, identifying and addressing poor bibliographies lacking scholarly resources, and appropriate times to refer the student to the library for a reference session. Entry-level databases, like Omnifile, Academic Search Premiere, and Web of Knowledge are demonstrated, the concepts of forwards and backwards citation searching are addressed, and the basic concepts of RefWorks, Claremont's chosen citation management tool, are explored. The writing center coordinators, tutors and librarians work to create a checklist of objectives for a research paper or project, such as locating sufficient scholarly information, creating a bibliography, mastering the assigned citation style, and producing multiple drafts. Librarians leave relevant handouts, business cards, links to chat widgets, and contact information for referrals during the sessions. Librarians also create bibliographies of sample papers for students to review. Tutors are made aware of the subject specialists and are provided a list of contact information and LibGuides links, and understand that the embedded librarian may have to delegate reference questions to the subject specialist if the content of the question is beyond a general scope. The tutors are encouraged to refer any student with issues of content and questions about resources to the embedded librarian as appropriate. The embedded librarian then handles the questions and interactions or refers as necessary.

Best practices for embedding in writing centers should be addressed with the writing center in question and tailored to the institution's culture. However, we have learned that ensuring access between the liaison librarian and writing center during peak hours is ideal. In some cases, the librarian is physically available and on site. In other cases, the librarian is available virtually via chat. Furthermore, the embedded librarians need to maintain regular contact with the tutors. Librarians in Claremont will join the tutors periodically during regular scheduled meeting times or by dropping in to say "Hi" during peak times in order to ensure that tutors feel adequately prepared to refer students as needed. Finally, librarians find "spin off" successes from embedding within the writing centers. Several tutors made follow-up appointments for assistance with their personal research projects and recommended meeting with the librarians to their friends and co-collaborators. Librarians noted requests from faculty for classroom instruction sessions after faculty learned about the assistance provided by the librarians through the writing centers.

Embedding in Sakai, our Learning Management System

In April 2006 the Claremont Colleges brought Sakai, an open source learning management system, online for all Claremont institutions, including the library. Sakai is a flexible LMS with several unique tools created by the contributing community. Sakai's greatest feature for libraries is the ability to create an open project site that is listed in a global, searchable directory. These project sites differ from course sites as course sites are created automatically from the registration data and are only accessible to enrolled students and faculty. Project sites are created by users and are very flexible. Many sites are open and joinable, similar to Facebook groups, while some are more restrictive and require the maintainer of the project site to manually invite individuals to participate.

Since 2006 the Sakai Administration Team has had a liaison librarian involved with the administration of the software and with the creation and completion of pedagogical objectives. Initially these ties were limited to exploring the interlinking of library resources into Sakai and using the expertise of a few instruction librarians to teach Sakai to the faculty and students. In early 2007 the first library site in Sakai was created. This Science Library site was born of a need to master Sakai and its tools in order to teach it to faculty and provide examples of the tools. However, when the site was used in instruction sessions, the faculty wanted to join the site in order to see how the learning management system tools were used, and both faculty and students wanted to join the site in order to benefit from the materials presented. At that time, the Science Library in Sakai project site was made publicly available and joinable to the entire Claremont community. It became obvious that the library could easily use Sakai's teaching structure to supply materials in a familiar way to users. The benefit of Sakai's open, joinable public sites listed in a searchable directory led the Claremont library to see the value of placing content within the LMS. Within a year, faculty began to see the expertise the librarians had in the LMS and started adding librarians as teaching faculty to traditional course sites, expanding the embedded program into the course specific arena.

The first major Sakai initiative was to create library sites in Sakai that were public and listed in the directory of open, joinable sites. The first two major sites in Sakai were the Science Library site and the Library 101 site. The Science Library site has over 450 students and faculty members; the majority of these individuals joined voluntarily after finding the site in the directory or learning of the site during an instruction session or reference appointment. These library sites take advantage of the structure of the LMS to present the same sort of materials handed out in instruction sessions, at reference desks, or found on library websites. The "Announcements" tool is used as often as needed, either to post a newsworthy blurb to the site or to email the entire group belonging to the site in question. Since the Sakai sites are focus specific, e.g., science-oriented or directed at new library users, the announcement is tailored for the interested group and not for the campus community as a whole. For example, when the sciences upgraded to the CAS web version of SciFinder Scholar, an announcement was sent to the members of the Science Library Sakai site prior to the general public announcement, allowing the Science Library community to explore the web version a few days before the rest of the community. In course sites, the Announcement tool is used to tell the class when the librarian is available for consultation, for example, or to notify the class when a resource or guide has been created.

Each Sakai site has a calendar, which is useful for providing focus-specific events in one place. In the Science Library site, the calendar is used to note the open office hours of the science librarian as well as the librarian's embedded times in the campus community and on service desks. Thus, the users of the site know where and when the li-

brarian is available to address research and library issues. Of course all open workshops regarding the instruction of research and citation management are included in the schedule so users can quickly locate times and topics for classes. In course sites, the calendar offers the same features, but the tool does allow for creative use. One brilliant librarian in Claremont working with a group of students in their senior seminar used it to arrange their required meetings. The faculty required that all the students in the seminar must meet with the librarian prior to declaring their thesis topic. In order to easily manage the meetings, the librarian used the calendar to block out her busy times, allowing the students to 'book' her time in the calendar by creating a calendar event. This novel approach enabled the librarian to set aside time when she could meet with the students, and let the students use their seminar course site calendar to book available times with little fuss. This also circumvented the "separate networks" problem that blocks students, faculty, staff, and librarians from sharing and seeing each other's calendars.

Other tools enable the uploading of handouts, database guides, and video tutorials. The "Resources" tool is perfect for hosting documents, links, and media files of all types in one convenient location. In addition to using folder structures like the "Resources" tool, Sakai allows for the creation of links as tools themselves that are then listed in the navigation of each course site. This is a perfect place for links to the library's website and relevant LibGuides. Sakai also has a "Glossary" tool, which is helpful for defining library jargon for users. The "Glossary" will export an XML file for distribution and importing of glossaries into other sites. The "Tests and Quizzes" tool aids in assessment and gauging current competencies of students before and after planned instruction sessions.

One big advantage of the flexible framework of Sakai is the ability to place a Meebo chat widget, or other such widget, directly into the course or project site. In the Science Library site, the Meebo widget is located on the front page of the project site and connects users directly to the science librarian. In the Library 101 site, the Meebo widget leads directly to the librarians logged into the Library H3lp, a library hosted instant message service chat pool. Placing a chat widget on a specific page is easy, but not the only option. One librarian used Sakai to create a webpage with a chat widget to their account and made the webpage a tool link. This tool then existed in the navigation of the course site, and reads "chat with the librarian" as the link name. Users click the link, and the page opens in a new browser window enabling communication while the user continues to work with the material in Sakai. This could easily become a tool added to each and every course site in all of Sakai immediately enabling all users to contact the library service points and librarians through chat service.

The primary benefit of having library materials in the LMS is convenience for users. Faculty members and students already log into the LMS for their daily course work and student/professor or student/student interaction. It is an easy step to simply click one tab over in the same browser window to have complete access to library materials related to their teaching and learning. The LMS structure provides a familiar continuity when used to organize library materials. For example, readings and handouts on research are in the same place, under "Resources." Scheduled classes and open office hours for librarians are in the same tool as the scheduled lectures and exams. The continuity of these tools ensures that faculty and students quickly know where to go when looking for an answer, or for a specific guide for research, bypassing the confusion of a disorderly or unfamiliar library website. Furthermore, Sakai enables the copying of materials across sites in a remarkably easy format. Faculty can copy links, guides, handouts, tutorials, files, and more and paste them directly into their course sites. This enables the faculty to easily incorporate library materials and resources into

their classes as necessary with only a few clicks. All materials are within easy reach and users, both faculty and students, are encouraged to take what they need and reuse it as it is applicable.

The ideal for open, joinable project sites is to enroll all members of a class, group, or college automatically at the beginning of the term. For example, creating a "Class of 2014" for all incoming freshman, or a subject specific site managed by the subject specialist for all declared seniors. Automatic enrollment allows librarians to develop content for a specific audience. If users are not automatically enrolled into a site, it can be promoted in appropriate LibGuides, contact pages, QR codes, business cards and more, and its value can be marketed during reference transactions and instruction sessions. It is imperative to make sure that all resources are kept up to date and that the tools are relevant to the teaching, learning, and pedagogical needs of the community. Hosting all files in one location and pointing to them either inside or outside of the learning management system streamlines workflows and cuts down on the "how many places do I need to modify this document" issue. In Claremont, all resources for the sciences are hosted in Sakai, and links to those objects exist in other places, like LibGuides and relevant web pages. Many learning management systems allow for file storage and for hosting all files in one, manageable location.

Once the Sakai project sites grew in popularity, faculty members began to add librarians to course sites, thereby incorporating librarians directly into courses. Professors typically add the librarians with the role of Instructor, allowing them to upload materials, such as readings or assignments, to the appropriate areas of the courses. Some instructors ask the librarians to enter into forum discussions about readings and research projects. Others ask the librarians to create assignments for library instruction, such as the three-step library research assignment. This assignment is designed to assess pre- and post-library instruction session competencies, as well as encourage the students to reflect on their experiences and what they learned in the instruction session as related to their research. Step one of this assignment is for the student to choose a topic, and search as they would normally search for resources, keeping a log of their progress. The logs are then uploaded to the drop box, and the librarian downloads and analyzes the logs in order to craft a library instruction session based on what the students already know and what they need to learn.

The second step is the instruction session itself, which includes examples of selected projects from the students' logs to illustrate search techniques. The final step is for the students to re-execute their search on their topic using the tools and techniques learned in the instruction session. The students again log their progress, and then write a reflection paper comparing their step one progress to their step three progress and reflecting on what they learned from the experience. Many students expressed that this compare/contrast helped them to realize the library instruction sessions provided superior searching techniques that positively influenced their research and discovery. The librarians also have the ability to follow up with students who still struggle with their research after step three, since the librarian has access to the step three logs and reflection papers.

Best practices for librarians integrating directly into course management sites revolve around effective time management. The workload of being involved with class work, discussions, library sessions, bulletin boards, and other class activities takes significant time and dedication, and it is best that a librarian restrict his or her activity to a manageable load of courses each term in order to provide the best service to the class community. Also important is working one-on-one with the course instructor to ensure that assignments and materials are relevant and important to the learning objectives of the class.

Embedding in the Campuses

Claremont librarians are challenged by the diverse and separate nature of the Claremont Colleges. Since each institution is independent of the other, the library is shared among them and not directly affiliated with any one school. As a result, librarians are often unintentionally excluded from lists, groups, communities, and places as a result of internal workflow processes. For example, email and computing network domains are all separate and created annually based on data from the registration system, and since list creation is domain-specific, librarians must work hard to be included in faculty, student, and staff lists as our domain is completely separate and distinct. Librarians also do not immediately gain access to learning areas on campus, as card swipe authentications are tied to campus specific ID cards, and the librarians have their own CUC ID cards. This additional hurdle makes embedding on-campus difficult, as well as much more necessary. Bridging the gap between the communities and the library is crucial, as the library is often not considered in any planning by campuses.

Beginning in 2002, I took over the Harvey Mudd College science library, Sprague Library. The building and services had been neglected for many years prior to my arrival, and the science community viewed the library in a negative light. Taking ownership, I began to attend faculty meetings, make "sales calls" to faculty offices, attend department gatherings and community events, and aggressively pursue information on how the library could support the teaching and learning for the faculty. Within a year the library building was repainted, new furniture purchased, and reference, instruction, and circulation statistics were up. The science community began to reassess the value of the library as a place for the librarian on its campus. Based on that work, Harvey Mudd College added "their" librarian to the faculty, staff, and student email lists, gave me an email alias with the school's domain, added me to the curriculum committee, and gave me unrestricted access to the campus and its community. I was accepted as a vital, integral part of life at Harvey Mudd College.

From this point, it was natural to explore how the other six schools would benefit from having their own librarian. In April of 2007 I wrote the "Definition of a Library Presence Without the Library" document, which outlined the perceived needs of a librarian presence without having traditional library space. The document was circulated among the library administrative staff and upper level librarian positions, and the Deans of Faculty at the Claremont Colleges. This document discussed the value of having posted "office hours" in a public area on campus away from the traditional reference desk, having space to work with users while exploring reference questions, maintaining a virtual library presence via IM and email, becoming involved with campus groups and committees, and creating ties to subject departments via meetings and networking. This document also brought to light the need for the campus community to collaborate and provide appropriate access to classrooms, teaching labs, computing networks, faculty and student email lists, and a to develop a respect for the role in teaching and learning the librarian provides. Previously, the Claremont Colleges did not regularly incorporate librarians into their communities, and this document began the push for that inclusion.

By fall of 2007 a group of outreach librarians began to meet to draft proposals for embedding librarians on each campus. We chose to define an embedded librarian as "an integral part to the whole," based on the geological definition of an embedded element. After long explorations, we decided to pair one librarian with each school, beginning a pilot program to one other institution besides Harvey Mudd College. By fall of 2009 the pilot program was finalized into an initiative and each school received their own embedded librarian. Below is the Embedded Librarian Initiative for the Claremont Colleges:

Embedded Librarian Initiative

The Claremont University Consortium Library is initiating a project to embed librarians out of the traditional library building and place librarians on the campuses and into programs to better integrate into the community, build relationships, and bridge the gap between teaching and research and library services and resources.

The Embedded Librarian, defined as "an integral part to the whole," will:

1. Commit time and energy to integrating into the community.
2. Spend significant time on the campus and with the community in question out of the main library building.
3. Teach classes on the campuses as appropriate.
4. Establish relationships with and work to share library resources and content with the community, as well as communicate back to the main library and library staff significant events.
5. Pursue participation on committees and campus groups of choice.
6. Offer reference assistance as requested.
7. Maintain an ongoing virtual presence to assist the community.
8. Serve one or two shifts on the Honnold/Mudd Library services desk.
9. Participate with library committees and groups as appropriate.
10. Act as a liaison to a subject or set of subjects.

The campus hosting the embedded Librarian should:

1. Provide the librarian with a consistent place to sit in order to make available regular, posted office hours or reference hours. The location should have enough space for collaborative work, electrical, and wifi access.
2. Subscribe the librarian to faculty, student, and staff lists, curriculum decision noti-

fications and other relevant communications in order to ensure library support and interaction with course work and faculty/student life.

3. The librarian should be able to reserve rooms and labs for teaching workshops and classes as needed.

4. The librarian needs to be included into committees, events, and groups.

In the fall of 2009, the formal Embedded Librarian Initiative began, with each campus hosting its own dedicated librarian. The campuses reacted quite positively and accommodated the librarians very well. A few of the librarians now have alias email addresses specific to a campus domain, for example, jez@hmc.edu. Domain-specific email addresses enable the librarians to post to the student and faculty lists, access the campus networks, log into the computer labs, and more importantly, provide a short, memorable email address for students and faculty members to use. The aliases point to the librarian's library email account.

Each librarian selected a space where they could be consistently available and posted office hours in order to communicate a guaranteed availability of their services to the campus community. These hours were emailed to the campus communities at the beginning of the term and posted in IT departments and writing centers, and reminders were shared at faculty meetings. Some librarians chose to hold office hours in the writing centers, as they are also the writing center liaisons, while others found spots in the campus café or in the campus IT departments or computing labs. The librarians took the liberty of exploring the campuses and getting to know key players in the community well before the fall semester in order to determine the best location for their embedded time.

Librarians work to include a brief library introductory session in orientation sessions for new students and faculty members on each campus. In one instance, all 250 incoming freshman for one college received a brief introduction to library resources. Almost all the new faculty members attend sessions where they learn about library services and collections.

Best practices for embedding into campus culture outside the traditional library buildings should include consistent and regular time spent in a highly visible location in order to meet the information needs for faculty and students. Writing centers work well, as do cafés and popular study areas. Computing labs work well, too, as long as the lab is highly used by the community. In my experience, the computing labs and IT departments are not as heavily traveled a thoroughfare as even a few years ago. More and more students have their own laptops and choose to work elsewhere. At Harvey Mudd College I have a small office in the IT area, but found that my interactions with faculty and students in that office were infrequent at best. Thus, I began to spend a few hours a week in each of the department areas, near the labs or near the department workspace. This time was much better spent as it increased my interactions with faculty and students.

Other best practices include aggressively acquiring time to introduce library resources or services at orientation sessions. Asking for a quick 10 or 15 minutes to simply introduce the faculty to the library instruction options, reference availability, and collections information at a new faculty orientation will go far in creating long-lasting relationships. New faculty frequently have many questions about the community and the available resources; acting as a welcoming mentor, answering questions and making connections will develop a deep friendship that enhances understanding of the library's place in teaching and learning.

Likewise, the same time spent at freshmen orientations and transfer student orientations places a face on the library, along with a concept of the available help the library will offer for research. For students, using the time to introduce yourself as the campus or class librarian and showing off a neat tool, like LibX or an iGoogle search box, is a quick way to get their attention and establish ties that will lead to follow up reference requests. New relationships made with key players can be leveraged to develop programs that benefit all departments. For example, at Harvey Mudd College I worked with the computing department to create a "Bite of Learning," short, thirty minute weekly lunch sessions where the librarians and the instructional technologists alternate sharing new tools and ideas. After a few very successful sessions, faculty and students asked to present at the Bite of Learning sessions, and attendance soared with user buy-in.

Finally, it is imperative to join faculty or student groups with whom you share similar interests. Book clubs, teaching and learning committees, family dining hours, knitting or sewing club, or tech exploration groups are great ways of getting to know community members and creating strong relationships. These important ties will lead to friendships and associations that will bring faculty and students to you for assistance with their information needs. Plus, it is not uncommon that a faculty member will bring up a new idea for a project or research problem while informally meeting out of 'work' time.

Concluding Suggestions

The Embedded Librarian Initiative required a high level of dedication to ensure success. The successes enjoyed in Claremont did not grow overnight, but slowly over time. When a library decides to embark on such a program, clear goals must be outlined, and with those goals, dedicated time needs to be set aside to make the program a success. Expect that the embedded librarian will spend X number of hours per week, month, etc., outside of the library, and this time needs to be respected and encouraged by administrations as the time commitment is essential for success. Be prepared to market the library with your "11 second elevator speech" at every opportunity, as you'll need to be aggressive in sharing the goals and objectives of your library's

program with every key player and faculty member you encounter.

Library administration support and buy-in is often necessary to encourage the development of the project. Library administrators are positioned to meet with the academic deans, presidents, and others in positions of authority in the campus community . Library administrators can make their own sales pitch of the project at administrative meetings to ensure that the academic deans will support the librarians on their campuses. This is imperative; an embedded librarian must be seen as integral to the central mission of the college.

The first step in establishing an embedded librarian initiative is to study the user community, taking a hard look at both current services and statistics. Developing relationships with instructional technologists and writing center directors will help identify what unmet needs they see with their students and faculty. Visiting the campus food-service cafés throughout the day helps determine peak use hours, and if it would be an approachable space for a librarian to host open office hours. Talking to student deans and student presidents can reveal what students like about current library services and what they would like to see. Visiting computing labs and other workspaces to observe how students are working and collaborating, and what tools they're using, is another good strategy. Studying such user behavior will determine how community members work and how they use library resources outside the library building. This knowledge will help your library in outlining key objectives for the program.

I suggest starting small and working up from small successes. Analyzing failures will help you learn what might have worked and whether the initiative did not match the community's needs. After identifying a community need, it is best to start a project by thinking of one, small way to make an impact. You might require that librarians begin by attending one event per week on the campus. Next, they can build on that experience by joining one campus committee or group. These small steps will create the relationships that begin integrating librarians into the community they serve.

The final step in planning an embedded librarian program is outlining assessment strategies. It is important to think ahead about how to gather statistics about time spent, classes taught, interactions had, connections made, questions answered, etc., for review each semester or each year. Embedded librarians might keep a journal or blog detailing their interactions and experiences in order to assess the successful ventures as well as failures. Setting a timeline for assessment and creating a rubric based on the initiatives' objectives to grade the progress of the project will promote a culture of assessment

By taking time to gauge the heartbeat of the user community, studying their habits and creating relationships with key players, it is easy to outline the structure for an embedded librarian initiative. Thinking of ways to meet existing needs based on the knowledge and observations of your users and the suggestions of other supporting networks is the first step. Creating goals and objectives while thinking about how assessment of the project will occur will ensure a thorough outline of your embedded project. Starting small and slowly building the initiative while gaining buy-in from administrations and users will also ensure success. With time and care, your library's embedded initiative will succeed.

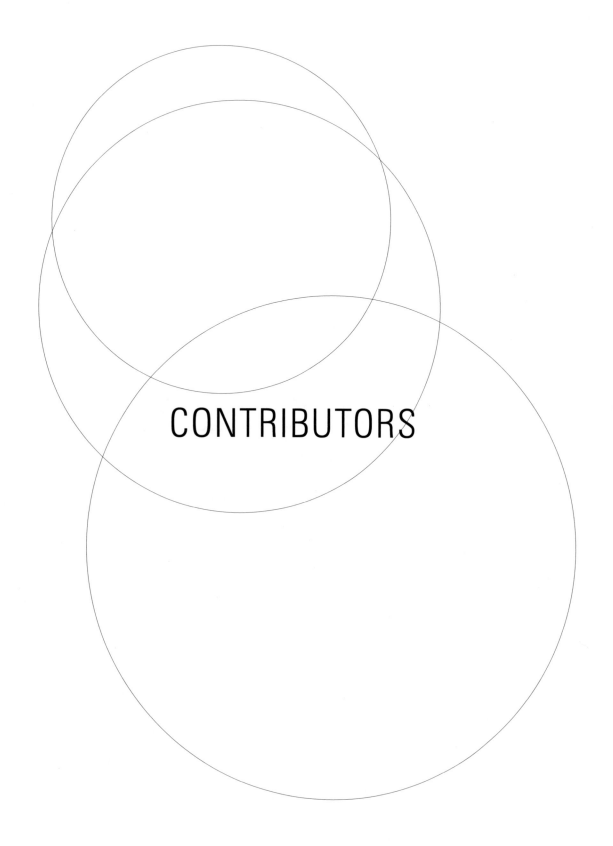

CONTRIBUTORS

Contributors

Camille Andrews is Learning Technologies and Assessment Librarian at Albert R. Mann Library at Cornell University. She teaches and creates learning objects, explores and assesses instructional technologies and learning spaces, provides reference services, and serves as liaison to the Education and Development Sociology departments. Camille is extremely interested in the intersection of library and information science, education, 21st century literacies and new technologies. Camille graduated from the College of William and Mary in 1996 with a BA in Literary and Cultural Studies (focused on Francophone African and Caribbean Literature) and from Simmons College in 2003 with a master's in Library and Information Science.

Laura Berdish is a reference librarian at the Kresge Business Administration Library at the University of Michigan. Laura holds an AMLS from the University of Michigan, and joined the Kresge Library staff in December 2006 following 20 years in Boston, working at a variety of corporate positions, including the former Digital Equipment Corporation, *Computerworld* (magazine) and internet startup TechTarget, as well as a brief but enjoyable stint as the Young Adult Librarian at the Belmont Public Library in greater Boston. Laura's reference duties at the Kresge Library include a role as coordinator of the Library's work with business school MAP teams.

Bojana Beric, MD, PhD, CHES is an Assistant Professor of Health Studies at Monmouth University in New Jersey, USA and a Visiting Professor at the Medical Faculty, University of Novi Sad, Serbia, Europe. Dr. Beric is a co-director of the Center for Human and Community Wellness: Community Campus Partnerships for Health and a co-chair of the Global Understanding Convention, both at Monmouth University in New Jersey.

Dr. Beric attained her PhD in Health Education from New York University and an MD degree from University of Novi Sad in Yugoslavia, practicing medicine in Yugoslavia before moving to United States in 1984 and working as a researcher at Baylor College of Medicine, Houston, Texas. Since 1994, Dr. Beric has been dedicated to health education and public health, living and working in New Jersey. Her research interests are in methods of communication of health information, in organizing a community of learners with the purpose of promoting health and preventing disease, participation in action, and in advancing health literacy.

Paul Betty is the Distance Learning Librarian at Regis University. His research interests include designing and distributing multimedia learning objects for libraries, synchronous and asynchronous online instruction, and open source music technology.

Matthew Brower is a Business Reference and Instruction Librarian at the University of Colorado at Boulder. He earned his BA degree at DePauw University, and received an MLS degree from Indiana University, Bloomington. He recently coauthored a book chapter on recruiting Information professionals, and has published reviews of business research databases. His other research interests include: emerging technologies and their application to instruction and reference services, research habits of scholars in the social science fields, and new models for developing research collections.

Lisa R. Coats, MA, MLIS is a Reference and Instruction Librarian at Monmouth University Library in West Long Branch, New Jersey. Ms. Coats attained her Master of Library & Information Science degree in 2004 at Rutgers University in New Brunswick, NJ, and she worked briefly in a public library before settling into academia at Monmouth University (MU) in 2006. At MU Library, Ms. Coats teaches library research to undergraduate and graduate students in library sessions and also conducts one-on-one reference instruction with students and faculty. She is the Library Liaison to the School of Nursing and Health Studies, the School of Education, the School of Social Work, and the Communication Department. She is a Part-Time Lecturer at her alma mater Rutgers' School of Communication & Information teaching a graduate-level reference course as needed. Ms Coats' research interests include student retention of information, information literacy, collaboration between faculty on campus and with outside institutions, instructional tools and teaching methods.

Emily Daly serves as the Coordinator of Upper Level Instruction at Duke University. Emily began her career in public and school libraries prior to joining Duke Libraries' Instruction and Outreach Department, where she has worked since August 2006. Her research interests include instructional design, user experience and usability studies.

Jezmynne Dene is currently the Director of the Portneuf District Library in Pocatello, Idaho. Previously, Jezmynne was a science librarian at the Claremont Colleges, in Claremont, California, where she was active in outreach and instruction. Jezmynne has a BA in Southwestern History from the University of New Mexico and an MLIS from the University of Illinois, Urbana-Champaign. Jezmynne continues to study Western American History and is a student in the Historical Resources Management MA program at Idaho State University.

Natalie Dollar, Associate Professor of Speech Communication, teaches upper division and graduate courses in intercultural and interpersonal communication, community dialogue, communication theory, youth communication outreach, and group communication. Before coming to OSU-Cascades in 2002, Natalie was a member of the Oregon State University faculty in Corvallis where she was named a College of Liberal Arts Master Teacher and awarded the College of Liberal Arts Dean Wilkins Faculty Development Award. Natalie received a Bachelor of Arts in Communication from Mississippi State University, a Masters of Arts in Communication Theory from Arizona State University, and a doctorate in Cultural Communication from the University of Washington.

Natalie's scholarship focuses on identity, culture, and communication. Her current research interests focus on dialogue as a means for co-constructing relationships among individuals or groups in conflict, teaching community dialogue, and negotiating identities in intracultural interactions

Rick Fisher earned both his B.A. and M.A. in English at the University of Wyoming. He currently teaches writing at UW, and he also conducts research on students' first-year and transitional experiences. He has presented research results at national conferences of librarians, composition faculty, and student affairs staff. Since 2005 he has also taught in the Synergy Program at UW, a nationally recognized program for conditionally admitted students; prior to that, he taught high-school English in a rural Nebraska school.

Martin Garnar is an associate professor of library science and the reference services librarian at Regis University in Denver, CO. He also teaches ethics for the University of Denver's Library and Information Science program, of which he is a proud alumnus. His research interests include intellectual freedom, ethics, and information literacy. He is an active presenter at state and national conferences and has served as president of the Colorado Association of Libraries and as chair of the American Library Association's Intellectual Freedom Committee. A native of New York, Martin lives in Denver's Berkeley neighborhood with his partner Mark and their adorable pair of miniature dachshunds.

Deborah S. Garson is Head of the Research and Instruction Services Department, Monroe C. Gutman Library and a lecturer at the Harvard Graduate School of Education. She has responsibility for the research and instruction services of the library and the Gutman Library Writing Services. She serves on the Harvard University Library Committee for Public Services, and is a member of the U. S. Department of Education ERIC Library Committee.

Kate Gronemyer is the Instruction Librarian for the Cascades Campus of Oregon State University, located in Bend, OR. In addition to work on collaborative information literacy instruction, her research interests include teaching undergraduate students about the value and purpose of scholarly work.

April Heaney directs the Synergy Program at the University of Wyoming, a first-year learning community for at-risk students. She leads several high school-to-college transition initiatives in Wyoming and directs supplemental instruction efforts for first-year college students. Her research interests focus on integrating critical pedagogies in writing classes and investigating the implications of admissions policies for academically at-risk students at public universities.

Baseema Banoo Krkoska is the International Projects Librarian at Albert R. Mann Library, Cornell University. She was formerly the business librarian at Mann library, when she created Mann's first embedded business information program for the users of business information in the College of Agriculture and Life Sciences, specifically catering to the information needs of the Applied Economics & Management department. She currently serves as the Project Director of The Essential Electronic Agricultural Library (http://teeal.org) aimed at improving access to scientific information in geographical regions where Internet is least accessible. She also travels periodically to Africa to provide in-person information literacy training to PhD scholars in the African Centers for Crop Improvement. She has an MBA from Hyderabad, India and moved to United States to earn a second masters in Communication from Cornell University. She is keenly interested in developing information literacy programs for users living in emerging economies.

Dallas Long recently accepted a new position as Assistant Professor and Head of Access Services at Illinois State University, where he hopes to forge a strong connection with the students. He holds master's degrees in Library & Information Science and Higher Education Administration from the University of Illinois at Urbana-Champaign and a bachelor's degree in Psychology from Webster University. He is currently a doctoral student in Higher Education Administration at Illinois State University.

Kristen Mastel is the Outreach and Instruction Librarian for the Agriculture, Biological and Environmental Sciences (ABES) department of the University of Minnesota Libraries where she is the liaison to Agricultural Education and the Colleges of Continuing Education and Extension. Kristen serves as the Chair of the Academic and Research Libraries Division of the Minnesota Library Association (local ACRL Chapter) and as the Chair-elect of the Art Libraries Society of North America – Twin Cities Chapter. Her degree in Library Science is from Indiana University – Bloomington. Kristen's research interests include: emerging technologies, building collaborative spaces, K2College continuum, and information literacy and instruction assessment.

Eileen McGowan is a Lecturer on Education and Director of the Field Experience Program at Harvard University's Graduate School of Education. Eileen's research focuses on the development of formal mentoring relationships within educational settings, whether in higher education or urban public school settings. As a faculty member associated with the Urban Superintendent's program, she runs mentoring seminars and supports their distance research groups.

Christopher A. Miller is Curator of the *e-kiNETx* and Cross-Cultural Dance Resources Collections in the Herberger Institute School of Dance at Arizona State University. Previously, he was ASU Libraries' bibliographer for Southeast Asia, a region in which he has worked extensively. Christopher's audiovisual and document digitization projects have received funding from the U.S. State Department Ambassadors Fund for Cultural Preservation (early Burmese recordings); the British Library Endangered Archives Programme (Pa'O Literary Archive); and the Center for Burma Studies (Burmese Field Recordings). Christopher holds a MA in Information Resources and Library Science from the University of Arizona; a MM degree in Music and Southeast Asian Studies from Northern Illinois University; and a Bachelor of Music degree from the North Carolina School of the Arts.

Craig Milne, BSc, *GradDipInfoLibStds*, AALIA (CP) has been a Liaison Librarian to the School of Urban Development and Faculty of Built Environment and Engineering at Queensland University of Technology since August 2006. His previous career was as a Hydrographic / Engineering Surveyor and he has been able to use this practical discipline knowledge in developing the library collection and in engaging with students and academics. Craig's most recent work has been as a Research Data Librarian working with researchers on data management. Other interests include Geographic Information Systems (GIS) and how libraries can support the use of spatial information as well as the application of GIS by libraries for strategic and operational planning and advocacy.

Jim Morris-Knower is currently an outreach and publicity librarian at Cornell's Mann Library, where he has worked since receiving his MLIS from the University of Michigan in 1996. In addition to being the liaison to the Communication department, he works closely with Cornell Cooperative Extension staff across the state, occasionally travelling to county offices to give training on library resources. In January 2011, he travelled to India as the librarian for an International Agriculture class at Cornell. After that, he's hoping that Richard Branson will need an embedded librarian for his Virgin Atlantic trips to space.

Ann Schroeder's library career spanned college libraries, small public libraries, and the Library of Congress. Twenty-two years of her career were spent at the Community College of Vermont (CCV), where she helped transform the library from small book collections at each site (pre-Internet) to an amazing array of online resources and services. She is best known for creating the College's very successful embedded librarian program in 2004. Ann retired from CCV in July 2010 and is enjoying the great outdoors of Vermont.

Corey Seeman is the Director of the Kresge Business Administration Library of the Ross School of Business at the University of Michigan. Corey has been at the library since November 2005 and previously worked as the Associate Dean for Resource and Systems Management at the University of Toledo (Ohio), Library Training Consultant, Innovative Interfaces, Inc., and Manager of Technical Services at the National Baseball Library at the National Baseball Hall of Fame and Museum, Inc. in Cooperstown. He holds a M.A.L.S. from Dominican University and an A.B. (from the University of Chicago (with a major in European History). He has written articles primarily in the areas such as library systems, cataloging (especially in the context of special library collections) and on collection development issues associated with autism. He will be focusing his writing on change management in the library and service issues associated with academic libraries.

David Shumaker has served as Clinical Associate Professor at the School of Library and Information Science, Catholic University of America, since August 2006. Dave's teaching interests include the role and future of librarians in society, the management of libraries and information services, marketing, information systems, and library public services. His research and writing focus on the changing roles of librarians in business and educational organizations.

Dave assumed his present position upon his retirement from the MITRE Corporation, where he worked for 27 years, rising to the position of Manager of Information Services. In this position he was responsible for MITRE's corporate library, records management, and archives operations. Earlier in his career, he was a Library of Congress Intern, a cataloger, and an automation specialist for the U.S. National Library Service for the Blind and Physically Handicapped. He holds graduate degrees from Drexel University and the University of Maryland. He blogs at http://embeddedlibrarian.wordpress.com.

Jennifer Thomas has been the Liaison Librarian for the School of Design, Faculty of Built Environment and Engineering at Queensland University of Technology (QUT) since 2007. She was recently seconded to QUT's flagship research institute where she provided research support services and published work on the academic library's role in e-research support. Jennifer's past publications have covered the topics of information literacy and federated resource discovery and other interests include advocacy and leadership within libraries. She is currently seconded to the State Library of Queensland to assist in building a collection on Asia-Pacific Design.